INSTRUCTOR'S MANUAL

and

TEST BANK

THE PRICE SYSTEM

AND RESOURCE ALLOCATION

Tenth Edition

INSTRUCTOR'S MANUAL

and

TEST BANK

THE PRICE SYSTEM

AND RESOURCE ALLOCATION

Tenth Edition

Ross D. Eckert
Claremont McKenna College

Richard H. Leftwich
Leftwich Associates

THE DRYDEN PRESS
Chicago   New York   San Francisco
Philadelphia   Montreal   Toronto
London   Sydney   Tokyo

ISBN 0-03-012532-4
Printed in the United States of America
789-066-987654321

Address orders:
111 Fifth Avenue
New York, NY 10003

Address editorial correspondence:
One Salt Creek Lane
Hinsdale, IL 60521

The Dryden Press
Holt, Rinehart and Winston
Saunders College Publishing

PREFACE

This Instructor's Manual serves three purposes. First, at the beginning of each chapter we highlight the chapter objectives and point out special problems we have observed in teaching the material over the years. We make suggestions for handling them which seem to have been successful for us. Second, we include a battery of questions that can be used in examinations and in developing student understanding of microeconomic concepts. It is made up of discussion questions and problems, true-false questions, and multiple-choice questions—all with solutions. Third, we provide solutions to the even-numbered end-of-chapter problems from the text. These solutions are presented in the same detail as the solutions to the odd-numbered problems that appear at the end of the text so that the instructor may use them as answer keys for examinations or class assignments. The manual should be viewed as an aid to persons who we assume are already competent instructors. In the development of questions, Professor Shirley Yu, Texas Tech University, has been most helpful.

A computerized version of the Test Bank for the IBM-PC is available through your local Dryden sales representative. This CTB will include sections on Problems and Questions for Discussion, Solutions to Problems and Questions for Discussion, True-False questions, and Multiple-Choice questions.

Ross D. Eckert
Richard H. Leftwich

CONTENTS

PART ONE

A REVIEW OF BASIC ECONOMIC ANALYSIS

Chapters 1 through 4, comprising Part One of the book, review basic concepts that students should have learned in their principles courses. They lay the foundation for an in-depth systematic development of microeconomic theory. If students in the class have been uniformly well trained in principles, these chapters can either be passed over quickly or omitted altogether. We find it useful to spend three to six class hours on them to establish a common base from which all students can work.

CHAPTER 1

ECONOMIC ACTIVITY AND ECONOMIC THEORY

Chapter Outline

Economic Activity
   Human Wants
   Resources
   Technology
Methodology
   The Construction of Economic Theory
   The Functions of Economic Theory
Price Theory and Economic Theory
Welfare

Application

How Would You Like Some "Free" Medical Care?

Chapter Objectives

This introductory chapter is intended to orient students. It
blocks out the nature of economic activity, shows how economic
theory evolves from economic activity, and explains the position
of microeconomics in the general body of economic theory. It
defines economic welfare, pointing to economic theory as a systematic way of examining the determinants of the level of welfare and of generating economic policies to raise welfare levels
over time. Welfare is a concept that we employ throughout the
book.

Suggestions for Teaching

First of all we review the nature of economic activity—the use
of scarce resources and available technology to satisfy unlimited
human wants to the greatest possible extent. Then we turn to
methodology—how theory is constructed and what it is good for.
It is important that students understand the role of theory in
the discipline of economics as well as how microeconomics fits
into the general theory framework. They should understand clearly the distinction between normative and positive economics. We
find it useful to make sure at this initial point in the study
of microeconomics that students understand the concept of Pareto
optimality. Finally, we insist that our students be able to
define all of the running glossary terms.

The application on zero-priced medical care illustrates the distorted incentives consumers have when goods are subsidized. The instructor may also use this application to draw the distinction between truly free resources and economic resources that have zero money prices artificially.

Problems and Questions for Discussion

1. Why is it that the population of any given country cannot secure the goods and services needed to satisfy all of its wants?

2. Analyze the following statement: "The government of India should pursue policies that will enable the entire population of that country to achieve adequate living standards."

3. Analyze the following statement: "The government of India should pursue policies that will enable the population of that country to achieve the highest living standards that its resources will permit."

4. Consider a brain surgeon and a butcher. As economic resources, what do they have in common? Analytically, would you classify them in the same or in different resource categories? Why?

5. Explain each of the steps involved in the construction of a theory.

6. The equation $s = 1/2gt^2$ is a famous law of physics. Based on a review of your course in introductory economics, can you think of any hypotheses from economic theory that have been known to be consistent with real-world events as often as this fundamental theorem of physics?

7. Explain the importance of each of the following criteria in evaluating a theory in economics or any other field (such as physics): whether the theory
   a. is logical or illogical.
   b. fits the evidence or is contradicted by evidence.
   c. contains simple or complex logic.
   d. contains only a few explanatory variables or many such variables.
   e. is testable or not.

8. Define and discuss the relationships between positive economics and normative economics.

9. What do we mean by "economic welfare"? How can we determine whether or not any event or activity increases the welfare of an individual? of a group of individuals?

10. Define "Pareto optimality."

11. Based on your own employment arrangements or those of your parents, which fringe benefits do you buy more of or shop less for because of a subsidized price? Could any of these choices have long-run effects on your health, safety, or well-being?

Solutions to Problems and Questions for Discussion

1. Because the wants of its population are unlimited, while its resources are scarce and its technology is limited.

2. The government of India cannot provide the labor skills or the capital needed to enable its population to achieve adequate living standards. Over a very long period of time it could pursue policies conducive to capital accumulation and the acquisition of higher skill levels.

3. This statement makes more sense over the foreseeable future. Any government should pursue policies that increase the efficiency with which its resources are used.

4. Both are classified as labor. Analytically, they have little in common and are best classed as two different resource categories.

5. See the text, pages 8 and 9.

6. The law of demand——that the quantity of a good that is purchased in a market is inversely related to the price of the good.

7. Each criterion matters to scientists, but most would probably agree that a, b, and e are critical.

8. Positive economics is concerned with what is, while normative economics is concerned with what ought to be; i.e., with policy making to convert what is into what ought to be. To be a competent normative economist one must be a good positive economist.

9. Economic welfare refers to economic well-being. If an individual tells us that an economic event increases her/his well-being, we understand that her/his welfare is improved, but this is not the case with a group. One person's gain may be at the expense of others. We can be sure of a gain in the welfare of a group only if at least one person gains while no one else loses.

10. Pareto optimality exists when no one can gain from an event without inflicting loss on someone else.

11. Depends on facts discovered.

True-False Questions

(F) _____ 1. Human wants for any specific good or service tend to be unlimited.

(T) _____ 2. The labor resources of an economy can be increased by education and training.

(F) _____ 3. Any economic system can be expected to provide a standard of living that is adequate for its entire population.

(F) _____ 4. The stock of capital of the United States economy consists to a substantial degree of its money supply.

(T) _____ 5. A can of beans on the grocer's shelf is a part of the grocer's capital resources.

(T) _____ 6. Techniques of production refer to the means, methods, and know-how available to convert resources into want-satisfying goods and services.

(F) _____ 7. If economic growth in the United States continues over the next twenty-five years as it has for the last twenty-five years, the wants of its population will likely be substantially satisfied.

(F) _____ 8. Economists are properly concerned with analysis, not with policy.

(F) _____ 9. To be a good normative economist, it is not necessary to be a good positive economist.

© 1988 The Dryden Press

(F)   ____   10.   The recession and unemployment that occurred in 1980 indicate that people in the United States economy are receiving on the average all the goods and services they need.

(T)   ____   11.   During the Civil War, it was possible for a person drafted into the Union Army to pay someone to go in his place. When this occurred, it can be presumed that the economic welfare of the society was increased by the transaction.

(F)   ____   12.   We would expect in most societies most of the time that income redistributions from the rich to the poor would constitute movements toward Pareto optimality.

(T)   ____   13.   It is unlikely that a good theory will contain all the details of the real world to which it applies, but it should explain the important causal relations that are at work.

(T)   ____   14.   To be useful, a hypothesis in economics (or any other field) must be logical and verified by available evidence.

(T)   ____   15.   A theory can never be proven, only refuted.

(F)   ____   16.   The forces that determine the mix of goods and services that comprise national income are explained by macroeconomic theory.

(T)   ____   17.   The causes of economic fluctuations are a part of the general body of macroeconomic theory.

(F)   ____   18.   The distortions introduced by subsidies in the application about "free" medical care are probably unique to medical care and have limited relevance either to other subsidized goods or to consumers outside Washington, D.C.

(T)   ____   19.   Subsidizing medical care for government officials in Washington, D.C. not only led them to spend less time comparing qualities of service but also led them to buy more of the subsidized service than otherwise.

Multiple-Choice Questions

(c) ____ 1. When unemployment occurs in an economy:
- a. the system can make up for it by using more capital.
- b. human wants have been satiated.
- c. the economic system is turning out less total product that it is capable of producing.
- d. it is a sign that technology is advancing at too rapid a pace.

(c) ____ 2. Which of the following is <u>not</u> an economic resource?
- a. the work of an economics professor
- b. iron ore
- c. a one-hundred share General Motors stock certificate
- d. the land occupied by the administration building at State University

(b) ____ 3. With regard to economic principles:
- a. Once they are established, they can generally be regarded as infallible.
- b. They are not necessarily absolute truths; they are subject to correction and refinement.
- c. They are tentative statements of causal relations.
- d. They are arrived at primarily through deductive reasoning.

(b) ____ 4. An economy's resources:
- a. tend to limit it to a more or less fixed set of product outputs.
- b. tend to be versatile or usable in producing a range of different product outputs.
- c. are usually unlimited in quantity.
- d. are not related to its living standards.

(a) ____ 5. A tentative statement of a causal relationship between two variables is called a(an):
- a. hypothesis.
- b. theory.
- c. edict.
- d. principle.

 © 1988 The Dryden Press

(c) ____ 6. The potential living standards of an economic system can be increased by:
  a. an increase in the purchasing power of its citizens.
  b. an increase in its population.
  c. an increase in its capital and its techniques of production.
  d. all of the above.

(d) ____ 7. Which of the following is <u>not</u> a hypothesis of economic theory?
  a. an increase in the legally enforced minimum wage lowers employment, all other factors held constant
  b. the higher the price, the lower the quantity demanded, all other factors held constant
  c. the higher the price, the higher the quantity supplied, all other factors held constant
  d. the higher the price of apples, the more apples growers may bring to market

(a) ____ 8. The phrase "all other factors held constant" was inserted in several of the possible answers to the previous question because:
  a. to test each hypothesis it is necessary to isolate the variable of concern from changes in other variables that could have caused opposite results.
  b. adding the statement is necessary to achieve Pareto optimality in each case.
  c. the phrase made each statement deductive rather than inductive.
  d. the phrase made each statement positive rather than normative.

(d) ____ 9. Pareto optimality is achieved when:
  a. the incomes of all persons are the same.
  b. goods and services are distributed in equal amounts to each consumer.
  c. no unemployment exists.
  d. no one can be made better off without making someone else worse off.

(d) ____ 10. Welfare in an economic sense refers to:
  a. aid to families with dependent children.
  b. social security.
  c. company pension funds.
  d. a state of economic well-being.

© 1988 The Dryden Press

(c) ____ 11. Positive economics is concerned with:
   a. getting points across in the classroom.
   b. economic policy making to achieve what ought to be.
   c. the determination of causal relations—what is.
   d. eliminating value judgments from decision making.

(c) ____ 12. Which of the following is not a microeconomic problem?
   a. determination of the wage rate of plumbers in Dallas, Texas
   b. the effects of farm price supports on the consumption of wheat
   c. the causes of inflation from 1966 through 1979
   d. the effects of the OPEC oil embargo on the price of oil in the United States in early 1974

(d) ____ 13. Which of the following does not appear to have been a consequence of subsidizing medical care for government officials in Washington, D.C.?
   a. Consumers were less prudent in choosing physicians.
   b. Consumers took more medical services than otherwise.
   c. More resources were devoted to medical services than otherwise.
   d. No consumer benefited from the subsidies.

CHAPTER 2

THE ORGANIZATION OF AN ECONOMIC SYSTEM

Chapter Outline

The Functions of an Economic System
   Determination of What to Produce
   Organization of Production
   Output Distribution
   Rationing in the Very Short Run
   Economic Maintenance and Growth
Ownership Rights and Resource Allocation
The Not-for-Profit Sector

Applications

Finders, Keepers
The Law of Capture
External Effects in Solar Energy and Dutch Toads
Suppressing Markets in Organ Transplants

Chapter Objectives

Students should understand that economic activity in every nation is organized as an economic system. We define an economic
system in this chapter and point out the principal characteristics of the two major types of systems in existence today—a
private enterprise system and a socialistic system. We emphasize
that the focus in this book is on a predominantly private enterprise system. Regardless of its type, every system must perform
certain functions. We classify the functions into five categories, but the number will depend on who is doing the classify-
ing. Then we discuss the role of a price system in a private
enterprise economy in performing those functions. How the price
system allocates resources depends in part on the legal resource
rights that owners have, so we explain here the important role of
property rights in an economic system. Since every student knows
that some production units are not price- and profit-oriented—
for example, schools and many hospitals—we introduce the not-
for-profit sector explicitly at this early juncture.

Suggestions for Teaching

First of all we try to make clear what an economic system is,
contrasting a <u>pure</u> socialistic system with a <u>pure</u> private enter-

© 1988 The Dryden Press

prise system. Next we nail down the functions that every system
must perform, using an intuitive discussion of how the market
mechanism—using prices and profits—performs them in a private
enterprise economy. This discussion anticipates the detailed
study of markets and prices that comprises most of the book.
Again, all of the running glossary definitions must be learned
by students.

Students usually think of goods as privately owned and allocated
through markets by the price system. This characterizes much
of the U.S. economy, but we can all think of exceptions. The applications to this chapter illustrate several important variations. How individuals compete and establish rights to unowned
goods is illustrated in the first two applications on lost-and-
found articles and mobile fish and game (often called either the
commons or the common-pool problem). The solar energy application illustrates how externalities can be internalized if con-
tracting costs are low, and the Dutch toad essay shows the difficulties involved when the external costs are borne by environmental species. The organ transplant application shows that some
of the most vital services in the U.S. economy are provided by
not-for-profit organizations through "markets" in which price is
purposely prevented from serving its usual function.

Problems and Questions for Discussion

1. Suppose that constant quantities of all goods and services
   available in an economy are placed on the market each month.
   A set of prices has been achieved that reflects consumer
   valuations of a unit of each one. Now suppose the government taxes the rich and gives subsidies to the poor. What
   will happen to the prices of (a) fur coats? (b) Cadillacs?
   (c) hamburger? (d) overalls? Indicate why in each case.

2. Over the years, as consumer demand turned away from rail
   transportation toward air transportation, what do you think
   happened to the comparative profits of the two industries?
   to the allocation of labor and capital between them? Explain how you think the process worked.

3. Explain why differences in income among individuals and
   among families occur in a private enterprise economic system. Do these differences mean that poverty must exist
   in such a system? Why or why not?

4. List and explain at least three means that can contribute
   to growth in an economy's output over time. Which of these
   would appear to be most promising for a lesser developed
   country such as Pakistan?

© 1988 The Dryden Press

5. "Since there is no central planning by the government for outputs and resource use in a private enterprise economy, it follows that the operation of the economy will be rather chaotic." Evaluate this statement critically.

6. Most private firms and many not-for-profit firms earn "profits" in the sense that their revenues exceed their costs. Claims of owners on these profits are very different between the two types of organizations. Explain these differences and the importance of them in determining the responsiveness of each type of organization to consumer demands.

7. Can you think of other situations in which rationing of the kidney type occurs? What about the rationing of blood for transfusion purposes when supplies are low (such as during holidays and vacation times during the year when people are "too busy" to donate)?

8. In desperation, the poorest of the poor in Brazil are turning to the sale of bodily organs as a device for getting themselves and their families out of poverty. One person is willing to sell a cornea for $100,000; another will sell a kidney for $30,000. Would you approve of such transactions if the sellers were fully informed about the medical consequences of their actions and buyers were willing to pay their prices? Do you think that you should be asked to approve such transactions since, strictly speaking, they only concern the two parties involved? Explain.

9. The taxpayer "rebellion" in California and other states has caused some states to issue securities to raise cash more often than they used to. These offerings are usually made through one of the investment banking firms on Wall Street, and the underwriting fees that these brokers negotiate with each state amount to a lot of money. State treasurers get to choose which Wall Street firm gets their state's business. The number of firms is large and most are highly skilled, so the market is very competitive. What means do you think the Wall Street firms use to get states as clients? Would any of the following surprise you? Chauffeured limousines when the treasurers visit New York? Campaign contributions to politicians in state governments? Can you think of others? (Tim Carrington and John J. Fialka, "Local Politicians Reap Big Crop of Cash Gifts from Wall Streeters," The Wall Street Journal, October 18, 1983.)

10. After the Mexico City earthquake in September 1985, the government expropriated 5,000 dilapidated apartment buildings and rental properties owned by Mexicans that suffered quake damage. The government's purpose was to hasten the replacement of run-down privately owned buildings housing thousands of poor city dwellers with new tenant-owned buildings. Owners were supposed to be compensated over a ten-year period. (Steve Frazier, "Mexican Property Seizures after Quake Infuriate Owners, Speed Flight of Capital," The Wall Street Journal, November 7, 1985.)

    a. What would you expect the effect of this government action to be on the rate at which new buildings are constructed?
    b. Do you see any connection between the government's action and the plunge in the value of the peso by about 30 percent relative to the U.S. dollar about the same time?

11. How would your community respond to an increase in the rate of burglaries and a decline in the confidence of regular police forces to prevent them? Can you think of any firms already in business that would store jewelry, oriental rugs, or cameras for a fee? What adjustments in resource allocation might occur?

12. Alaska's Kenai River is the world's most productive salmon fishery. Fish in excess of 50 pounds make it popular among sportsmen and profitable for 350 commercial boats that take about 60 percent of the $30-million annual catch. But the catch is declining. The sportsmen say this is due to too little "conservation" and too much commercial fishing. The commercial fishermen say that the real issue is their livelihoods. Alaska cut the fishing season but not fishing licenses, which have tripled over ten years. Both groups of fishermen oppose tighter limits on gear or catches. (Ken Wells, "Prized Salmon in Alaska Stir Bitter Battle," The Wall Street Journal, August 6, 1984.) The key economic issue in this debate is not conservation versus livelihoods. What basic economic issue is at stake?

Solutions to Problems and Questions for Discussion

1. a. Decline because rich people have less to spend.
   b. Decline for the same reason as a.
   c. Increase because poor people have more to spend.
   d. Increase for the same reason as c.

2. Profits increased relatively in the air transportation
    industry. Labor and capital were attracted out of the less
    profitable rail industry into the more profitable air in-
    dustry because the latter, wanting to expand, became willing
    to pay more for their services and the former, wanting to
    contract, was willing to purchase their services only at
    lower prices.

3. Because individual and family incomes depend on the labor
    and capital resources owned by each one. Different ones own
    different qualities and different quantities of resources.
    Poverty is not inevitable. A private enterprise system can
    transfer as much income as it desires from the more wealthy
    to those at the lower end of the income scale.

4. (a) Capital accumulation. (b) Improvements in technology.
    (c) Upgrade in labor education and skills. All three would
    be important, but (c) probably should have the highest pri-
    ority. An educated and skilled population will have greater
    success in accomplishing (a) and (b) than an illiterate and
    unskilled population.

5. The quotation confuses predictability with chaos. Planners
    may determine with rigid certainty the amounts of resources
    going into the production of certain goods but wind up with
    either too many or too few of these goods relative to what
    consumers want (e.g., the normal shortages of consumer goods
    in Eastern Bloc countries). In capitalist economies, most
    of the planning is done by private individuals in the course
    of their normal profit-making activities. The amounts of
    resources that are devoted to production of each good or
    service may not be predictable in advance, but shortages or
    surpluses should not persist unless government intervenes
    to fix prices at nonmarket-clearing levels. We do not view
    this as chaos. Profits and prices organize the private
    enterprise economy.

6. In general, for-profit firms will respond better to consumer
    demands. This is because their owners can capture the
    residual profits that occur when revenues exceed costs. The
    things consumers demand most will have the higher prices
    relative to costs, and therefore will be the most profitable
    to produce. Resource owners, in the interests of their
    incomes, will direct their firms toward the production of
    these articles. In many not-for-profit organizations,
    owners and managers cannot take home in personal income as
    much of the profits that are generated by responding to
    consumer demands. Therefore, not-for-profit firms usually
    have weaker incentives to respond to consumer demands unless
    they face competitors or their survival is at stake.

7. Blood is obtained from donors rather than sellers. Too much blood is available relative to the amount demanded at times of the year donors find convenient to give. The "excess" over what is used for hospitalized patients is sold to pharmaceutical companies for processing into commercial products. Too little blood is obtained when donors are too busy to give. At such times inventories of blood decline and some surgeries may be postponed. These problems could be reduced by relying on the price system rather than donations to determine the quantity of blood available.

8. Such exchanges are purely voluntary and each party benefits as long as all the risks are understood by both. We would approve such exchanges. This is a normative judgment, however, that each voter must make individually.

9. Such forms of competition do not surprise us. The state treasurers have valuable business to offer and it must be allocated among the investment banking firms in some manner. The treasurers are prohibited from accepting money payments in exchange, so they or their associates capture personal benefits in less direct ways.

10. a. Investors will be reluctant to construct new buildings for fear they will be expropriated. More future housing will have to be provided by the government than it anticipated.
    b. The connection is logical, but one would have to research the matter to determine if other contemporaneous events could have prompted the flight into dollars from pesos.

11. Private storage firms would spring up if enough families had valuables worth protecting. In Rome, Italy, where burglaries were common in the 1970s, security services were provided by pawnshops (especially during the summer vacation months). Pawnshops make loans on valuables for a specified period at agreed interest rates. The loan is less than the resale value of the item, which the pawnbroker holds as collateral for sale at a profit if the loan is not paid on time. Pawnshops have iron bars on the windows and strong vaults. They can rent vault space implicitly via the interest they charge on the loan. In Rome, only 2 to 3 percent of the items stored at pawnshops are not redeemed. (William Tuohy, "Pawnshop Serves Wealthy Romans as a Safe Storage Place," Los Angeles Times, July 10, 1977.)

12. The fundamental issue is whether property rights or regulations will limit fishing by either group sufficiently to preserve the stock of fish. "Conservation" versus "livelihoods," in this case, appear to be mere catchwords in the political debate over whose share of an overfished fishery declines least.

True-False Questions

(F) _____ 1. Business receipts in a private enterprise economic system usually result from the exploitation of customers by business firms.

(T) _____ 2. In a private enterprise system, consumers are left relatively free to spend their incomes on whatever they desire to purchase.

(F) _____ 3. In a private enterprise system, the organization of production is largely determined by the directors of the 200 largest corporations.

(T) _____ 4. Relative prices and profits made in different lines of endeavor guide the organization of production in a private enterprise economy.

(F) _____ 5. The basic cause of poverty is laziness on the part of the poor.

(F) _____ 6. A private enterprise economic system is less likely to produce what consumers want than is a socialistic system.

(T) _____ 7. A poor person has less "voting power" in the marketplace than does a rich person.

(F) _____ 8. Poverty of some part of the society is an essential characteristic of the market system.

(F) _____ 9. Economic efficiency is more or less the same concept as mechanical efficiency.

(T) _____ 10. Resource owners tend to employ their resources in those uses where they contribute most to consumer welfare.

(F) _____ 11. The incomes of people who do not work are generally obtained at the expense of income for those who do work.

(F) ____ 12. A private enterprise economy would likely provide higher living standards if business firms were forbidden to make profits.

(T) ____ 13. The sale of overripe bananas by a grocer at a relatively low price provides an example of a very short-run situation.

(T) ____ 14. A given supply of a product can be rationed among consumers so that every consumer gets all he wants to buy if the price of the product is free to move up or down.

(F) ____ 15. An increase in a country's population should serve to increase its per capita income.

(T) ____ 16. Economic growth generally results from improvements in the quality of the labor force, capital accumulation, and improvements in production techniques.

(F) ____ 17. Speculative activity in an economy is generally wasteful and should therefore be suppressed.

(F) ____ 18. Not-for-profit firms and organizations are superior to for-profit enterprises because the former group has been able to suppress human greed completely.

(F) ____ 19. Governmental agencies are almost always more responsive to the demands of taxpayers than private firms are to the demands of their customers because people can vote directly at election times for what they want their government to do, whereas their relationships with private firms are limited to particular transactions.

(F) ____ 20. The right of access to sunlight should always be given to the party who was harmed.

(F) ____ 21. The right of access to sunlight should always be given to the party whose property or solar device was constructed earliest.

(T) ____ 22. Parties to a dispute over externalities generally should be allowed to attempt to resolve their differences through bargaining before courts or legislatures attempt to resolve the dispute.

(T) ____ 23. Property rights are likely to affect both the distribution of income and the allocation of resources through the price system.

(F) ____ 24. In the application on property rights to abandoned goods, the judge appears to have taken into account the incentives his ruling would create for finding and reporting other abandoned articles.

(F) ____ 25. Property rights to goods on the high seas are established in essentially the same manner as for articles on land in the United States.

(T) ____ 26. Allowing a market in organ transplants not only would increase the supply available but probably allocate that supply differently than now occurs through noncompetitive charities.

Multiple-Choice Questions

(a) ____ 1. In a market economy, the price system:
   a. guides and directs economic activity.
   b. generally results in an inefficient organization of production capacity.
   c. can be depended upon to bring about an equitable distribution of income.
   d. is not able to limit demand for goods and services to the supplies available.

(b) ____ 2. Every economy must have some mechanism for determining what goods and services are to be produced and the quantity of each because:
   a. a price system cannot be depended upon to solve the complex problems involved.
   b. the resources available are insufficient to completely satisfy all human wants.
   c. consumers are not capable of determining what they ought to have—they are likely to demand the wrong things.
   d. of the needs for national defense.

© 1988 The Dryden Press

(c) ____ 3. In a private enterprise system, production is organized by:
a. means of target production quotas set by the government.
b. persuasive advertising on the part of a few large corporations.
c. the prices of goods and resources and by profits and losses.
d. labor unions.

(d) ____ 4. Individual (family) income is determined by:
a. the quantities and qualities of the resources it owns.
b. the prices it receives for its resources.
c. the contributions it makes to the economy's output.
d. all of the above.

(d) ____ 5. Which of the following legal rules for an externalities dispute such as solar access strike you as being likely to maximize the value of the resources involved?
a. to prohibit the new activity and protect the old activity
b. to prohibit any vegetation or construction that interferes with solar access
c. to grant rights of solar access to owners of solar energy devices no matter what the consequences might be for owners of neighboring property
d. to try to assign the property right to the higher-valued use but to permit exchange and sale of the right via the price system in case someone else values it more

(a) ____ 6. Which of the following is not an externality involved in the production of a good or service?
a. It makes me unhappy to see you smoke cigarettes.
b. The noise from a nearby railroad causes dairy cows to give less milk.
c. The smell of chickens from a nearby farm nauseates the homeowners in a nice residential neighborhood and forces them to stay indoors.
d. An upstream steel mill dumps dirty effluent into a river that is used as a source of water for downstream wheat farmers.

(a) ____ 7. Private property rights typically have the following features:
a. exclusivity and full transferability
b. common pool situations
c. ownership established by first-come, first-
served
d. the right to use but not to sell

(d) ____ 8. Assume your parents could live in their present
home for as long as they live but could not sell
it and must relinquish it to the local housing
authority when they moved or died. Which of the
following probably would <u>not</u> be the result of
this bundle of property rights?
a. refusing to spend their own money to add
a new room as the family increased in size
b. refusing to make major repairs during
retirement years
c. maintaining the appearance of the front yard
to the average quality of the rest of the
houses on the block, all of which are presumed
to be private property and owner occupied
d. buying good double-bolt locks for the doors

(b) ____ 9. Over a century ago, ownership of raw land in
Western America was established under the Home-
stead Act, which gave a person 160 acres of land
provided the land was physically occupied and was
"improved" by constructing a dwelling. Which of
the following would you predict to result from
these property rights?
a. more equality in the distribution of income
b. devoting more resources to occupying land
sooner and constructing dwellings sooner than
if owners could obtain property rights by
simply purchasing land
c. maximizing the value of production from
scarce resources including land
d. inflation

(d) ____ 10. Which of the following groups probably would not gain if an organ market were allowed to develop by permitting sick persons to buy cadaver organs from next of kin?
a. persons who were next of kin to the deceased
b. persons who would die without organ replacements
c. surgeons and hospitals who did organ transplants
d. nonprofit organizations that now allocate the available organ supply

THE PURELY COMPETITIVE MARKET MODEL

Chapter Outline

Pure Competition
    The Necessary Conditions for Pure Competition
    "Pure" and "Perfect" Competition
    Pure Competition in Economic Analysis
Demand
    Demand Schedules and Demand Curves
    A Movement Along a Given Demand Curve versus a
        Change in Demand
Supply
Market Price
    Market Price Determination
    Changes in Demand and Supply
Price Elasticity of Demand
    Measurement of Price Elasticity
    Arc Elasticity
    Point Elasticity
    Elasticity and Total Money Outlays
    Factors Influencing Price Elasticity
    Cross Elasticity

Applications

Demand versus Quantity Demanded
An Empirical Supply Curve for Blood
Ticket Shortages and Scalping at the 1984 Olympics

Chapter Objectives

The concepts reviewed in this chapter are the bedrock on which microeconomic analysis is built and the student who does not understand them thoroughly may as well hang up his or her books!

Demand and supply must be understood as functional relationships between prices and quantities of an item with "other things being equal" as parameters in the demand and supply equations. Quantities must be thought of as <u>flows</u> per unit of time.

Price determination results from the interactions of buyers and sellers, not merely from the intersections of curves. Surpluses and shortages provide the motivations for movements of the price of an item toward an equilibrium level.

© 1988 The Dryden Press

Three points regarding price elasticity of demand are important. First, how is it measured? Second, what forces determine or affect it? Third, what are its implications for total spending on an item?

Suggestions for Teaching

We like to introduce concepts as they are needed to enable students to proceed with analysis. Consequently, since the principles of demand, supply, and market price determination are presented in this chapter (and in other textbooks) in a purely competitive context, we discuss explicitly the conditions underlying a purely competitive market structure. Other market structures will be introduced as they become relevant.

One major problem that students have with demand and supply concepts is that of seeing each as a functional relationship between variables—like Adam Smith they tend to see them as points instead of curves. It helps if we emphasize the difference between movements along a curve and shifts of the curve itself in response to changes in the "other things being equal." The application on demand versus quantity demanded demonstrates vividly how financial writers who are not economists confuse the two concepts—and their readers as well! The application on an empirical supply curve for blood helps relate the concepts to the real world.

We drill our students a good bit on the effects of changes in demand or supply on the equilibrium price of an item, in each case showing that at the original price level the change generates a shortage or a surplus that in turn motivates buyers or sellers to push the price up or lower it. The 1984 Olympics provides a case study in price fixing, shortages, and how people are motivated by the shortages.

The elasticity concept seems especially troublesome to many students and requires careful special treatment. We use many arithmetic, as well as geometric, examples to help them see the relationships among elasticity, price changes, and total spending on an item. Once more, the running glossary items are important!

© 1988 The Dryden Press

Problems and Questions for Discussion

1. With appropriate demand and supply diagrams, show and explain what happens to the price and quantity exchanged of a product if:
   a. demand increases and supply remains the same.
   b. demand decreases and supply remains the same.
   c. supply increases and demand remains the same.
   d. supply decreases and demand remains the same.
   e. both demand and supply increase.
   f. both demand and supply decrease.

2. Consider the demand for and supply of unskilled labor.
   a. Under purely competitive conditions, show the equilibrium wage rate and level of employment.
   b. Suppose that all labor in this market is unionized and succeeds in obtaining an increase in wage rates. Under what circumstances will the <u>total wage bill</u>:
      (1) increase?
      (2) decrease?
      (3) remain constant?
   c. What happens to the level of employment in (b)?

3. Draw a demand curve that is convex toward the origin of the diagram. Locate a point at random and determine whether demand is price elastic, inelastic, or of unitary elasticity at the point. How many different geometric ratios can you find to measure price elasticity at the point?

4. For each of the following goods, indicate whether demand is likely to be rather price elastic or rather price inelastic. Explain why in each case.
   a. beer
   b. Schlitz beer
   c. salt
   d. beige slacks
   e. Wonder bread
   f. gasoline

5. Suppose the price of gasoline is $1.50 per gallon and that 1,000,000 gallons per day are consumed at that price. How much of a price increase would be necessary to reduce consumption to 900,000 gallons per day if the average elasticity of demand for the price increase is .4?

© 1988 The Dryden Press

6. For product X, given the demand function, p = 30 - 2x/3, and the supply function, p = 3 + x/3:
   a. Determine the equilibrium price and quantity exchanged.
   b. Calculate the price elasticity of demand at the equilibrium point.
   c. If the price of X is set at $10, calculate the surplus or shortage.
   d. Indicate the direction of change in total spending on X if the price of X is changed from the equilibrium level to $14.
   e. According to (d), is demand price elastic? Why or why not?

7. Did it strike you as odd that some of the college students in the article about blood donations were willing to give away their blood but not to sell it? Have you previously assumed that people always behave in strict accordance with pecuniary rewards? Did you believe that economists make that assumption? Are you surprised to learn that economics does allow for charitable or nonselfish behavior, for the very reason that we often see such behavior in the real world and that any sensible theory of human behavior must allow for such conduct?

8. Do you think that the nations that boycotted the 1984 Olympic Games should get a refund on the tickets that they had previously ordered and paid for? Giving a refund makes the tickets available for sale or distribution to other persons. What would you predict that the Olympic Committee decides about this issue?

9. An Olympics "patron" who paid $25,000 for two premium tickets to each Games day in effect donated money to buy seats for 50 youths, handicapped people, or senior citizens who could not otherwise have afforded to attend the Games. How does this differ from pricing of goods and services in for-profit markets? Do people who buy Cadillacs thereby provide bus transportation for low-income urban dwellers? Why is charity of the Olympics kind more common in nonprofit organizations?

© 1988 The Dryden Press

10. In 1985, the U.S. Supreme Court struck down a New Hampshire law requiring that attorneys be residents for a specified period to practice law there regularly. Some 40 states impose residency requirements to take the state's bar examination. The Court said that it was unconstitutional for a state to grant residents privileges or immunities superior to those of nonresidents. Residency rules required a big law firm that did not employ residents of a state to hire local firms to act as "local counsel" for its clients. (Stephen Wermiel, "States' Residency Rules for Lawyers Found Unconstitutional by Top Court," The Wall Street Journal, March 5, 1985.)
    a. Who benefits and who loses from the Supreme Court's ruling? Explain.
    b. What would you predict states like New Hampshire will do in the wake of this ruling?

11. In 1985, a chain of specialty food stores in the Los Angeles area advertised a close-out sale on "bonus" bottles of a national brand of salad dressing. Each bonus bottle contained 25 percent more than the standard bottle. The standard bottle sold for $1.21 but the bonus bottle sold for only $.69 including a coupon worth $.10 off the purchase price of a standard bottle. What would you expect to be the reason behind this exceptional offer?

12. The bus fare in Los Angeles County was raised in July 1985 from $.50 per trip to $.85, the first increase in three years. The decline in ridership was estimated at 5 to 9%. "On balance," a bus system official said, "what it tells us is that the demand for transit in this urban area is greater than we expected." (Victor Merina, "Fare Hike Cuts RTD Ridership Less Than 10%," Los Angeles Times, July 12, 1985.)
    a. Calculate the price elasticity of demand using the assumption that the decline in quantity demanded was 7%.
    b. Evaluate the economics of the official's comment.

Solutions to Problems and Questions for Discussion

1. a. Both increase.
   b. Both decrease.
   c. Price decreases and quantity increases.
   d. Price increases and quantity decreases.
   e. Quantity increases. Price may increase or decrease, depending on whether the demand curve shifts more or less to the right than does the supply curve.
   f. Quantity decreases. Price may increase or decrease, depending on whether the demand curve shifts less or more to the left than does the supply curve.

2. a. These occur at the intersection point of the demand and supply curves—the wage level at which employers demand the same quantity that desires employment.
   b. (1) If elasticity of demand is less than one.
      (2) If elasticity of demand is greater than one.
      (3) If elasticity of demand is equal to one.
   c. Decreases.

3.

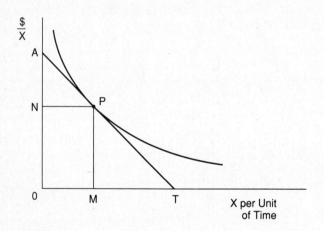

Depends on the ratio of MT/OM. In the above case $\varepsilon > 1$. MT/OM = PT/AP = ON/NA.

4. a. Inelastic. Good substitutes are not available.
   b. Elastic. Other brands are good substitutes.
   c. Inelastic. No good substitutes. Small proportion of consumers' incomes spent on it.
   d. Elastic. Good substitutes are available.
   e. Elastic. Other brands are good substitutes.
   f. Inelastic. No good substitutes.

5. $0.375. Solve: $.4 = 1/10 \times 1.5/x$.

6. a. Solving the two equations simultaneously, $p = 12$; $x = 27$.
   b. Using the demand equation and increasing price by 1 unit, elasticity $= .667$.
   c. Solving both equations for $p = 10$, the shortage is 9 units.
   d. TR increases.
   e. Demand is inelastic. Percentage change in x is less than percentage change in p.

7. It did not strike us as odd. We do not assume that people are motivated by money only, and few economists make such assumptions. We are not surprised to see economics account for charitable behavior, gifts between family members and friends, and other nonmarket "transactions."

8. We would refund their money for all tickets that were subsequently resold. It does not seem to us to be fair to collect money for the same ticket twice. We would predict that the committee returned the money. After all, someday the tables might be turned again with the United States being the boycotter.

9. It differs. This pricing tactic is sometimes called a tie-in, a package deal, or bundling. In this case, its purpose is cross-subsidization: to transfer resources from high-income to low-income groups. It is rare in the unregulated private sector but common among nonprofit organizations. Often such organizations are created in the first place to stimulate such transfers, and their "owners" usually do not lose income if profits are not maximized. (Such tie-ins also may make all or some of the price of the tickets tax deductible.)

10. a. Local attorneys lose; outside attorneys gain. Local consumers gain by having more attorneys to choose from.
    b. They might require all attorneys to take an examination on local law, for which local attorneys have an advantage.

11. The advertisement acknowledged that the bonus bottle gave the appearance of being smaller than the standard bottle rather than 25 percent larger. Apparently some customers were too hurried to read labels, so it behooves manufacturers to choose package sizes and shapes to convey information accurately. The chain wanted to get the misleading "bonus" bottles off the market.

12. a. Using equation 3.3, the percentage change in quantity demanded is 7 and the percentage change in price is 70. Elasticity is 0.1.
    b. The official thinks that an inelastic demand is the same as a "greater" demand—the old story of confusing a movement along a demand curve with a shift.

True-False Questions

(F) ____ 1. Pure competition is most likely to occur in markets where sellers engage in extreme rivalry and constantly try to take each other's market shares.

(T) ____ 2. The concept of mobility implies that buyers can buy from any seller they choose and sellers can sell to any buyer they choose.

(T) ____ 3. A demand schedule or curve for a product shows the quantities per unit of time that all buyers in the market would take at all alternative prices.

(T) ____ 4. The quantities shown by a demand schedule or a supply schedule are properly thought of as <u>rates</u> of purchase or sale.

(F) ____ 5. An improvement in the techniques of producing a good will cause a movement to the right along its supply schedule.

(F) ____ 6. An increase in demand for a product, given supply, will increase the price but usually will not affect the quantity exchanged.

(T) ____ 7. A decrease in the supply of a product, given demand, will increase its price and decrease the quantity exchanged.

(T) _____ 8. If the major trading countries of the world get together and establish a minimum price for crude oil that is higher than the world equilibrium price, the result will be a surplus of oil.

(F) _____ 9. Price elasticity of demand is measured by the slope of the demand curve.

(T) _____ 10. Milk producers, dissatisfied with the price they receive for their products, may find that if they destroy a part of the supplies they produce, the price received will be higher but their collective total receipts will be lower.

(F) _____ 11. If consumers will purchase 200 units per day of a product at $1.00 per unit, and at $0.90 they will purchase 240 units, demand is inelastic for the price change.

(F) _____ 12. A linear demand curve has a constant price elasticity throughout its length.

(T) _____ 13. Usually the most important factor causing demand for a product to be elastic is the availability of substitutes for the product.

(T) _____ 14. A demand curve that is a rectangular hyperbola has an elasticity of minus one at all price levels.

(F) _____ 15. High positive cross elasticities of demand among products indicate that they are complements to each other.

(F) _____ 16. An arc elasticity measurement is usually more accurate than a point elasticity measurement.

(F) _____ 17. At the equilibrium price for a product, elasticity of demand is unitary.

(F) _____ 18. A seller can usually increase total receipts by increasing the price of the product.

(T) _____ 19. For a linear demand curve, total receipts from sale of a product are maximum at the price at which elasticity equals one.

(F) _____ 20. Altruistic or charitable behavior is outside the scope of economics and economic theorizing.

(T) ____ 21. The elasticity of market supply will tend to increase over the long run as producers have more time to enter the market in response to a higher price.

(T) ____ 22. The elasticity of demand for a product is usually greater the longer the period of time allowed when a price change occurs, since it allows for more consumers to adapt to the price change.

(F) ____ 23. A rise in the price of coffee will reduce the demand for coffee.

(T) ____ 24. A rise in the price of coffee will reduce the demand for sugar.

(T) ____ 25. The allocation of Olympics tickets by the committee supports the theory that nonprofit organizations have different incentives structures than for-profit organizations.

(F) ____ 26. The Olympics Committee could have captured additional revenues if it had not underpriced seats of average quality.

Multiple-Choice Questions

(d) ____ 1. Which of the following is <u>not</u> a requisite for pure competition?
   a. smallness of any individual seller and any individual buyer of the product
   b. an absence of artificial restraints on price movements
   c. mobility of goods and services and of resources
   d. rivalry among the sellers of the product

(c) ____ 2. Pure competition:
   a. does not exist in product markets in the United States.
   b. is too unrealistic to be of value in economic analysis.
   c. is the economic counterpart of frictionless mechanics in physics.
   d. all of the above

© 1988 The Dryden Press

(b) ____ 3. Market demand for a product or service refers to:
   a. the quantities that will be placed on the market at alternative prices, other things being equal.
   b. the rates at which consumers will be willing to purchase the product at alternative prices, other things being equal.
   c. the quantity that consumers will take at the prevailing price, other things being equal.
   d. the rates at which consumers will be willing to purchase the product at alternative income levels, other things being equal.

(b) ____ 4. A change in demand:
   a. is defined as a movement from one point to another on a given demand curve.
   b. is defined as a shift in an entire demand curve.
   c. usually results from a change in supply.
   d. both (b) and (c) above

(a) ____ 5. An increase in both demand and supply will:
   a. increase quantity exchanged but may or may not change the price of a product.
   b. increase the price of a product but may or may not change the quantity exchanged.
   c. decrease both the price and the quantity exchanged of the product.
   d. decrease the quantity exchanged and increase the price.

(d) ____ 6. Which of the following will not cause a shift in the supply curve for some product?
   a. a change in the technology that is best for producing it
   b. a reduction in the cost of an input that is important for its production
   c. an environmental control that makes its production more expensive for every level of output
   d. a change in the elasticity of supply because of a price change

(d) ____ 7. Which of the following will <u>not</u> cause a shift in the demand curve for a product?
   a. a change in consumers' preferences for the good
   b. a change in consumers' money incomes
   c. a change in the prices of closely related goods
   d. a change in the elasticity of demand resulting from a price change

(c) ____ 8. Which of the following would <u>not</u> cause a change in demand for coffee?
   a. an increase in the price of tea
   b. an increase in consumers' incomes
   c. an increase in the supply of coffee
   d. publication of strong evidence that coffee consumption increases the incidence of heart disease

(d) ____ 9. Letting x represent the quantity per unit of time of a product and P represent its price, which of the following measures the price elasticity of demand?

   a. $\Delta x / \Delta P$

   b. $\dfrac{\Delta x}{x} \div \Delta P$

   c. $\dfrac{\Delta P}{P} \div \dfrac{\Delta x}{x}$

   d. $\dfrac{\Delta x}{\Delta P} \times \dfrac{P}{x}$

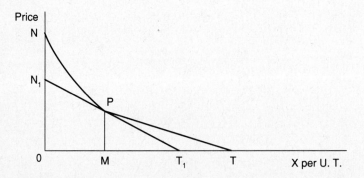

(b) ____ 10. In the preceding diagram in which NT represents a demand curve, the price elasticity of demand at point P is measured by:
   a. ON_1/OT_1.
   b. MT_1/OM.
   c. MT/OM.
   d. PT/PN.

(d) ____ 11. An increase in the prices of the resources necessary to produce a product will cause:
   a. the supply curve to shift upward.
   b. a decrease in supply.
   c. a movement to the left along the supply curve.
   d. both (a) and (b) above.

(c) ____ 12. If the price elasticity of demand for a product is greater than one:
   a. it will pay suppliers to restrict supply.
   b. suppliers can increase their receipts by securing a price floor that lies above the equilibrium level.
   c. suppliers can increase their total receipts if they can devise technology that will increase supply.
   d. suppliers can increase their total receipts by securing a price ceiling that is below the equilibrium level.

(a) ____ 13. On a linear demand curve, price elasticity is:
   a. greater than one on the upper half of the curve and less than one on the lower half of the curve.
   b. less than one on the upper half of the curve and greater than one on the lower half of the curve.
   c. greatest at the midpoint of the curve.
   d. equal to one at all points on the curve.

(d) ____ 14. Total receipts of sellers of a product are maximum at that point on a demand curve where price elasticity is:
   a. greatest.
   b. least.
   c. increasing.
   d. unitary.

(b) ____ 15. Which of the following products is likely to have an elastic demand?
   a. tobacco
   b. Ford Tauruses
   c. salt
   d. beer

(a) ____ 16. If demand for a product is inelastic, an increase in its price will:
   a. reduce the quantity taken and increase the total expenditures for it.
   b. increase the quantity taken and increase the total expenditures for it.
   c. reduce the quantity taken and decrease the total expenditures for it.
   d. reduce the quantity taken and leave the total expenditures for it unchanged.

(c) ____ 17. Which of the following revisions to the title of the article from The Wall Street Journal about the prices of beef and pork uses economic definitions correctly?
   a. "Strong Pork Demand, Due to Low Beef Prices, May Indicate Permanent Shift from Beef"
   b. "Strong Pork Demand, Due to Low Pork Prices, May Indicate Permanent Shift from Beef"
   c. "Strong Quantity of Pork Demanded, Due to Low Pork Prices, May Indicate Permanent Shift from Beef"
   d. "Strong Pork Demand, Due to High Beef Prices, May Indicate Permanent Shift to Beef"

(c) ____ 18. The application on blood supply demonstrated that the students in the sample group were motivated to donate:
   a. only by money.
   b. only by altruism.
   c. generally by money, although not at very low prices.
   d. generally by money, although not at very high prices.

(c) ____ 19. Which of the following groups would not benefit from ticket scalping?
   a. buyers of tickets
   b. sellers of tickets
   c. the Olympics Committee
   d. people who decide late that they want to see the event

(b) ____ 20. Which of the following is <u>not</u> a valid observation about the way the Olympics tickets were sold and distributed?

a. The best seats were underpriced.

b. All the ticket speculators lost money.

c. Demand for tickets during the few weeks just before the Olympics turned out to be very difficult to predict.

d. Ticket sales were not organized to maximize convenience for consumers.

CHAPTER 4

POLICY APPLICATIONS OF THE MODEL

Chapter Outline

Agricultural Price Supports
Oil and Gasoline Price Ceilings
    Consequences of Price Ceilings
    Consequences of Price Decontrol
Economic Effects of an Excise Tax
"Pricing" M.B.A. Classes

Chapter Objectives

There is no new theory in this chapter. It has two objectives.
The first is to whet students' appetites for further study of
microeconomics by applying what they have learned to interesting
current issues and problems. The second is to demonstrate that
simple demand-supply theory can tell us much about the effects
of present-day actual and proposed economic policies.

Suggestions for Teaching

The issues we have chosen to discuss are farm price supports,
energy price controls, the incidence of excise taxes, and the use
of play money to allocate spaces in popular M.B.A. classes rather
than the arbitrary techniques commonly used at most institutions.
There is nothing sacred about this set. Any instructor should
feel free to deviate from them, presenting whatever alternative
applications he or she thinks will do the job. We believe that
this is an important point in the intermediate course to try hard
to spark student interest—while the theory is still simple and
before getting into the more complex intricacies of microeconomics beginning with Chapter 5.

Problems and Questions for Discussion

1. With demand-supply analysis, examine the implications of
   restricting or reducing the supply of milk through quotas
   placed by law on the amount that milk producers can market.
   What happens to the price? the quantity sold? total receipts of all producers? total receipts of individual
   producers? the welfare of the general public?

© 1988 The Dryden Press

2. Experience with price support programs in agriculture has convinced many economists that these programs are unwise. The price support yields an excess supply which causes the government to restrict acreage. That encourages farmers to cultivate other acres more intensively, leading the government to put quotas on production, which farmers then attempt to circumvent through a seemingly never-ending series of actions to keep "one step ahead" of the regulators. Go to your library and read up on the history of governmental attempts to support the prices of just one commodity, such as sugar beets or soybeans or some other crop that is grown in your state. Does your research tend to support the skepticism of economists?

3. The U.S. government since 1949 has supported the price of honey and made low-interest loans to beekeepers. Would it surprise you to learn that the government buys about half the nation's output of honey? What would be your best guess regarding: (a) the level of the price support relative to the cost of producing honey in the United States; (b) the level of the price support relative to the foreign price of honey; (c) the growth in honey imports by the United States since the program came about; (d) the growth in the number of beekeepers in the United States since the program began?

4. What would be the effect of each of the following changes in the PIK program on the supply curve of wheat in Figure 4.1 in the text?
   a. fewer acres planted but a greater-than-proportional increase in per acre yield owing to extra use of fertilizer
   b. removing only the least productive acres from plantings
   c. errors by government employees in the U.S. Department of Agriculture in determining the number of acres of wheat that were eligible for planting

5. Consumers' demand for gasoline became more elastic during the 1970s. What probable effects would this have had on the enthusiasm of oil companies for a much talked about special per gallon tax on gasoline favored by many politicians?

6. Do you favor a government-imposed maximum price for natural gas in the United States, assuming that the price would be set below the market price that would otherwise prevail? What would be the effects on production? consumption? the relation between the amount produced and the amount demanded?

7. Would price ceilings on gasoline assure that the poor would be better off than they would be without them?

8. Would you prefer that unit sales taxes be added to the price of a product and paid by buyers or that they be included in the price and be absorbed by sellers? Explain your reasoning.

9. Draw the necessary diagrams to demonstrate the point that, generally, buyers bear a greater proportion of an excise tax the less elastic the demand curve or the more elastic the supply curve in the neighborhood of the price change.

10. Would you favor a policy of paying market-clearing wages to jurors just as we do for physicians or college professors? Presumably individuals who were professional jurors would attempt to establish reputations for fairness and conscientiousness that courts would be willing to pay more for. Perhaps firms such as Sears would offer jury services just as they offer house-painting services that many people trust and buy. Do you think that there would be "better" incentives for jurors to do a higher-quality job under a price-system approach than under the conscription approach discussed in the text?

11. Droughts are not confined to the "Sun Belt." In 1981, hundreds of communities in New England and the mid-Atlantic states rationed water, and New York City fined users who did not cut consumption. ("Water Shortage in the Northeastern States Clouds Business Prospects for the Region," The Wall Street Journal, February 25, 1981.)
   a. Why are water prices usually held constant during shortages? (Is water in your community supplied by a private firm, a government-regulated firm, or a public agency? Ask how prices are determined and what would be required to raise them.)
   b. Water-rationing officials often define car washing and lawn watering to be "nonessential" uses. What would be "essential uses" if water were rationed by the price system?
   c. Some communities charge users a fixed monthly fee regardless of the amount of water used. Can water be rationed by the price system without water meters?

© 1988 The Dryden Press

12. Finding an apartment in Santa Monica, a beach community with rents about two-thirds those of adjacent Los Angeles, has been likened to a treasure hunt. As many as 400 people inquire about each vacancy, and tenants rarely move. (Alan Citron, "Santa Monica—Only the Elite Need Apply," Los Angeles Times, April 8, 1984; Dave Larsen, "Quest for Shelter Where the Mountains Meet No-Vacancies-by-the-Sea," Los Angeles Times, May 4, 1986.)
    a. Some tenants compete for apartments by raising owners' incomes but without paying rents above the legal ceiling. How?
    b. Santa Monica does not allow rents to be raised to market-clearing levels when vacancies occur. Compared to the pre-control tenant population, average tenant income increased, the percentage of tenants in the 18 to 20 and the 45 to 54 age groups fell, and couples in their 20s and 30s were thought by apartment owners to be ideal tenants. Why?
    c. Santa Monica has a "black market" where brokers are paid finders' fees by prospective tenants ranging from $300 to $3,000. Who would collect these payments absent rent controls?
    d. How much of each dollar in time and gasoline costs spent searching for a rent-controlled apartment would the renter have been willing to spend in higher rents if rent controls were removed? How much of each dollar in legal fees and lobbying costs to eliminate controls would apartment owners have been willing to spend in maintenance, renovation, and new construction?

13. Many people seem to believe that the enactment and enforcement of minimum housing standards in a given city will be in the best interests of slum dwellers. What effects will the adoption of such standards have on the quality, quantity, and price of available housing?

14. Price supports have induced the federal government to buy and store some 2.9 billion pounds of dairy products—enough milk and cheese to cover 65 football fields with piles 17 feet high or to fill a freight train stretching from New York City to Toledo, says Jeffrey Birnbaum (in "Congress at a Cattle Crossing," The Wall Street Journal, June 14, 1983). Using demand and supply diagrams, analyze each of the following proposals:
    a. To pay dairy farmers not to milk as many cows, using a fund created by assessing them $.50 per 100 pounds sold
    b. To lower price supports gradually, accepting the fact that some dairies will not survive

© 1988 The Dryden Press

Solutions to Problems and Questions for Discussion

1. The market supply curve becomes vertical at the maximum amount that milk producers can sell. The price rises and the quantity sold declines. Total receipts of all producers increase (decrease) if demand is inelastic (elastic). What happens to individual producers depends on how the reduction in output is apportioned among them. The public loses welfare from buying smaller amounts and by paying higher prices for them.

2. Subjecting a commodity to price supports that are effective and above market-clearing levels usually will yield one or more of these consequences. If you find one that does not appear to fit the pattern, check to see what the market-clearing price was before the minimum price was instituted or whether it appears that the law is being effectively enforced.

3. a. By law the price support level is indexed to inflation and exceeded average production cost by about 50 percent in 1982.
   b. Foreign prices were about 20 percent less in 1982.
   c. Foreign production and U.S. imports of honey were rising rapidly in 1982, due also to the strong dollar.
   d. The number of U.S. beekeepers has remained level for a decade at fewer than 300, but the number of colonies has declined about 20 percent to 4 million. The U.S. loan program for honey, like that for wheat, keeps up the price and generates huge government stockpiles—100 million pounds worth in 1982. Honey is so expensive relative to other sweeteners and imports are growing so much that the long-run outlook for the industry is unclear. (Michael A. Hiltzik, "Honey Price: Sweet Deal or a Sting," Los Angeles Times, December 27, 1982.)

4. a. Supply would shift to the right.
   b. Supply would shift to the left, but by less than would occur if the acres that were removed from production were of average productivity.
   c. Supply would shift to the left if the number of acres of average productivity that were planted declines. The shift would be relatively great if the government erred on the side of allowing fewer acres to be planted than were eligible, and it would be relatively small if the government erred on the side of allowing more acres to be planted than were eligible. We would expect the U.S.D.A. more often to err on the side of allowing more acres to be planted, which is what happened.

5. Oil companies would be less enthusiastic for a per gallon
    tax on gasoline as the price elasticity of demand for gas-
    oline increase. Demand elasticity will rise as consumers
    find more substitutes for gasoline, such as smaller cars,
    shorter commutes, and more housing insulation. As the sup-
    ply curve in text Figure 4.3 shifts upward by the amount
    of the per gallon tax, the price increase to consumers is
    smaller the greater the elasticity of demand. The smaller
    the proportion of the price increase that consumers bear,
    the greater the tax incidence that falls on sellers. (A
    perfectly elastic demand curve would cause 100 percent of
    the incidence to fall on sellers.)

6. We would oppose controls on the price of natural gas. Pro-
    duction would decline. The amount consumed would decline
    because it cannot exceed the amount produced. The amount
    that consumers demand, however, would increase, and the dif-
    ference between the amount demanded and the amount produced
    at the controlled price would determine the extent of the
    shortage.

7. It depends on how much gasoline is supplied after controls
    are imposed and how it is rationed. If rationed by first-
    come, first-served, the advantage goes to people who arrive
    early. People with low incomes find waiting less expen-
    sive than those with high incomes, so rationing by waiting
    might benefit the poor. Allocating each family coupons
    to buy a fixed amount of gasoline each month at controlled
    prices would benefit the poor even more if they could sell
    them to higher-income persons. Even so, the poor would be
    worse off if the amount of gasoline they obtained at con-
    trolled prices was less than the amount they would have
    preferred to buy at market-clearing prices.

8. The argument accompanying text Figure 4.3 suggests that
    the incidence of a given tax will be the same whether it is
    collected from sellers or buyers.

9. Draw a supply-and-demand diagram and shift the supply curve
    upward by the amount of the unit tax. If the demand curve
    is vertical (perfectly inelastic), the price increase equals
    the tax, so 100 percent of the tax's incidence is borne by
    consumers. If the demand curve is horizontal (perfectly
    elastic), the price increase is zero, so 100 percent of the
    tax's incidence is borne by sellers.

10. We would favor it, and we would expect that professional
    jurors would have stronger incentives for rendering better
    decisions if their future income depended on it.

11. a. Water rates are usually regulated by public agencies and can not be adjusted quickly or easily. Usually public hearings and legal proceedings are required. Some water suppliers are governmental agencies, are sensitive to charges of gouging, and managers cannot personally benefit from higher prices.
    b. What are "essential uses" under the price system are those uses that consumers are willing to purchase water for at equilibrium prices.
    c. We doubt it.

12. a. They offer to pay for repairs or redecoration that stay with the apartment—paint, draperies, fixtures, or carpets.
    b. Landlords hope they will be allowed eventually to raise rents to market-clearing levels when vacancies occur. Therefore, they want young, higher-income tenants who will want to buy homes before long.
    c. The owners would.
    d. All the search costs could have been paid in rents, and all the legal costs could have been paid in improvements.

13. Higher standards raise the quality and the cost of housing and therefore shift supply to the left. Landlords may abandon units that are not worth improving, and higher construction costs may cause the private sector to reduce future supply. Higher costs mean higher rents but a smaller quantity demanded of the higher-quality units. Thus, some tenants will shift to inferior but less expensive housing in other communities. Improving the lot of some tenants may occur at the cost of making others worse off.

14. a. Taxing the amount of milk produced will push the supply of milk to the left, as will paying dairies to reduce herds.
    b. This step is illustrated in text Figure 4.1. As the quantity supplied declines, some dairies will exit the industry.

True-False Questions

(F) _____ 1. A support-price for an item that is below the equilibrium price will cause a surplus.

(F) _____ 2. Farm price supports have not caused increases in the income of farmers because the price elasticity of demand for farm products has generally been less than one.

© 1988 The Dryden Press

(T) _____ 3. Effective price supports can be expected generally to cause overproduction of the items supported.

(F) _____ 4. Raising the level of the federal minimum wage is an excellent means of combatting unemployment.

(F) _____ 5. If the wage rates of part-time student employees on the campus at State University were increased substantially, there should be no substantial decrease in the number of students employed.

(T) _____ 6. Rent controls are likely to cause the quantity of housing available to the poor to be less than it would be in the absence of such controls.

(F) _____ 7. If the United States government limits the imports of crude oil from abroad, domestic producers will be encouraged to increase their outputs and the price is likely to fall.

(T) _____ 8. The imposition of an excise tax on a product can be viewed either as shifting the demand curve downward by the amount of the tax or the supply curve upward by the amount of the tax.

(T) _____ 9. With regard to the incidence of an excise tax on sellers and buyers, it makes no difference whether the tax is collected from buyers or sellers.

(T) _____ 10. Given the supply curve, the more elastic the demand curve when an excise tax is imposed, the greater will be the incidence of the tax on the seller.

(F) _____ 11. Price controls on gasoline is a fairer way to allocate scarce supplies (as opposed to letting prices alone clear the market) because every buyer has an equal chance of arriving early in the day to obtain a favorable position in the queue.

(F) _____ 12. Farm bankruptcies in the 1980s were caused by price supports and the surpluses they engendered.

(F) _____ 13. All U.S. agriculture, including growers who sell at roadside stands, benefits from crop subsidies.

(T) _____ 14. Many M.B.A. students at the University of Chicago benefited from using play money to allocate popular classes rather than a more traditional system of class registration, although it is not possible to say that every student was better off.

(T) _____ 15. Rationing student enrollments in popular classes alphabetically or by first-come, first-served is necessary at most colleges because rationing by money or play money rationing is not utilized.

(F) _____ 16. At most colleges and universities the most important services to students are rationed by prices and the least important services are rationed by waiting or some other nonprice method.

Multiple-Choice Questions

(d) _____ 1. A price floor placed by the federal government under all crude oil sold in the United States would, if effective, result in:
    a. greater domestic production than would occur without it and, therefore, greater consumption of petroleum products.
    b. smaller domestic production than would occur without it and, therefore, increased conservation of U.S. oil reserves.
    c. increased imports and smaller domestic output.
    d. surpluses of crude oil.

(c) _____ 2. If the Social Security payroll tax were levied entirely on employers:
    a. employers would pass the entire tax on to either workers or consumers.
    b. workers would benefit.
    c. the incidence of the tax on workers and employers would not be changed.
    d. payroll tax collections would increase.

(b) ____ 3. Which of the following is <u>not</u> correct with regard to effective price controls on a product accompanied by first-come, first-served policies on the part of sellers?
   a. Consumers who buy the product pay a lower money price than would be the case without the controls.
   b. The economic cost to consumers cannot exceed the controlled price of the product.
   c. It causes economic wastes in terms of labor power used in searching and queuing to obtain the product.
   d. It prevents available supplies of the product from being placed in their most valuable uses.

(b) ____ 4. Ordinarily an increase in the level of the minimum wage would be expected to:
   a. increase the total wages paid to the group of workers who formerly received less than the new wage level.
   b. reduce employment.
   c. have no effects on the employment level.
   d. decrease the total wages paid to the group of workers who formerly received less than the new wage level.

(a) ____ 5. If the price of any given agricultural product should be supported, the total cost to the government—that is, total government outlays—required to maintain the price at a given support level will be smaller under a subsidy plan than under a storage and loan plan (government purchase of surpluses at the support price level) if:
   a. demand for the product is elastic.
   b. demand for the product is inelastic.
   c. demand for the product has unitary elasticity.
   d. supply is inelastic.

(c) ____ 6. If a law were passed requiring that all university and college teachers must have Ph.D. degrees:
   a. the total salary bill of all colleges and universities together would rise.
   b. the total salary bill of all colleges and universities together would fall.
   c. the average salary of employed university professors would rise.
   d. both (a) and (c)

(c) ____ 7. Effective price controls (ceilings) for a product will insure that:
   a. poor people will be able to obtain greater quantities of it than before.
   b. the welfare of poor people will be increased.
   c. shortages will occur.
   d. both (a) and (b)

(a) ____ 8. A national health insurance program would be expected to cause:
   a. an increase in demand for health services and a rise in their prices.
   b. an increase in supply of health services and a decrease in their prices.
   c. an increase in both demand and supply with an indeterminate effect on prices.
   d. no essential change in either demand or supply.

(b) ____ 9. The effects of implementing a housing code that increases substantially the minimum housing standards permitted in a city are:
   a. better housing for all of the poor people of the city who had been living in substandard housing.
   b. a decrease in supply and an increase in price of the housing available to the poor.
   c. a shortage of housing.
   d. a surplus of housing.

(d) ____ 10. An excise tax on gasoline will raise the price of gasoline to consumers by an amount:
   a. equal to the tax if demand is inelastic but elasticity is greater than zero.
   b. equal to the tax if demand is elastic but elasticity is less than infinity.
   c. less than the tax if supply has an elasticity of zero.
   d. less than the tax if the elasticities of demand and supply are less than infinity but greater than zero.

(a) ____ 11. During the 1970s debate over oil price decontrol, the advocates of decontrol were implicitly
assuming that:
a. the demand and supply of oil were relatively
elastic.
b. the demand was relatively elastic but the
supply inelastic.
c. the demand was relatively inelastic but the
supply elastic.
d. none of the above

(c) ____ 12. During the 1970s debate over oil price decontrol,
the opponents of decontrol were implicitly assuming that:
a. the demand for oil was relatively inelastic
but the supply was elastic.
b. the demand was relatively elastic but the
supply was inelastic.
c. the demand and supply were both relatively
inelastic.
d. none of the above

(e) ____ 13. Price controls can be expected to produce which of
the following types of behavior among either consumers or producers or government officials?
a. disputes and conflicts among consumers as
to who gets the goods at the controlled price
b. tendencies among producers to produce less
output than formerly
c. tendencies among both consumers and producers
to engage in black markets
d. increased discretionary power among government
officials
e. all of the above

(a) ____ 14. The long-run solution to the U.S. farm problem
requires:
a. letting the price system operate to encourage
farmers to leave farming for other jobs.
b. cutting each subsidy program by 10 percent.
c. idling fewer acres of farmland.
d. idling more acres of farmland.

© 1988 The Dryden Press

(b) ____ 15. Which of the following groups of students is likely to benefit least from using play money to ration popular courses?
 a. students who are willing to bid the most
 b. students who are willing to bid the most but would have gotten most of their preferred classes under the previous rationing system
 c. first-year students
 d. seniors

(d) ____ 16. Which of the following is not a typical method used by colleges and universities for rationing entry to popular classes?
 a. "needs" of students for their major or to graduate
 b. first-come, first-served
 c. the alphabet
 d. dollar contributions to the student scholar-ship fund

PART TWO

THE UNDERPINNINGS OF DEMAND

In Part Two we begin the systematic development of microeconomic
principles at the intermediate level. Since the ultimate goal
of economic activity is the satisfaction of human wants, it is
logical to begin with the theory of demand. The modern theory of
demand, based on indifference curve analysis, is contained in
Chapters 5 and 6. Chapter 7 on utility analysis is in many ways
redundant and can be omitted without loss of continuity. We
include it as a special case of the more general theory of demand
partly as a matter of historical interest but mainly because
almost every journal article on demand theory makes reference to
it. We believe the neophyte's tool kit needs it.

The transition from demand as originated by consumers to demand
as viewed by sellers is made in Chapter 8.

CHAPTER 5

THE MODERN THEORY OF CONSUMER CHOICE

Chapter Outline

The Consumer's Preferences
   The Consumer's Indifference Map
   Indifference Curve Characteristics
   Complementary and Substitute Relationships
Constraints on the Consumer
   The Budget Line
   Shifts in the Budget Line
Maximization of Consumer Satisfaction
Price Index Numbers
   The Laspeyres Price Index
   The Paasche Price Index

Applications

Index Numbers in Practice
The Hazards of Artificial Sweeteners
Income in Kind versus Income in Cash

Chapter Objectives

The theory of choice that underlies a large part of economic
analysis is developed in this chapter. First, we examine the
decision-maker's preference structure or preference function
—what the decision-maker would like to do if unconstrained.
Second, the constraints on a consumer's behavior and how the
consumer responds to those constraints are brought into the
picture. Obviously we are presenting a constrained maximum
problem and a simplified solution to it.

Some of the strengths and weaknesses of measuring general
price level changes with price index numbers are demonstrated
by applying the theory of choice to their construction and
an evaluation of them.

Suggestions for Teaching

Our experience indicates that several pitfalls await students
learning indifference techniques. Some are confused about what
the axes of an indifference curve diagram measure. We find it
necessary to drill them on the fact that each axis measures

© 1988 The Dryden Press

physical quantities of a good or service—that the Y-axis <u>does</u> <u>not</u> measure price. Later on we show them that one axis, say the X-axis, can measure quantities of one product and the other axis can measure quantities of all other products using dollar's worths as a quantity common denominator. Some have difficulty grasping the independence of budget lines from the indifference map. The application on the hazards of artificial sweeteners is useful in separating the forces that affect the indifference map from those that affect the budget line.

The measurement problem arises again as we consider budget lines. Again, drill is needed on what happens to budget lines as the price of one product changes, as the prices of both products change, and as the consumer's income changes. Some students, accustomed to measuring the price of a good on the vertical axis of a demand diagram, find it particularly diffi- cult to visualize the slope of the budget line as a measure of the relative prices of the two goods. The income in kind versus income in cash application provides excellent drill on the determinants of a budget line.

Given the indifference map and the budget of the consumer, there is little difficulty in finding the satisfaction maximiz- ing combination of products—the tangency point provides an intuitively correct answer. The problem students have is in understanding <u>why</u> this answer is correct. We find it helpful to compare various points of <u>intersection</u> between indifference curves and the budget line with the <u>tangency</u> point in terms of the consumer's MRS_{xy} and the tradeoffs the market will permit.

The application on index numbers in practice gives meaning and direction to what otherwise might be the esoteric theory of Laspeyres and Paasche price index numbers. We use it to show, among other things, how much in the economy rides on founda- tions that are somewhat shaky.

Most of our students find intermediate price theory one of the hardest undergraduate courses they take. Learning becomes much more palatable when we show them constantly how theory applies to issues and problems of the day. We think the applications here are very helpful in this respect, but the good instructor will always be on the lookout for additional ones.

Don't forget the glossary items.

© 1988 The Dryden Press

Problems and Questions for Discussion

1. Using food (F) and clothes (C) as goods consumed, draw a representative set of indifference curves for a consumer, placing units of F on the vertical axis and units of C on the horizontal axis.

   a. Why did you draw them downward sloping to the right? If the curves were to turn upward as we consider larger and larger quantities of C, what would the upward slopes mean?

   b. Why are your curves nonintersecting?

   c. Locate two points close together on one of the curves. Define and explain the MRS_{fc} between the two points.

   d. Why are they convex to the origin?

2. Draw a consumer's budget line for food and clothes.

   a. What does each axis of the diagram measure?

   b. Explain what determines the position and slope of the budget line.

   c. What happens to the budget line if the consumer's income increases?

3. Draw a consumer's budget line and set of indifference curves for food and clothes on the same diagram, with one of the indifference curves tangent to the budget line.

   a. Select a point where the budget line <u>intersects</u> an indifference curve. What motivates the consumer to move away from this combination? (Hint: What is the consumer just <u>willing</u> to do as compared with what he is <u>able</u> to do in the marketplace?)

   b. Show the consumer's most preferred combination of food and clothes. How do you know that it is the most preferred?

4. a. Assume that the prices of X and Y are $3 and $5, respectively; Smith's income is $150, and his preference function is U = xy. Find the combination of X and Y that maximizes his satisfaction.

   b. If the price of X is raised to $5, other things remaining the same, what will the satisfaction-maximizing combination of X and Y be?

5. Use indifference maps to diagram and explain the consequences for consumer behavior of the following issues that
have received national attention during the past few years:
(a) research findings that for a time suggested that the
nitrites used in processed pork and delicatessen meats might
be hazardous; (b) the possibility that birth control pills
could cause blood clots and other serious side effects; and
(c) the possibility that the U.S. Food and Drug Administration has too much power in its ability to prevent any drug
from being used in the United States until the FDA believes
it is safe (in contrast to a weaker type of regulation that
would allow certain drugs to be used as long as manufacturers provided consumers with detailed warnings).

6. Draw the indifference map and budget line of a consumer who
purchases good X. Let the Y-axis show income available for
purchasing goods and services other than X. Show the amount
of X consumed when the consumer is maximizing satisfaction.
How much is being spent on X, and how much is available for
the purchase of other goods and services?

7. For two goods, say soft drinks and orange juice, discuss
the likelihood of concavity to the origin of a consumer's
indifference curves. If the curves were concave, what kind
of economic behavior would be required to maximize satisfaction? Diagram your answer.

8. Assume that two individuals have the same indifference maps
for choices between pizzas and hamburgers, but each prefers
to consume a different combination of the two goods than the
other. Does this mean that one of the persons is irrational? Explain.

9. Diagram and explain a consumer's satisfaction-maximizing
choice between two goods that are perfect substitutes when:
a. the consumer's MRS_{xy} is <u>not</u> equal to P_x/P_y; and
b. the consumer's MRS_{xy} is equal to P_x/P_y.

© 1988 The Dryden Press

10. The principal idea behind the Tax Reform Act of 1986 was to
lower tax rates on ordinary income by closing "loopholes"
on investments that had previously been given favorable tax
treatment—for example, in natural resources, real estate,
tax-exempt bonds, solid-waste facilities, and steel. Two of
the most influential authors of the legislation, and strenu-
ous advocates of tax reform, were Senator Robert Packwood
(Republican, Oregon) and Senator Bill Bradley (Democrat,
New Jersey). Although each favored closing many loopholes,
Packwood managed to preserve several tax advantages for the
timber industry, which is important in Oregon. Bradley,
"one of the founding fathers of tax overhaul, made sure tax-
exempt bonds for solid-waste and hazardous-waste disposal
facilities—important to his state—not only were kept
whole but were exempted from limits placed on other kinds
of bonds" (Anne Swardson, "And Just in Case You Thought You
Could Kiss Loopholes Goodbye...," Washington Post, National
Weekly Ed., September 1, 1986). Draw each senator's apparent preference map for trade-offs between closing loopholes and preserving loopholes, and explain each senator's
satisfaction-maximizing choice.

Solutions to Problems and Questions for Discussion

1. a. Because consumers prefer more to less, thus requiring
more of C to compensate for less of F. Upward slope
would mean that larger quantities of C reduce the
consumer's satisfaction level, thus requiring larger
quantities of F to compensate.
   b. Because intersection violates the transitivity postulate.
   c. The MRS_{fc} measures the amount of food the consumer would
be willing to give up to obtain each unit of the additional amount of clothes.
   d. Because the more clothes and the less food the consumer
has, the less food he/she would be willing to give up
for an additional unit of clothes.

2. a. Units of food and units of clothes.
   b. Its intersection with the food axis is determined by
the consumer's income and the price of food. Intersection with the clothes axis is similarly determined. The
slope equals the price of clothes divided by the price
of food.
   c. It shifts to the right parallel to itself.

© 1988 The Dryden Press

3. a. The consumer is willing to give up more food for an
        additional unit of clothes than the market requires.
    b. The point of tangency between the budget line and an
        indifference curve. This indifference curve is the
        highest that the budget will allow the consumer to
        reach.

4. a. At $x = 25$ and $y = 15$. Each indifference curve has an
        elasticity of one at all points on it. Therefore, at
        its point of tangency with the budget line, the latter
        must also have an elasticity of one since this would
        occur at the midpoint of the budget line.
    b. At $x = 15$ and $y = 15$ for the same reasons.

5. a. and b. Assume that the hazardous product per unit
               of time is plotted along the vertical axis and
               its substitute along the horizontal. Once
               the warning is published, a typical consumer's
               marginal rate of substitution between the two
               goods would increase in the manner portrayed
               in text Figure 5.10.
           c. A prohibition of the hazardous product rather
               than warning consumers about its possible
               side effects affects the slope of the consum-
               er's budget line in the manner portrayed in
               text Figure 5.11.

6. Refer to an indifference diagram such as text Figure
    5.12, where income per month is plotted along the verti-
    cal axis and medical insurance per month is plotted along
    the horizontal. At combination G_2 the consumer buys OM_2
    of medical insurance per month and has OC_2 of income per
    month to spend on other things. I_2C_2 is the amount of
    income per month sacrificed to buy OM_2 of medical insur-
    ance.

7. We suspect that it would be rare for an individual to
    have concave indifference curves for these two goods.
    But should it occur, the satisfaction-maximizing combi-
    nations would be a corner solution along one axis or
    the other depending on the budget line's slope.

8. Neither is necessarily irrational. Each could have a
    different income and budget line or could be in a differ-
    ent market and therefore face different relative prices
    of the two goods.

9. a. The indifference curves are straight lines and satisfaction is maximized at a corner solution on one axis or the other—on the Y-axis if the budget line's slope exceeds the indifference line's, and the X-axis if the budget line's slope is less.
   b. Here the budget line and the indifference line overlap, so the result is indeterminate.

10. Each senator's indifference map between closing loopholes and preserving loopholes appears to be of the normal, convex shape. Each maximizes satisfaction by "purchasing" some amount of each.

True-False Questions

(F) ____ 1. The nonsatiation assumption means that if a consumer prefers a bowl of Wheaties to a bowl of Rice Krispies and a bowl of Rice Krispies to a bowl of Cheerios, he/she prefers a bowl of Wheaties to a bowl of Cheerios.

(F) ____ 2. Indifference curves forming a consumer's indifference map are equidistant from each other because of the nonintersection assumption.

(T) ____ 3. An indifference curve shows combinations of items among which a consumer is indifferent.

(T) ____ 4. Indifference curves slope downward to the right if the nonsatiation assumption holds.

(F) ____ 5. The marginal rate of substitution of one product for another indicates the rate at which the market requires a consumer to exchange the second product for the first.

(F) ____ 6. If an indifference curve is to be convex to the origin, the marginal rate of substitution between the goods for which it is drawn must be increasing in absolute value.

(F) ____ 7. Two goods are substitutes if an increase in the consumption of one, holding the consumer's preference level constant, increases the marginal rate of substitution of the other for money.

(T) ____ 8. A consumer's budget line shows what the consumer is able to do in the marketplace; i.e., it shows the market constraints on the person.

(F) ____ 9. The most preferred position for a consumer is a combination of goods on the budget line at which $MRS_{xy} > P_x/P_y$.

(F) ____ 10. If the fringe benefits given an employee are greater than would be purchased if the employee were given the cash value of the benefits instead, this is evidence that the employee is better off with the fringe benefits than with their equivalent cash value.

(T) ____ 11. The Laspeyres price index provides the maximum estimate of increases in the cost of living; it may actually be less than the index shows.

(F) ____ 12. The Paasche price index provides the maximum estimate of increases in the cost of living; it may actually be less than the index shows.

(F) ____ 13. The issuance of warnings that a product may be hazardous to consumers' health will affect a consumer's budget line but will have no impact on the consumer's indifference map.

(F) ____ 14. An increase in the price of good Y will cause a consumer's budget line to intersect the Y-axis of the budget line diagram at a point farther from the origin.

(F) ____ 15. With regard to a given drug with substantial possibilities of side effects, consumers will usually be indifferent as to whether the government prohibits its use or permits it to be sold with a warning on the label.

(F) ____ 16. The only way a consumer will display a "corner solution" to a two-good model (where he/she consumes either all X or all Y) is if the indifference curves are concave to the origin.

(T) ____ 17. When the Consumer Price Index rises you can bet confidently that it has overstated the actual increase in the cost of living for a given person.

(T) ____ 18. The Consumer Price Index is merely an index of prices rather than a true index of changes in the cost of a given standard of living.

(F) ____ 19. Taxes should not be included in the Consumer Price Index because they bear no relationship to the prices of other consumer goods that the index tracks.

(T) ____ 20. The PCE Deflator index is based on weights that are assigned somewhat arbitrarily by the government economists who construct it.

Multiple-Choice Questions

(c) ____ 1. An indifference curve shows:
    a. the maximum combinations of two products that a consumer prefers.
    b. the minimum combinations of two products that a consumer prefers.
    c. the combinations of two products among which the consumer has no preference.
    d. the actual combinations of two products that a consumer will choose.

(a) ____ 2. Two indifference curves of a consumer usually cannot intersect because:
    a. the transitivity principle usually applies to consumer choices.
    b. the nonsatiation principle usually applies to consumer choices.
    c. of the general theory of the second best.
    d. the convexity principle usually applies to consumer choices.

(b) ____ 3. If the marginal rate of substitution of coffee for tea is four, this means the consumer:
    a. would want to give up coffee for tea.
    b. would be willing to give up four units of tea for one unit of coffee.
    c. has too much tea.
    d. can sell four units of tea and use the money to buy one unit of coffee.

(a) ____ 4. If a consumer were to increase his/her consumption of breakfast cereal, one would expect which of the following?
a. an increase in the marginal rate of substitution of sugar for money
b. a decrease in the marginal rate of substitution of sugar for money
c. no change in the marginal rate of substitution of sugar for money
d. a decrease in the marginal rate of substitution of cereal for sugar

(b) ____ 5. Let the vertical axis of a diagram measure cans of beer while the horizontal axis measures hamburgers. If the price of beer is $.50 per can and the price of a hamburger is $1.50, the slope of the budget line of a consumer for these two products is:
a. 1/3.
b. 3.
c. 1 1/2.
d. 5.

(a) ____ 6. In question 5, an increase in the price of beer will cause the budget line to:
a. rotate counterclockwise from its intersection with the hamburger axis.
b. rotate clockwise from its intersection with the hamburger axis.
c. rotate counterclockwise from its intersection with the beer axis.
d. rotate clockwise from its intersection with the beer axis.

(b) ____ 7. A fringe benefit in the form of company housing as compared with a money payment of the same value to an employee, ignoring the impact of income taxes and assuming that housing units are available:
a. is always preferable.
b. is never preferable and in the best of circumstances will yield equivalent satisfaction.
c. is never preferable and in the best of circumstances will yield smaller satisfaction.
d. is sometimes preferable and sometimes not.

(b) ____ 8. The Laspeyres and the Paasche price index numbers:
   a. both measure changes in the cost of living, but the Laspeyres is more accurate than the Paasche.
   b. establish the maximum and minimum limits, respectively, within which the cost of living changes.
   c. both measure changes in the cost of living, but the Paasche is more accurate than the Laspeyres.
   d. both measure changes in the cost of living accurately.

(a) ____ 9. Consumers will always prefer a warning statement to a prohibition because:
   a. the warning statement gives them additional degrees of freedom, since those who would prefer to bear risks may continue to consume the product.
   b. all consumers think of themselves as needing protection from dangerous products and choices.
   c. most consumers do not trust their government.
   d. most goods nowadays are too complex for consumers to judge competently.

© 1988 The Dryden Press

CHAPTER 6

ENGEL CURVES, DEMAND CURVES, AND EXCHANGE

Chapter Outline

Engel Curves
   From Indifference Analysis to Engel Curves
   Income Elasticity of Demand
Demand Curves
   From Indifference Analysis to Demand Curves
   Corner Solutions
   Price Elasticity of Demand and the Price Consumption Curve
   Income Effects and Substitution Effects
   Constant Real Income Demand Curves
   Consumer's Surplus
   The Giffen Paradox
   Market Demand Curves
Exchange and Welfare

Applications

The Case of Amtrak
The Demand for Refuse Collection
The Rolls-Royce Demand Curve Is Also Downward-Sloping

Chapter Objectives

The chapter title states its major objectives—to build Engel curves, demand curves, and the fundamental basis of exchange as logical extensions of the theory of consumer choice. The Engel curves and demand curves are for one individual consumer and must be summed to obtain their market counterparts. In addition, we develop in this chapter various special aspects of the demand relationship that should broaden and deepen students' understanding and appreciation of what it is and of its usefulness. We hope, too, that students will come to understand that any voluntary exchange will increase the economic well-being of <u>all</u> parties to that exchange—a little understood point in the world today!

Suggestions for Teaching

There are at least three pairs of concepts in this chapter that confuse many students. First, they may confuse an income-consumption curve with the Engel curves that it generates.

© 1988 The Dryden Press

Second, they may confuse a price-consumption curve with its corresponding demand curve. Third, it is very common for students to confuse demand curves with indifference curves. At the bottom of fuzzy thinking on these points is a failure to understand what is being measured on the axes for each one of the curves involved. This is a good place to stress again exactly what it is that we measure on the axes of our diagrams. We find it useful to drill students again and again on deriving Engel curves and demand curves from indifference maps and budget lines. The applications on Amtrak and the demand curve for refuse will help students shift gears between the demand curves of theory and empirical demand curves.

Most students at the intermediate level find the separation of income effects and substitution effects of a price change for a product hard to grasp—consequently, they also have difficulty with the constant real income demand curve. Most of the problem is an inadequate understanding of budget lines and how they shift as prices and incomes are changed. The Rolls-Royce demand curve application makes practical use of the separation. Some instructors may want to skip the constant real income demand curve since it is rarely used empirically and since most economists' attention is focused on constant money income demand curves. It is not essential to our development of a price theory framework; however, it does help students understand that the usual measurement of consumer's surplus is an approximation.

The Giffen Paradox also can be omitted without great loss. We include it to improve the student's grasp of graphic analytical tools—not because we believe it to be an important real world phenomenon. It is doubtful that the phenomenon ever existed.

The Edgeworth box presentation showing the gains from exchange is a part of the bedrock foundation of price theory—or of economic theory in general for that matter. It demonstrates why economic activity takes place among individuals, and it is essential that students understand this point since it is utilized at several junctures later in the book.

Problems and Questions for Discussion

1. Show with a diagram and explain each of the following:
   a. a price-consumption curve
   b. an income-consumption curve

2. Demonstrate diagrammatically and explain how points on the consumer's demand curve for food can be determined. Now show and explain the determination of points for the Engel curve for clothes.

© 1988 The Dryden Press

3. Suppose that a consumer purchases only two products, X and
    Y, and that the Engel curve for one of them is inelastic.
    What can you say about the elasticity of the Engel curve for
    the other? Can you draw any general conclusions from this
    exercise?

4. Suppose that two products—food and clothing—are shower-
    ed down from Heaven in fixed monthly quantities. Consumer
    Smith always receives the same monthly quantity of each.
    So does consumer Jones. However, the amounts of each re-
    ceived by Smith are not the same as those received by Jones.
    The total quantity of food and total quantity of clothing
    initially available to the two of them together cannot be
    changed.
    a. Diagram and explain in terms of Pareto optimality the
        situation that they find themselves in if no exchange
        is permitted.
    b. Now suppose the government sets a price P_{f_1} on food
        and P_{c_1} on clothing. These prices are arbitrarily
        chosen and at point F exhaust the combined incomes of
        Smith and Jones. Show on your diagram and explain what
        each consumer would want to do; what exchanges would
        actually take place; whether shortages or surpluses
        occur; and whether or not Pareto optimality would be
        achieved.
    c. Now let the price of each good be free to move. Ex-
        plain what happens assuming that each consumer is a
        pure competitor in the purchase of each product. Is
        Pareto optimality achieved?
    d. What can you say about the distribution of products
        between the two consumers? Is it equitable or not?
        Explain.

5. Assume that two goods, X and Y, are distributed between two
    persons, S and J. Let the utility function of S be:

    $$U^S = x_s y_s;$$

    and let the utility function of J be:

    $$U^J = x_j y_j;$$
    $$x_s + x_j = 100;$$
    $$\text{and } y_s + y_j = 80.$$

    Show that the diagonal of an Edgeworth box locates the con-
    tract curve.

6. Draw the Engel curves implicit in the arguments of the rail
    enthusiasts who wanted to see the Amtrak system expanded.
    Do the same for the economists who argued that it should be
    cut back. Which of these estimates appears to be borne out
    by experience based on actual Amtrak ridership? Which has
    the government tended to adopt in its funding decisions for
    Amtrak? What would you estimate the shapes of the Engel
    curves for air and automobile travel to be in comparison to
    that for rail travel? Ship travel for luxury cruises?

7. What would be your reaction, as an economist, to a report
    by a national polling organization that 60 percent of Ameri-
    cans in its sample preferred a stronger national defense?
    Would you have any economic reasons for being skeptical of
    these findings even if they were corroborated by another
    national polling organization? What additional questions
    would you want to ask of the persons who were sampled be-
    fore you accept or reject the conclusions that the nation
    should buy a more elaborate defense system?

8. Try to draw the combined income and substitution effects
    of a price change and a "snob" effect of the price change
    so that the snob demand curve is upward-sloping rather than
    downward-sloping. What basic assumptions of consumer behav-
    ior that you have made will be ruled out by a snob demand
    curve that is upward-sloping? Explain.

9. In text Figure 6.8(b), identify the substitution and income
    effects in terms of the quantity of X purchased as price
    declines from p_{x1} to p_{x2} along:
    a. the constant money income demand curve d_m; and
    b. the constant real income demand curve d_r.

10. Using text Figure 6.8 as a model, draw a consumer's indif-
    ference map showing the income and substitution effects for
    an increase in the price of X. Draw the consumer's constant
    money income and constant real income demand curves in a
    diagram below the indifference map. At the higher price,
    label the quantity on the constant money income demand curve
    "a" and the quantity on the constant real income demand
    curve "b". Label the intersection of the two demand curves
    "c".
    a. At the higher price, is the consumer's satisfaction
        level highest at a or at b?
    b. Compare the satisfaction levels at a, b, and c.
        Explain.

© 1988 The Dryden Press

11. In the figure that you drew for the previous question, identify the substitution and income effects in terms of the quantity of X purchased as price rises from p_{x1} to p_{x0} for:
   a. the constant money income demand curve $d_m d_m$; and
   b. the constant real income demand curve $d_r d_r$.

Solutions to Problems and Questions for Discussion

1. a. See text, pp. 142-145.
   b. See text, pp. 146-148.

2. See text, pp. 142-148.

3. It must be elastic. If an increase in income increases one of the two goods by a smaller percentage than the percentage increase in income, it must increase the other by a greater percentage than the percentage increase in income. The income elasticity for all goods together must be one.

4. a. At the initial distribution F in the following diagram, Smith is willing to give up more food to obtain an additional unit of clothing than Jones would require. Either or both could get on higher indifference curves thus moving toward Pareto optimality.

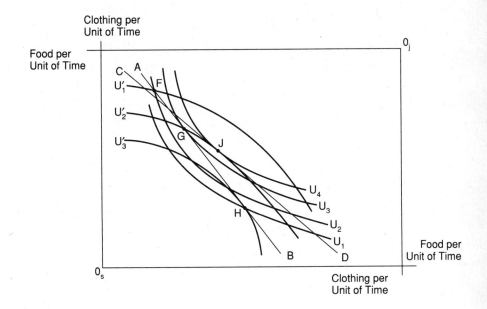

© 1988 The Dryden Press

b. The budget of both is shown by AB which passes through F and has a slope of p_c/p_f. Smith would want combination G and Jones would want combination H. There is a shortage of food and a surplus of clothing. Pareto optimality would not be achieved since at either G or H, or any point in between, at least one consumer could get on a higher indifference curve without forcing the other to a lower.

c. The price of food would rise and the price of clothing would fall, decreasing the slope of the budget line until it passes through a point of tangency between an indifference curve of Smith and an indifference curve of Jones. This distribution of goods at J is Pareto optimal.

d. We cannot say anything about the equity of the distribution. We can only say that given the distribution of income between the two consumers, the distribution of goods at J is Pareto optimal.

5. Both utility functions are made up of indifference curves that are rectangular hyperbolas; consequently, each indifference curve of each consumer has an elasticity of one at every point on it. The exact center of any straight line from the Y- to the X-axis will be tangent to an indifference curve of each person, thus the indifference curves of the two parties are also tangent at such a point. Moving from the lower left corner of the Edgeworth Box to the upper right corner must therefore bisect the Box into two equal halves (triangles). The height and width of the Box (80 and 100) are immaterial.

© 1988 The Dryden Press

6. The Engel curves in either text Figure 6.1(b) or Figure 6.1(c) appear to be consistent with the enthusiasts' argument that improving the quality of rail service would make it more attractive to middle- and higher-income groups. Figure 6.1(b) would be consistent with the argument that rail service is only a weakly superior good, where the increase in consumption becomes smaller and smaller relative to the increase in income. Figure 6.1(c) would be the curve consistent with the even less plausible argument that rail service was a strongly superior good, where the increase in consumption becomes greater and greater relative to the increase in income. The Engel curve in text Figure 6.2 is consistent with the argument of economists that rail service is an inferior good. The data in text Tables 6.1, 6.2, and 6.3 support the economists' position. It is not clear to us whether the government has increased funding for Amtrak based on the position of the rail enthusiasts or as a result of political pressures from certain blocs of voters who benefit from Amtrak. In either event, funding has been insufficient to reverse the trends in ridership. In contrast to travel by rail, travel by air, automobile, and luxury cruise ships all appear to be strongly superior goods with Engel curves like text Figure 6.1(c).

7. We would be skeptical for two reasons. First, such polls do not indicate the intensity of preference. Polls rarely reveal by how much more voters prefer spending another dollar on subsidies for transportation relative to subsidies for housing. Second, polls usually do not attach price tags to the items in question. How much would people favor buying more defense if its cost was expected to be $10 billion versus $100 billion? Polls by other polling organizations are likely to have the same defects, but corroborating results do suggest that a broad group of voters is concerned about certain issues.

8. For a snob good to be a Giffen good as well and have an upward-sloping demand curve, it is necessary for the snob effect to exceed the combined income and substitute effects of a price change. The key to understanding this point is to distinguish between movements along a demand curve versus shifts in the demand curve. Assume a decrease in price caused the quantity demanded of the snob good to decrease rather than increase. As total quantity demanded of a snob good falls, however, the more snobs want to buy and the more new snobs enter the market. This causes the Σd_a demand curve in text Figure 6.16 to shift to the right. Since the Σd curves can not shift to the left as price declines, a snob good can not be a Giffen good as well.

9. a. The substitution effect is from x_1 to x_3 and the income effect is from x_3 to x_2.
   b. The substitution effect is from x_1 to x_3 and the income effect is zero.

10. a. At b in the following diagram, the consumer is on a higher indifference curve.

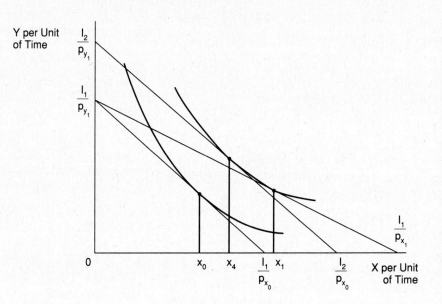

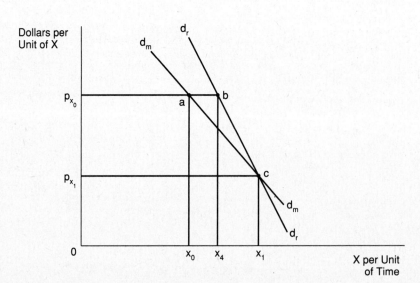

b. The same at b and c since at both the consumer is on
the same indifference curve. Lower at a since the consumer is on a lower indifference curve, i.e., has not
been compensated for the increase in the price of X.

11. a. The substitution effect is from x_1 to x_4 and the income
effect is from x_4 to x_0.
b. The substitution effect is from x_1 to x_4 and the income
effect is zero.

True-False Questions

(F) ____ 1. The income effect of a price change works in the
same direction as the substitution effect for both
inferior and normal goods.

(F) ____ 2. Ordinarily it would be expected that, for an
increase in the price of steak, the income effect
would be more important than the substitution
effect.

(F) ____ 3. The demand curve and the price-consumption curve
for a consumer are identical in most cases.

(T) ____ 4. The price-consumption curve for most decreases in
the price of hamburger would be expected to slope
downward to the right, indicating that demand for
hamburger is elastic.

(T) ____ 5. The Engel curve for beer probably slopes upward to
the left above some income level, indicating that
above that income level it is an inferior good.

(F) ____ 6. An indifference curve is essentially the same concept as a demand curve.

(T) ____ 7. If the price consumption curve for product X
slopes downward to the right, demand for that
product is elastic.

(T) ____ 8. A corner solution to a consumer's maximization
problem provides information on where the consumer's demand curve for one product intersects the
price axis.

(T) ____ 9. If a tangent to an Engel curve cuts the quantity axis to the left of the origin, the income
elasticity of demand at the point of tangency
is greater than one.

(F) ____ 10. In the Giffen case, income effects of a change in the price of the good are in the opposite direction from the substitution effects, but the substitution effects prevail.

(T) ____ 11. If the distribution of two goods between two consumers is such that the marginal rates of substitution between them are not the same for the two consumers, an exchange of goods between the consumers can benefit both and harm no one.

(T) ____ 12. If the distribution of two goods between two consumers lies on the contract curve, no exchange of goods can be made between them without making one party worse off.

(F) ____ 13. Giffen goods are all inferior goods, and all inferior goods are Giffen goods.

(T) ____ 14. The results of the study of refuse-collection services in the text were generally consistent with basic demand theory.

(F) ____ 15. Two individuals who have the same incomes and face the same market prices for commodities X and Y will ordinarily consume equal amounts of each product.

(F) ____ 16. The constant money income demand curve and the constant real income demand curve are identical only when consumer's surplus is zero.

(T) ____ 17. The Giffen Paradox has almost no likelihood of being found in the real world because strongly inferior goods are rarely a large portion of the consumer's budget.

(F) ____ 18. The demand curve for a bandwagon good is usually less elastic than the demand curve for a snob good.

(F) ____ 19. Exchange between two individuals with equal income endowments will never occur.

(F) ____ 20. The concept of consumer's surplus is best represented by the area under the indifference curve that is tangent to the consumer's budget line.

(T) ____ 21. The available economic evidence suggests that use of most Amtrak trains in recent years has been an inferior good.

(F) ____ 22. The snob effect works to make the demand curve for snob goods rise upward to the right.

Multiple-Choice Questions

(a) ____ 1. During a period of expanding income and economic activity, sellers would prefer that:
a. Engel curves for their products be elastic.
b. Engel curves for their products be inelastic.
c. individual consumer demand curves for their products be elastic.
d. market demand curves for their products be elastic.

(c) ____ 2. An individual consumer demand curve for a good will slope downward to the right if:
a. the good is a Giffen good.
b. the income effect of a price change is in the opposite direction from and outweighs the substitution effect.
c. the substitution effect of a price change is in the opposite direction from and outweighs the income effect.
d. both b and c

(c) ____ 3. To determine an individual's demand curve for one good we should:
a. change the consumer's income, while holding the prices of the goods and the consumer's tastes and preferences constant, and observe the quantities of it the consumer will take.
b. change the consumer's tastes and preferences, while holding income and product prices constant, and observe the quantities of it the consumer will take.
c. hold the consumer's income and tastes and preferences constant, change the price of one good, and observe the quantities of it the consumer will take.
d. hold the consumer's income and tastes and preferences constant, change the prices of all goods, and observe the quantities of it the consumer will take.

© 1988 The Dryden Press

(a) ____ 4. To determine an individual's Engel curve for one
good, we should:

    a. change the consumer's income, while holding
the prices of the goods and the consumer's
tastes and preferences constant, and observe
the quantities of it the consumer will take.

    b. change the consumer's tastes and preferences,
while holding income and product prices constant, and observe the quantities of it the
consumer will take.

    c. hold the consumer's income and tastes and
preferences constant, change the price of one
good, and observe the quantities of it the
consumer will take.

    d. hold the consumer's income and tastes and
preferences constant, change the prices of all
goods, and observe the quantities of it the
consumer will take.

The following diagram is for Questions 5 and 6:

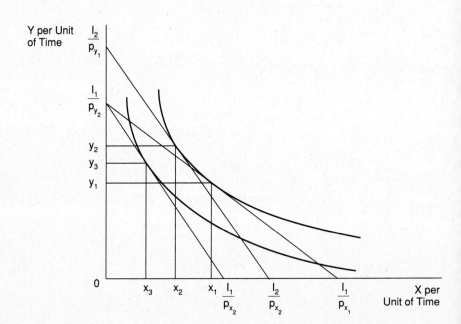

(b) ____ 5. The income effect of the change in p_x from p_{x_1} to p_{x_2} is:
a. $x_2 x_1$.
b. $x_3 x_2$.
c. $x_3 x_1$.
d. $y_1 y_3$.

(a) ____ 6. For the price change from p_{x_1} to p_{x_2}, the elasticity of demand:
a. is greater than one.
b. is less than one.
c. is equal to one.
d. cannot be determined.

(d) ____ 7. For a Pareto optimal distribution of two goods, X and Y, between two consumers, S and J, it is necessary that:

a. $MRS_{xy}^{S} = MRS_{xy}^{J}$.

b. the distribution be at a tangency point of an indifference curve of S with an indifference curve of J.

c. that both consumers be on the contract curve.

d. all of the above

(a) ____ 8. On an Edgeworth box diagram for two goods, X and Y, the origin of consumer S at the lower left-hand corner and origin of consumer J at the upper right-hand corner:

a. if $MRS_{xy}^{S} > MRS_{xy}^{J}$, there is an incentive for S to trade Y to J for X and for J to trade X to S for Y.

b. if $MRS_{xy}^{S} = MRS_{xy}^{J}$ but the distribution of goods is closer to the origin of S, there is an incentive for J to trade both X and Y to S.

c. if $MRS_{xy}^{S} > MRS_{xy}^{J}$, there is an incentive for S to trade X to J for Y and for J to trade Y to S for X.

d. if $MRS_{xy}^{S} > MRS_{xy}^{J}$, there is an incentive for S to trade X to J for Y but J has no incentive to trade.

© 1988 The Dryden Press

(a) ____ 9. Which of the following is a compensated demand curve?
   a. the constant real income demand curve
   b. the constant money income demand curve
   c. the consumer's satisfaction-maximizing indifference curve before the change in price
   d. the consumer's satisfaction-maximizing indifference curve after the change in price

(b) ____ 10. Which of the following is probably the best approximation to the correct measure of consumer's surplus?
   a. the area under a constant money income demand curve above the price that the consumer is charged
   b. the area under a constant real income demand curve above the price that the consumer is charged
   c. the area under the indifference curve that is tangent to the budget line
   d. the area between (i) the indifference curve that is tangent to the original budget line and (ii) the indifference curve that is tangent to the budget line that reflects a compensated decrease in income

(d) ____ 11. The available evidence suggests that Amtrak service is:
   a. a Giffen good.
   b. a normal good.
   c. a superior good.
   d. an inferior good.

(a) ____ 12. The evidence presented in the application on refuse collection supports which of the following propositions:
   a. The demand curve for refuse collection slopes downward to the right.
   b. Refuse collection is an inferior good.
   c. The demand for refuse collection has a substitution effect only.
   d. The demand for refuse collection varies too much among families to make any valid generalization.

© 1988 The Dryden Press

(a) _____ 13. The demand curve for Rolls-Royces does not rise upward to the right because:

  a. it would imply that the snob effect exceeds the combined income and substitution effects, and therefore that snobs enter the market as total quantity falls.

  b. it would imply that a Rolls-Royce is an inferior good.

  c. it would imply that a Rolls-Royce has a negative income elasticity.

  d. it would imply that consumers fail to understand the concepts of income effects, substitution effects, and snob effects.

© 1988 The Dryden Press

CHAPTER 7

THE UTILITY APPROACH TO CONSUMER CHOICE
AND DEMAND—A SPECIAL CASE

Chapter Outline

The Utility Concept
   Cardinal versus Ordinal Measurement
   Nonrelated Goods and Services
   Related Goods and Services
Indifference Curves
Consumer Choice
   Objectives and Constraints
   Maximization of Utility
Demand Curves
   The Demand Curve for X
   Quantities Taken of Other Goods
Exchange and Welfare

Applications

Value in Use and Value in Exchange
Charitable Giving

Chapter Objectives

Classical utility analysis tells us little that is new about consumer choice and demand—it is a special case of the more general theory of the last two chapters. It can be omitted without leaving breaks in the framework of price theory. We include it for two reasons. First, it has historical importance—it was the initial formulation of a more or less complete theory of consumer choice and demand. The modern theory grew out of its limitations. Second, despite criticisms leveled at its awkwardness and limitations, economists almost invariably refer to it and use it in their research and writings on consumer choice and demand. We think it is important that our students be familiar with its outlines. Certainly it will add to their understanding of demand theory.

Suggestions for Teaching

Students were introduced to the marginal rate of substitution of one product for another in Chapter 5. The relationship between a consumer's total utility and marginal utility

   © 1988 The Dryden Press

from a product should further extend their grasp of the marginal concept by putting it in its usual mathematical form. The classic diamond-water paradox in the application on value in use and value in exchange reinforces students' grasp of the concept and the importance of it. We use the utility surface device to move from a cardinal to an ordinal measurement. Once we have established that equal-utility contour lines can be drawn around a cardinal utility surface and projected to the XY plane as indifference curves, the exact distances that they lie above the plane become immaterial. It is important only that those farther from the origin be higher than those that lie closer. The utility surface also enables us to take the <u>relatedness</u> of products into account. Externalities in a consumer's utility function are demonstrated in the application on charitable giving. Still, in deriving an individual's demand curve for a product using the Walrasian approach, it is much simpler and easier to assume that utility is measurable cardinally—and this assumption does no violence to the end results. They are valid whether or not utility is measurable cardinally.

Problems and Questions for Discussion

1. Mr. Smith has diabetes and Mrs. Smith loves houseplants of all types. Assuming that houseplants can be measured in homogeneous units, draw and explain the household's marginal utility curve for insulin and for houseplants.

2. Explain and illustrate with a diagram the evolution of indifference curve analysis from the old cardinal utility analysis of consumer choice.

3. For a consumer of food (F) and clothing (C), explain by means of utility analysis the determination of two points on his/her demand curve for food.

4. Air is much more useful to the average person than caviar. Yet the air that is breathed has a zero cost per cubic foot while caviar is so expensive that most people do not buy it. How would you explain this situation?

5. Do you think that the principle of diminishing marginal utility is applicable to additional quantities of each of the following: (a) peanuts; (b) beers; (c) income; (d) children; (e) remaining coins or stamps that make up a complete set for a collector?

© 1988 The Dryden Press

6. Suppose Mr. A has an income of $100 per day; the prices of product X and Y are $10 and $30, respectively; and his daily marginal utility schedules are as follows:

Units of Product	Product X Marginal Utility (Utils)	Product Y Marginal Utility (Utils)
1	10	24
2	9	21
3	8	18
4	7	15
5	6	9

What quantities of X and Y will Mr. A purchase in maximizing his satisfaction?

7. With given supplies of all goods and services, will the achievement of a Pareto optimum for consumers require inter-personal comparisons of satisfaction? Explain.

8. Consider a point on a consumer's utility surface. Explain what each of the following means in economic terms:
    a. the slope of the surface moving in the X direction
    b. the slope of the surface moving in the Y direction
    c. the slope of the contour line through the point with respect to the X- and Y-axes

9. Practice your facility with the total utility and marginal utility curves of Figure 7.6 in the text by assuming that a group of persons receives a windfall gain instead of incurring a disaster. How do the curves shift now and what are the results? Are they consistent with what you see in the world (e.g., the reductions in foreign aid given by the United States to countries that have found larger-than-expected deposits of petroleum or other minerals)?

10. Redraw your answer to text Problem 10 on the assumption that you must transfer income to X through your own efforts only at a price p_x' that is higher than the price p_x that pertained when you transferred income through a charitable organization. Explain the effect of the higher price p_x' on the amount of income you transfer following the disaster.

© 1988 The Dryden Press

Solutions to Problems and Questions for Discussion

1. The marginal utility curve for houseplants probably reflects diminishing marginal utility, as in text Figure 7.1. The marginal utility curve for insulin has different characteristics. It is probably undefined at zero units of insulin per day, which would imply death for many persons with diabetes. The marginal utility of whatever number of units of insulin were required to stabilize the person with diabetes would be extremely high and constant unless substitutions between insulin and diet were possible, out to the optimum quantity to control diabetes. It would fall to zero at that quantity.

2. Originally utility was treated as though it were cardinal and as though goods were independent. Problems of relatedness—substitutes and complements—made the analysis unwieldy, leading to formulation of utility functions in ordinal terms. Projection of contour lines to a two-dimensional plane translated utility analysis into indifference curve terms. See text pages 180-188 for a more complete examination and diagrammatics.

3. See text, pp. 192-195.

4. We could call this the air-caviar paradox. However more useful air may be than caviar, air is generally so plentiful that one can get all one wants at a zero price. The total value in use of air is enormous even though its total value in exchange is zero. Caviar is not sufficiently common to satisfy everyone at a zero price, so it is an economic good. The total value in use of caviar relative to its total value in exchange is small compared to air.

5. We suspect that marginal utility for each of these goods increases over some range of quantities for many consumers but not all consumers. For some, having the first unit of each of these commodities makes them want the second unit even more. We also suspect, however, that for each commodity diminishing marginal utility eventually sets in at some quantity for most people.

6. He will purchase 4 units of X and 2 units of Y, for which he spends his daily income of $100. At this combination, the ratio between the marginal utilities of X and Y is 21 to 7 or 3 to 1, and the ratio between their prices is also 3 to 1.

7. No. Each consumer makes his or her own calculations
    without knowing the change in utility of the other person.
    Trade continues naturally and voluntarily as long as each
    party concludes that an additional transaction produces a
    net utility gain. A Pareto optimum is achieved when <u>both</u>
    parties no longer gain from further exchange.

8. a. MU_x
    b. MU_y
    c. MRS_{xy}

9. Using the analysis in text Figure 7.6, assume that B
    gets an unanticipated inheritance. Marginal utility for
    A of making gifts to B per unit of time still diminishes.
    But owing to the <u>rise</u> in B's income, the total utility
    curve shifts down from TU_1^A to TU_2^A and the marginal util-
    ity curve shifts down from MU_1^A to MU_2^A (rather than up as
    in the case when B was hit by a disaster). That is, the
    marginal utility per dollar given by A, shown in panel
    (b), is now less the better off B is. In the following
    adaptation of text Figure 7.6, the total utility of A's
    gifts in the amount of g_3 declines from T_3 to T_4, and the
    marginal utility declines from M_3 to M_4. This leads A
    to reallocate his income in such a way that gifts decline
    to some smaller amount g_2 dollars.

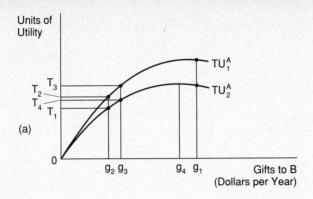

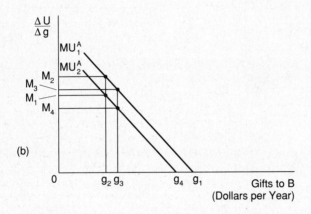

10. In the figure accompanying the solution to text Problem 10, the slope of line gpj reflected p_X, the price of transferring income to X through a charitable organization. At a higher price p_X' of transferring income to X through your own efforts only, the slope of the new budget line through g is now steeper than gpj. The new budget line through f is also steeper and has the same slope as the new budget line through g. Owing to the higher transfer price p_X', A makes fewer gifts to B both before and after the disaster, and A achieves a lower level of satisfaction.

True-False Questions

(F) _____ 1. A consumer's saturation point for a good occurs at the consumption level at which the marginal utility for the good is greatest.

© 1988 The Dryden Press

(T) _____ 2. Logically one would expect the marginal utility of a good to a consumer to be decreasing in the neighborhood of the saturation point.

(F) _____ 3. If bacon and eggs are important variables in a consumer's utility function, it would be generally correct to write the function: $U = b(b) + e(e) + \ldots$.

(F) _____ 4. The problem in using the ordinal concept of utility is that it does not permit the consumer's utility function to be translated into an indifference map.

(F) _____ 5. An increase in the price of one good, given the price of other goods and the consumer's income, would be expected to increase the marginal utility of money.

(F) _____ 6. In order to maximize satisfaction, a consumer must allocate his/her income among different goods so as to maximize the marginal utility of each good purchased.

(F) _____ 7. A consumer maximizes satisfaction by purchasing those quantities of different goods and services at which their marginal utilities are equal.

(T) _____ 8. If a consumer is maximizing satisfaction and the price of one good falls, it will be necessary to transfer dollars from other goods toward the one in order to restore the consumer to an equilibrium position.

(T) _____ 9. If for two consumers of products X and Y the MU_x/MU_y of one is equal to the MU_x/MU_y of the other, no incentive exists for exchange.

(T) _____ 10. To locate points on a consumer's demand curve for one product, we vary the price of the product and at each price we note the quantity of the product the consumer takes when he/she is in full equilibrium.

(F) _____ 11. Pearls are expensive because the total use value of them to consumers is very large.

(T) _____ 12. If voluntary exchange of products among individuals occurs, it is reasonably certain that all parties to the exchange gain.

(T) ____ 13. Economic theory can be used to help explain behavior involving charity, love, and other unsel-
fish actions in the same manner and with the same
analytical apparatus as are used to explain consumer purchases of automobiles, vacations, and
other goods.

(T) ____ 14. The total use value of water exceeds the total use
value of diamonds or any other rare stone.

(F) ____ 15. A convex indifference curve has a diminishing
marginal rate of substitution between X and Y such
that the ratio MU_X/MU_Y is declining. This implies
that both X and Y have diminishing marginal utilities.

Multiple-Choice Questions

(c) ____ 1. The marginal utility of a good to a consumer
refers to:
a. a situation in which the consumer has doubts
about whether the good is useful to him/her or
not.
b. the saturation point of the goods.
c. the change in the consumer's total utility per
unit change in her/his consumption level.
d. the excess of what the consumer must pay over
what the consumer is required to pay.

(a) ____ 2. When the measurement of utility was thought of in
cardinal terms, with increases in consumption by a
consumer, marginal utility was generally thought
to be:
a. diminishing.
b. first diminishing then increasing.
c. increasing.
d. constant.

(a) ____ 3. Which of the following is not an ordinal measurement?
a. age
b. degree of difficulty of examination questions
c. quality
d. beauty

(b) ____ 4. Which of the following is the reason why economists usually assume that utility is measurable
ordinally but not cardinally?
a. Ordinal measurement is simpler.
b. They can get most of the same implications
from a theory using ordinal utility measurement without making the unrealistic assumptions that cardinal utility requires.
c. The assumption of cardinal utility only applies to certain countries.
d. Cardinal measurements convey intensity of
rankings as well as order whereas ordinal
measurement conveys only the latter.

(b) ____ 5. For an inveterate beer drinker starting the eve-
ning in the local pub, it would be expected that:
a. the marginal utility of beer would at first
decrease.
b. the marginal utility of beer would at first
increase.
c. the total utility of beer would soon reach a
maximum.
d. the total utility of beer would decrease.

(d) ____ 6. A consumer maximizes satisfaction, or is in equilibrium, when spending her/his income in such a
way that:
a. the total utility from each good is maximum.
b. the total utility from each good is equal.
c. the marginal utility from each good is equal.
d. the marginal utility per dollar's worth of
each good is equal.

(c) ____ 7. If the utility function is of the form U =
F(x,y,...):
a. goods X and Y must be unrelated.
b. goods X and Y are definitely related.
c. goods X and Y may or may not be related.
d. marginal utility of X must be diminishing.

(c) ____ 8. In constructing a utility surface:
a. utility of both goods must be ordinal in
nature.
b. the goods used must be unrelated.
c. there is ordinarily a different total utility
curve for one good for each different quantity of the other.
d. saturation points cannot be shown.

(a) ____ 9. The contour lines of a utility surface:
  a. projected downward to the product plane form the consumer's indifference map.
  b. show the respective marginal utilities of the goods.
  c. show different levels of utility in a cardinal sense only.
  d. usually form a straight line.

(c) ____ 10. For a consumer spending his/her entire income in such a way that satisfaction is maximized, a rise in the price of one good with no change in the consumption level of the other good will:
  a. cause a change in the amount spent on the good.
  b. decrease the marginal utility of the good.
  c. increase the marginal utility of the good.
  d. increase the marginal utility of other goods.

(d) ____ 11. Voluntary exchange between two individuals will:
  a. increase the welfare of one at the expense of the other.
  b. leave the welfare of both relatively un-changed.
  c. decrease the welfare of both.
  d. increase the welfare of both.

(b) ____ 12. Points on an individual consumer's demand curve for one good can be determined by:
  a. holding the quantities of all other goods constant, varying the price of the good and observing the quantities of it that will be taken.
  b. holding the prices of all other goods con-stant, together with the consumer's income and tastes, varying the price of the good and observing the quantities that will be taken when the consumer is in equilibrium at each price.
  c. changing the consumer's money income, together with the price of the good, and assessing the impacts of the substitution effects and the income effects.
  d. dividing the market demand curve by the num-ber of consumers in the market.

(a) ____ 13. In the diamond-water paradox, the high price of
diamonds relative to water is explained by:
a. The value in exchange of diamonds exceeds
the value in exchange of water even though the
value in use of water exceeds the value in use
of diamonds.
b. The value in exchange of diamonds exceeds the
value in use of water even though the value in
exchange of water exceeds the value in use of
diamonds.
c. The value in use of diamonds exceeds the value in use of water and the value in exchange
of water exceeds the value in exchange of diamonds.
d. Neither commodity typically is a superior
good.

(d) ____ 14. Economic theory generally applies to which of the
following:
a. transactions in which money is used for exchange
b. barter transactions
c. charitable gifts and nonpecuniary exchanges
d. all of the above

(d) ____ 15. In the application on charitable giving, A's
increased gift to B after disaster struck B was
illustrated by:
a. a movement along A's total utility curve.
b. a shift in B's total utility curve.
c. a movement along B's total utility curve.
d. a shift in A's total utility curve.

CHAPTER 8

MARKET CLASSIFICATIONS AND DEMAND AS VIEWED BY THE SELLER

Chapter Outline

Pure Competition
   The Demand Curve
   Influence of the Firm on Demand, Price, and Output
Pure Monopoly
   The Demand Curve
   Influence of the Firm on Demand, Price, and Output
Imperfect Competition
   The Demand Curve
   Influence of the Firm on Demand, Price, and Output

Applications

Market Structure in the United States: A Broad Tableau

Chapter Objectives

Demand can be viewed from two vantage points: (1) that of the
demanders themselves and (2) that of the sellers of products.
The orientation of the preceding three chapters is around the
former. In Part Four, Prices and Output Levels of Goods and
Services, it will be necessary to understand the latter. Consequently, we believe it is desirable to introduce the second
viewpoint in Part Two, The Underpinnings of Demand, so that the
way sellers view demand can be contrasted with the way buyers
view demand. We want our students to see both in juxtaposition
in order to put them in proper perspective.

This chapter also classifies selling markets. Each type is
defined thoroughly and the three classifications are compared
in a straightforward manner. The application on market structures in the United States ties the theoretical classification
and the real world together.

Suggestions for Teaching

We like to make a clear distinction among three types of demand
curves: (1) individual consumer's demand curves, (2) market
demand curves, and (3) demand curves faced by individual sellers
or firms. A market demand curve for a product is, of course,
simply the horizontal summation of the individual consumer

demand curves for it. The demand curve faced by a seller is distinctly different. It is not, as many students tend to think, the result of disaggregation of a market demand curve. We think this point is made most forcefully for students by discussing market structures and the demand curve facing a seller right on the heels of the theory of consumer choice and demand.

Not all of our users and reviewers agree with our placement of this material, however, and our advice to dissenters is to use it in whatever way makes your teaching most effective.

Problems and Questions for Discussion

1. a. Draw hypothetical demand curves for each of three consumers for hamburger. If these three consumers were the only demanders, how would you arrive at the market demand curve? Do it graphically.
   b. Now draw a hypothetical market supply curve for hamburger and identify the equilibrium price and quantity. (Act as though the three consumers of part (a) are enough to make the market one of pure competition.)
   c. Assuming that the market is one of pure competition, show from part (b) the determination of the demand curve facing a single firm. Explain the demand curve carefully.

2. Explain the relationship between the demand curve facing the single firm and the market demand curve in each of the following cases:
   a. pure monopoly
   b. oligopoly
   c. monopolistic competition

3. Why is it that the demand curve facing an oligopolist may be hard to determine with precision?

4. What causes the demand curve facing the firm in a market of monopolistic competition to slope downward to the right?

5. How would you classify each of the following products in terms of the market-classification scheme developed in Chapter 8?
   a. the dial-a-ride service in your town
   b. "Sunkist" oranges
   c. computer software
   d. urban land
   e. downtown land in prime locations
   f. rural land

6. Do you think it would be possible for a private company to obtain a monopoly of land? What about prime land in downtown locations? Explain.

7. What would be the effect of advertising on the demand curve of a pure competitor? Explain.

8. Referring to Table 8.1 in the text, what do you think are the reasons for the four-firm concentration ratio for the cereal breakfast food industry being much higher than for the cement industry when it is well known that local cement firms are often monopolies or near monopolies? Explain.

9. Which is more important—the size of the eight-firm concentration ratio or the size distribution of the eight firms (that is, whether they are equal in size or one is much larger than the others)?

10. Data on the number of firms and their market shares are often incomplete in competitive industries with many small firms. Does this mean that concentration ratios for such industries are useless? Explain.

11. Canada has a smaller population than the United States, but the production techniques and optimal firm sizes are probably about the same in each country. Which country would have the smaller nationwide concentration ratios?

12. In most communities, hospitals have been independent, not-for-profit organizations. Recently, for-profit firms have begun to form nationwide hospital chains. As a result, national concentration ratios will rise. Does this suggest to you that competition among local hospitals will have declined? Explain.

Solutions to Problems and Questions for Discussion

1. a. By summing them horizontally.
   b. Equilibrium price and quantity are identified at the intersection of the market demand and market supply curves.
   c. The demand curve facing the single purely competitive firm is horizontal at the equilibrium market price.

2. a. A pure monopolist's demand curve is the market demand
        curve. The absence of similar products means that the
        firm has the market all to itself.
    b. An oligopolist has rivals, so its demand curve is not
        the market demand curve. An oligopolist's demand curve
        is downward-sloping, but its precise shape is difficult
        to estimate owing to uncertainty over how rivals will
        react to the oligopolist's actions.
    c. A firm in a monopolistically competitive industry will
        face a downward-sloping demand curve owing to product
        differentiation. It is likely to be relatively elastic,
        however, because of the large number of other firms
        that sell good substitutes.

3. The reasons are two. First, oligopoly situations vary
    widely in terms of the number of sellers and the nature of
    the product, so generalization to a typical case is just
    about impossible. Second, even if the number of firms and
    the nature of the product can be specified, the reactions of
    each of several rivals to changes in price or product con-
    figurations are impossible to predict or generalize.

4. Product differentiation is the primary factor separating
    monopolistic from pure competition. With it, consumers
    become attached to particular sellers with varying degrees
    of tightness. Thus a small decrease in one seller's price
    may attract marginal customers from other sellers but so few
    from each one that none of the other sellers notices the
    loss. An increase in the seller's price causes its marginal
    customers to go to other sellers but, again, so few to any
    one seller that none notices the gain. Therefore, what
    would have been a perfectly elastic demand curve facing the
    firm takes on a downward tilt.

5. a. It is probably a government-licensed monopolist of dial-a-ride services, although it may compete to a degree with taxicab and bus services, thus becoming oligopolistic.

   b. "Sunkist" is the trade name for an association of citrus growers in California and Arizona that sells a large share of the citrus crop. It is one of the largest sellers in an oligopolistic market that includes other associations and many smaller rivals.

   c. Computer software is probably still an oligopoly, although the number of sellers is increasing rapidly.

   d. Urban land markets tend to be monopolistically competitive. It is rare for huge amounts of acreage in a given area to be owned by a single entity.

   e. Unique locations may be oligopolistic and raise land values, but the lower prices that other parcels can fetch act as a brake on how much prices (or economic rent) on the prime parcels can rise.

   f. Monopoly elements should be relatively rare for rural land. The market for wheat farms of given size and productivity in, say, Nebraska or Minnesota, should be competitive.

6. Obtaining a monopoly of prime downtown land would be possible but it would be expensive and unlikely in most cases. In downtown areas, it would require purchasing many parcels. Attempting to buy them quickly and openly induces present owners to "hold out" for higher prices, and buying them slowly as each parcel comes on the market postpones whatever monopoly gains might be obtained. High land prices in one downtown area tend to stimulate competitive development in adjacent areas, so an attempt at monopolization would usually be self-defeating.

7. A pure competitor has a horizontal demand curve. It can sell its whole production at the going market price without advertising, so it has no incentives to advertise.

8. Concentration ratios are calculated on a nationwide basis. Therefore, even a cement producer that has a monopoly in the nation's largest metropolitan area will produce only a small fraction of all the nation's cement. Cereal producers sell nationally and therefore have higher nationwide concentration ratios even though none of them has a monopoly in any city.

9. Economic theory gives no general answer to this question. A case-by-case, empirical approach is necessary.

10. No. Analysts recognize that it is expensive to gather information about every firm in an industry. Thus, analysts use the four- or eight-firm ratios and recognize their limitations.

11. The ratios should be higher in Canada than in the United States. Apparently, they are higher in Canada and several small European countries. (Douglas F. Greer, Industrial Organization and Public Policy [New York: Macmillan, 1980], 131.)

12. No. Hospital markets are primarily local because of the convenience to patients of being hospitalized close to home and the cost of searching for better facilities in other communities. The formation of chains will increase nation-wide concentration ratios but will probably make all hospitals more competitive in communities where chains operate. This will benefit consumers.

True-False Questions

(T) _____ 1. For the pure monopolist, the market demand curve and the demand curve facing the firm are identical.

(F) _____ 2. For the monopolistic competitor, the market demand curve and the demand curve facing the firm are identical.

(T) _____ 3. Automobile service stations in most cities of 25,000 or more provide an example of differentiated oligopoly.

(T) _____ 4. The automobile industry is an example of differentiated oligopoly.

(T) _____ 5. The demand curve facing the firm in a purely competitive market appears horizontal at the equilibrium market price level.

(F) _____ 6. Since a monopolist has no rivals, there is no incentive for the firm to engage in sales promotion activities.

(T) _____ 7. An oligopolist engages in sales promotion activities in order to encroach on the markets of rival firms.

© 1988 The Dryden Press

(F) ____ 8. The downward slope of the demand curve facing a monopolistic competitor stems from the downward slope of the market demand curve for the product.

(T) ____ 9. An oligopolistic firm may have difficulty determining where its demand curve lies because of uncertainties regarding the reactions of rivals to the activities of the one.

(F) ____ 10. The demand curve facing monopolists are for the most part inelastic.

(T) ____ 11. The use of four- and eight-firm concentration ratios by economists is purely a matter of convenience and has no basis in market theory.

(F) ____ 12. Concentration ratios are widely used by economists because they unambiguously give accurate information on the degree of competition in a particular market.

(F) ____ 13. Household refrigerators and freezers are clearly the most concentrated market according to the concentration ratios in Table 8.3 in the text, and therefore, this market is also the most effective oligopoly of any of the industries listed in the table.

(F) ____ 14. The market for haircuts in a large city would be purely competitive, even if a governmental regulation limits entry, as long as the number of sellers remains very large.

Multiple-Choice Questions

(c) ____ 1. A seller in a purely competitive market faces a demand curve that:
   a. is the same as the market demand curve.
   b. is a proportional part of the market demand curve.
   c. is horizontal at the level of the equilibrium market price.
   d. is perfectly inelastic.

© 1988 The Dryden Press

(a) ____ 2. Under conditions of pure competition:
   a. no rivalries among sellers exist.
   b. each seller can be expected to react to the market actions of any other sellers.
   c. cutthroat competition frequently occurs.
   d. cartel arrangements are common.

(d) ____ 3. An increase in supply in a purely competitive market will:
   a. not change the demand curve facing the firm.
   b. shift the market demand curve downward.
   c. shift the demand curve facing the firm upward.
   d. shift the demand curve facing the firm downward.

(d) ____ 4. Purely competitive markets do not contain which of the following characteristics:
   a. sellers having locational advantages over competitors
   b. government marketing orders
   c. sellers who charge more to some buyers than to others
   d. all of the above

(b) ____ 5. The telephone company in a given locality faces:
   a. a horizontal demand curve.
   b. the market demand curve.
   c. a vertical demand curve.
   d. a downward-sloping demand curve that is more elastic at each price level than the market demand curve.

(b) ____ 6. Monopolists frequently engage in:
   a. product differentiation.
   b. sales promotion activities.
   c. rivalry with other firms in the market.
   d. price wars.

(b) ____ 7. In an oligopolistic industry, there are:
   a. many sellers of a product which may or may not be differentiated.
   b. few sellers of a product which may or may not be differentiated.
   c. no sales promotion activities.
   d. no rivalries among sellers.

(c) ____ 8. In order for General Motors to be able to determine the U.S. demand curve for Oldsmobiles, it:
a. can ignore the output of Mercuries in the
United States.
b. must take into account the sales of Mercedes
in Europe.
c. must take into account sales policies of all
firms that market automobiles in the United
States.
d. can ignore the advertising done by Chrysler
Corporation for Imperials.

(e) ____ 9. Which of the following is not a defect of using
concentration ratios to measure the degree of
competition or monopoly in a market?
a. The ratios exclude exports and imports.
b. Industries are defined according to production
characteristics rather than demand characteristics.
c. Some industries are defined in national terms
when, in fact, they are highly localized.
d. The ratios ignore recycle and scrap markets.
e. all of the above

(d) ____ 10. If United States Steel Corporation raises the
price per ton of basic steel that it sells, it
will:
a. increase its share of the market if other
steel producers raise their prices by a smaller percentage.
b. increase its share of the market if other producers match the price increase.
c. decrease its share of the market if other
firms raise their prices by a larger percentage.
d. increase its share of the market if other
firms raise their prices by a larger percentage.

(d) ____ 11. Product differentiation in the barbering trade:
a. does not occur.
b. is partly the result of supposed differences
in the skills of different barbers.
c. may be based on the locational advantages or
disadvantages of barber shops.
d. both (b) and (c)

(b) _____ 12. Which of the following is an example of monopolistic competition?
a. gasoline retailing in a town of 1,000 people
b. the retail grocery trade in a city of 500,000
c. the competition among automobile producers in the United States
d. the sale of wheat

(b) _____ 13. The demand curve facing a monopolistic competitor:
a. is downward-sloping to the right because the market demand curve is downward-sloping to the right.
b. is downward-sloping to the right because of product differentiation.
c. is horizontal at the equilibrium market price.
d. is the same as the market demand curve.

(a) _____ 14. Which of the following statements accurately describes the information contained in a four-firm concentration ratio?
a. It shows the combined market share of the four largest firms in the industry.
b. It shows the relative sizes of the four largest firms.
c. It shows changes in the composition over time of the four largest firms.
d. It tells you at least something about the importance of the industry's four smallest firms.

(d) _____ 15. Which of the following is information that the four-firm concentration ratio does not contain?
a. data on level of entry barriers in the industry
b. whether the market is primarily national or local
c. the fraction of market sales that the four biggest firms account for
d. (a) and (b)

PART THREE

THE FOUNDATIONS OF COSTS AND SUPPLY

In this part of the book, as in Chapter 8, attention is concentrated on an individual firm rather than on consumer units.
In Chapter 9 we develop the principles governing a firm in
combining resource inputs to produce product final goods or
services. In Chapter 10 these principles of production are
translated into the cost curves of a firm. The type of market
in which a firm sells is not important in Part Three since it
does not affect either the principles of production or the
construction of the firm's cost curves.

CHAPTER 9

THE PRINCIPLES OF PRODUCTION

Chapter Outline

Producer Choice and Consumer Choice: A Comparison
The Production Function
    The Concept
    The Production Surface
    Product Curves
The Law of Diminishing Returns
Product Curves and Technical Efficiency
    The Three Stages for Labor
    The Three Stages for Capital
    Stage II Combinations
    A Generalized Stage II
    The Least-Cost Resource Combination
Production Possibilities for the Economy
    Resource Allocation among Products
    Transformation Curves

Applications

Technological Change at Coca-Cola
Road Salt Use in Midwestern Cities

Chapter Objectives

This chapter has two main facets: (1) exposition of the physical production function of a firm and (2) the theory of choice among alternative resource combinations by a firm. The firm's production function shows the relationships between its product output and its resource inputs. The theory of choice deals with which of the many resource combinations available to the firm it should use.

Suggestions for Teaching

The material of this chapter becomes much easier for students if they are able to see first of all that the theory of choice for a firm in using resources to yield product parallels that of a consumer using products to yield satisfaction. So we begin with a comparison of the two. Then we use a production surface to illustrate a firm's production function. A physical model of a production surface that can be taken apart is very helpful at this point in visualizing the production function. Then the step from the production surface to an isoquant map is an easy one. Alternatively, an isoquant map can be built up directly without the aid of a production surface.

We explain the construction of product curves for a resource—total, average, and marginal—as a cross section of the production surface. It is of critical importance to get across the fact that the horizontal axis measures <u>ratios of variable resources</u> in the general case. Most students, many instructors, and some textbook writers miss this crucial point. As a <u>special case</u>, it is, of course, correct to measure units of a variable resource per some fixed quantities of fixed resources on the horizontal axis. But note that this special case is of no importance in the theory of choice of economically correct variable resource combinations.

There are several major end results of the study of product curves. First, Stage III for any resource involves negative marginal physical product for that resource, making the Stage III quantities of it redundant. Second, Stage I for any resource is Stage III for some other resource, making quantities of that other resource redundant in that Stage. Third, Stage II is common to both resources and contains all economically relevant combinations of the two variable resources for which the cross section is constructed. In Stage II the law of diminishing returns is operating for both resources. Fourth, the <u>total product curve</u> of the resource shown in the numerator of the ratio of quantities shows the efficiency with which the resource shown in the denominator is used for various combinations. Fifth, the <u>average product curve</u> of the numerator resource shows the efficiency with which that resource is used. After discussing these important points, we go back to the firm's isoquant map—the full production function—and show that combinations lying outside the ridge lines are those containing redundant quantities of one resource or the other.

A family of isocost curves, correct combinations of resources for each cost level, and the firm's expansion path create no special problems. Spacing isocosts by equal cost outlay intervals, one can readily show the different isoquant patterns that lead to increasing returns to size, decreasing returns to size, and constant returns to size. The application on road salt use shows the effects of changes in resource prices on isocosts and expansion paths. The one of technological change at Coca-Cola illustrates the effects of such changes on a firm's isoquant map.

© 1988 The Dryden Press

If the Edgeworth box was learned thoroughly in Chapter 5, it should give no trouble here. The movement from the contract curve to the production possibilities curve is sticky for some students. Units of measurement on the axes of the two diagrams are often not understood. Neither is the concavity to the origin of the transformation curve. These concepts usually require special emphasis in the classroom.

Problems and Questions for Discussion

1. From the following per day information for a firm:
   a. compute the average and marginal physical product curves for labor.
   b. plot the total average and marginal physical product curves. Identify and explain each of the three stages for labor.

Capital ($1,000 worth)	Labor (Man-hours)	Total Product (Shirts)
1	1	20
1	2	42
1	3	66
1	4	88
1	5	108
1	6	124
1	7	136
1	8	144
1	9	148
1	10	148
1	11	144
1	12	136

2. Draw a hypothetical isoquant map for a firm that uses labor and capital to produce units of clothing. Draw and explain the ridge lines. Select a quantity of capital that lies outside the ridge line nearest the capital axis. Now, show and explain the impact on output of larger and larger quantities of labor used with that quantity of capital. Explain as fully as you can the shape of the total product curve that would emerge.

3. Draw and explain an isocost curve for a firm that uses only labor and capital to produce its product. What would make it shift? What would cause its slope to change?

© 1988 The Dryden Press

4. For a firm with two resource inputs, A and B, one product output, X, and a production function homogeneous of degree one:
   a. explain the symmetry of Stage I for A and Stage III for B, Stage III for A and Stage I for B, and Stage II for both resources.
   b. starting with a Stage I ratio of A to B, explain what happens to the efficiency with which each A and B is used as the ratio of A to B is increased through Stage I, Stage II, and into Stage III for A.
   c. in which stage would you expect the firm to operate? Why?

5. A wheat farmer and a road construction firm have a fixed amount of labor and a fixed amount of gasoline to be allocated between them each month. Suppose that initially the government allocates gasoline between the two users on a 50-50 basis. Illustrating with an Edgeworth box:
   a. under what circumstances would you expect that the allocation would not be efficient?
   b. what would it take to make the allocation efficient? Why?

6. From question (5), explain how a transformation curve for wheat and miles of highway can be constructed.

7. Given a firm's production function, its total cost outlay, and the prices of the resources that it uses, explain and illustrate the conditions for maximum output of the firm's product. How can the firm's expansion path be generated?

8. Rework the road salt problem assuming that the price of salt declines instead of rises. Draw the diagrams and describe the adjustments for each of the three cities, indicating the amounts of inputs purchased and the levels of road safety achieved. How do your results differ from those in Figures 9.10, 9.11, and 9.12 in the text?

© 1988 The Dryden Press

9. Go through last week's issues of The Wall Street Journal or the financial pages of a major newspaper in your state to find a case in which a reporter is explaining the consequences of some change in input prices; for example, the price of lumber required to build houses, the price of sugar used to produce syrups for colas and other beverages, the price of grain used to feed livestock, and so forth. Draw isoquant-isocost diagrams consistent with the facts that the reporter describes just as we did for road salts. These articles are very common in newspapers since the consequences of these prices produce large wealth effects on the firms involved and thus their stock prices, and working through the diagrams will test your understanding of the basic concepts.

10. Discuss the major similarities and differences between the theory of consumer choice and the theory of producer choice.

11. Assume that your college doubles the number of classrooms and the number of professors but the number of students increases by only 50 percent. Does this situation imply operation of the law of diminishing returns? Why or why not?

12. Rotterdam, Holland, has some of the world's biggest oil refineries. Most were built to produce heavier products such as fuel oil and industrial heating oil in the era when crude was cheap. But the demands for these goods fell as higher crude prices stimulated coal and natural gas production. Refineries can be modified to make lighter distillates such as gasoline, diesel, and aviation fuel that have fewer market substitutes. These costly modifications became economical after demands changed markedly. ("Oil Glut Forces Big Changes at Rotterdam's Refineries," Los Angeles Times, September 18, 1981.)
   a. Which diagram in the text illustrates the alternative products that a refinery could produce?
   b. Which concept explains the rate at which substitutions between the two types of products are made with given technology?
   c. Show the before-and-after changes in output for the Rotterdam refinery. What is plotted on each axis of the diagram?

© 1988 The Dryden Press

13. By 1982, Campbell Soup Co. had invested $10 million in genetic research to develop a "super tomato" that resists disease, is impervious to rot, strong enough not to crush under the weight of other fruit, and sufficiently flavorful for soup, ketchup, sauce, and juices. (Betsy Morris, "Campbell Soup Is Looking for 'Super' Tomato," The Wall Street Journal, April 2, 1982.)

   a. Draw before-and-after diagrams to show the change in isoquants for substitutions between ordinary tomatoes and super tomatoes in the production of soup. Assume super tomatoes become commercial. Show the short-run and long-run expansion paths.

   b. What determines the degree to which super tomatoes replace regular tomatoes? Explain.

14. Solar water-heating manufacturers enjoyed good residential sales in the early 1980s owing to federal energy tax credits that reimbursed the buyer for 40 percent of the expenditure up to $10,000. These credits, adopted in 1978 when energy prices were rising, were due to expire December 31, 1985. The manufacturers told Congress that solar sales would decline in an era of steady electricity and natural gas prices unless the tax credits were maintained. (Nancy Rivera, "Solar Tax Credit Extension Sought," Los Angeles Times, March 12, 1985.)

   a. Draw an isoquant-isocost diagram between solar versus conventional energy to show the effect of expiring tax credits. Assume a family that would purchase some solar energy without credits.

   b. Draw the diagram for a family that would purchase only conventional energy without credits.

Solutions to Problems and Questions for Discussion

1. a.

Units of Labor	Average Product of Labor	Marginal Product of Labor
1	20	20
2	21	22
3	22	24
4	22	22
5	21.6	20
6	20.7	16
7	19.4	12
8	18	8
9	16.4	4
10	14.8	0
11	13.1	-4
12	11.3	-8

b. Stage I for labor ends (and Stage II for labor begins) at 4 units of labor, where the marginal product and average product of labor are equal (holding capital fixed at one unit). Stage II for labor ends (and Stage III for labor begins) at 10 units of labor, where the marginal product of labor is zero.

2. Use text Figures 9.5 and 9.2 for reference. Assume that B is capital and A is labor. Draw a set of isoquants like those of Figure 9.5. Ridge line OC is made up of the vertical points of the isoquants while OD is made up of the horizontal points. Select a point such as b_1 of capital and draw a horizontal line such as KJ, labelling the isoquant to which it is tangent, x_6. Reference to Figure 9.2 may help at this juncture. Larger and larger quantities of labor, used with b_1 of capital, cause TP_1 to increase out to the quantity of labor at which KJ is tangent to x_6. For further increases in labor, it will decrease. To the left of OC, MPP_c will be negative and Stage I for labor will exist; i.e., AP_1 will be rising as you move to the right. MPP_1 will peak at a quantity of labor to the left of OD. Thus the TP_1 curve will be rising at an increasing rate to that quantity of labor at which MPP_1 peaks, then at a decreasing rate to the quantity at which KJ is tangent to x_6, and will decrease at still larger quantities of labor.

3. Review the discussion of text Figure 9.6. The isocost
    curve would shift parallel to itself if the cost outlay
    available to the firm changes (absent a change in the rel-
    ative prices between the two inputs). It would shift to
    the right if total cost outlay increases and would shift
    to the left if cost outlay decreases. The slope of the
    isocost curve would change if the relative prices between
    the two inputs change.

4. See text, pp. 237-248.

5. a. Review the discussion of the Edgeworth box in text
        Figure 9.7. The allocation would be inefficient if the
        marginal rate of technical substitution between gaso-
        line and labor in the production of wheat were different
        from that for the construction of new miles of highway.
    b. The two producers should be allowed to exchange labor
        and gasoline voluntarily until they achieved a combina-
        tion lying on the contract curve of the Edgeworth box.
        This would be a point such as K in Figure 9.7.

6. Review the discussion of text Figure 9.8. The transfor-
    mation curve is generated from the quantities of wheat pro-
    duced and highway miles constructed as indicated on the
    isoquants of an Edgeworth box along the contract curve, mov-
    ing from the lower left origin to the upper right origin.

7. Review the discussion of text Figure 9.6. The expansion
    path is generated on an isoquant map as the firm's cost
    outlay changes and the isocost curve shifts parallel to
    itself. The expansion path consists of the locus of com-
    binations of the two resources generated by the tangencies
    between each isocost and the highest possible isoquant.

8. The analysis is basically reversed. Redraw each figure to make the slopes of the isocost curves flatter as a result of the decrease in the sale price. The generally correct result is for each city to use more salt relative to sand than previously. However, assume that each city's reaction to the decline in the price of salt parallels its reaction to the rise in price. Cincinnati's reaction to the rise in the price of salt was correct, so its reaction to the decline would be correct. It would use more salt relative to sand, and thereby achieve the same level of safety for a smaller budget (total outlay). Chicago would achieve an inefficient result again if it reacts to the decline in the price of salt in the same manner as it reacted to the price rise. Buying the same amount of salt regardless of the price means that Chicago would forego the increase in safety that could be obtained if the same budget were spent differently. McKeesport would also achieve an inefficient result again if it selects a corner solution by purchasing zero sand as a result of the decline in the price of salt, rather than by purchasing some combination of the two resources as Cincinnati does.

9. Articles of this kind are relatively common, and the instructor should be able to find them without difficulty if students cannot. They can be brought to class for discussion in class or be distributed for take-home assignments. Often the article suggests particular responses by firms that can easily be adapted to the isoquant-isocost framework.

10. Review the table on p. 228.

11. No. The concept of diminishing returns applies to the change in output that occurs when one resource used (such as classrooms) increases relative to the other (such as professors). The concept of returns to size applies to the change in output when all resources used change in the same proportion.

12. a. Either text Figure 9.7 or 9.8, or both.
    b. A transformation curve such as MN in text Figure 9.8 shows the marginal rate of transformation between lighter products and heavier products for an oil refinery.
    c. Plot heavy oil products per unit of time along the vertical axis and light products along the horizontal. Moving from R to S in Figure 9.8 shows an adjustment from heavy to light products.

13. a. Draw diagrams patterned after those in text Figure 9.9.
    b. It depends on the shapes of the isoquants and the slopes of the isocost lines; that is, the degree of substitutability between them and their relative prices.

14. a. Following text Figure 9.10, plot solar energy per unit of time along the X-axis and conventional energy per unit of time along the Y-axis. Removing the tax credit raises the price of solar energy relative to conventional energy. Thus, if T_1 is the total outlay, the new isocost line rotates inward from AB to AC. The expansion path adjusts from one like GH to one like SJ as more conventional energy is used relative to solar energy for each output rate and total outlay. A diagram like Figure 9.10 would show a family that purchased some solar energy without the tax credit.
    b. A diagram like Figure 9.12 would show a family that purchased zero solar energy without the tax credit.

True-False Questions

(F) _____ 1. One shortcoming of the concept of a production function is that it ignores technology.

(T) _____ 2. A production function takes cognizance of the possibilities of substitution among resources by a firm and also the possibility that some resources used may be complementary to others.

(T) _____ 3. At alternative possible output levels, a firm may use different production techniques.

(T) _____ 4. A given production function may be represented graphically by an entire isoquant map.

(F) _____ 5. A production function that is homogeneous of degree one precludes operation of the law of diminishing returns.

(F) _____ 6. Diminishing returns for a resource begin at the employment level at which its total product begins to decrease.

(T) _____ 7. The resource employment level at which total product of the resource is maximum is also the one at which its marginal physical product is zero.

© 1988 The Dryden Press

(F) _____ 8. The law of diminishing returns for a resource becomes effective at the Stage I-Stage II boundary for that resource.

(T) _____ 9. If a firm uses one hundred resources and combines them efficiently, it will be in Stage II for each of those resources.

(T) _____ 10. If a firm uses one hundred resources and combines them efficiently, an increase in the use of any one of those resources will result in diminishing marginal physical product for it.

(T) _____ 11. On the ridge lines of an isoquant diagram, the marginal physical product of one of the resources is zero.

(F) _____ 12. The marginal rate of technical substitution between two resources is always measured by the slope of the firm's isocost curve for them.

(F) _____ 13. The slope of an isocost curve is determined by the ratio of the marginal physical products of the resources for which it is drawn.

(T) _____ 14. A least-cost combination of resources is one at which the marginal physical product per dollar's worth of any one resource used by the firm is equal to the marginal physical product per dollar's worth of any other resource that it uses.

(T) _____ 15. A least-cost combination of resources is one at which the marginal rate of technical substitution of one resource for another is equal to the ratio of their prices.

(F) _____ 16. Generally speaking, there is only one efficient allocation of two resources between two products produced by those resources.

(F) _____ 17. There is no way to obtain a transformation curve for two products from the contract curve for them.

(T) _____ 18. A production function, $x = f(a,b)$, is homogeneous if $\lambda^n x = f(\lambda a, \lambda b)$.

(T) ____ 19. Chicago's behavior after the rise in road salt prices is economically rational only if one presumes that the city simultaneously wants to increase the level of road safety for its residents relative to previous levels.

(F) ____ 20. The Stage II concept for variable resources can be illustrated on a total product diagram but not on an isoquant diagram.

(F) ____ 21. Technological change cannot be illustrated on an isoquant diagram.

(F) ____ 22. The transformation curve of a firm is derived logically from its total product curves.

(T) ____ 23. Coca-Cola's experimentation with different sweeteners for Coke was initially stimulated by changes in input prices.

(F) ____ 24. Changes in the mix of sweeteners used in the production of soft drinks can be illustrated by changes in the shapes of isoquant curves only.

Multiple-Choice Questions

(b) ____ 1. Which of the following is not a characteristic of a production function?
   a. It shows input-input relationships.
   b. It shows output-cost relationships.
   c. It shows input-output relationships.
   d. It may show output-output relationships.

(c) ____ 2. An isoquant map shows:
   a. the resource combinations that a firm can purchase with a given cost outlay, given the resource prices.
   b. the combinations of products that can be produced with given quantities of a resource.
   c. the combinations of resources that are necessary to produce given outputs of a product.
   d. the least-cost combination of resources.

(a) ____ 3. The law of diminishing returns refers to those employment levels of a resource at which its:
   a. marginal physical product declines.
   b. total product declines.
   c. average product declines.
   d. transformation curve declines.

(d) _____ 4. The amount of common labor that a building construction company will use if it operates efficiently is one at which:
a. the marginal physical product of the labor is
maximum.
b. the marginal physical product of the labor is
minimum.
c. the marginal physical product of the labor is
zero.
d. the marginal physical product of the labor is
declining.

(d) _____ 5. If a firm's isocost curve is tangent to one of its
isoquants:
a. maximum output is being obtained from a given
cost outlay.
b. a given amount of product is being obtained at
the least possible cost.
c. the marginal physical product of a dollar's
worth of one resource used equals the marginal
physical product of a dollar's worth of the
other.
d. all of the above

(c) _____ 6. For a production function that is linearly homogeneous:
a. diminishing returns for any one resource are
not possible.
b. Stage I and Stage III for any one resource do
not exist.
c. Stage I for one resource must be Stage III for
some other resource or resources.
d. resources must be used in fixed proportions.

(a) _____ 7. The efficiency with which any given resource is
used by a firm is reflected by the resource:
a. average product curve.
b. total product curve.
c. marginal physical product curve.
d. price.

(a) _____ 8. The marginal rate of technical substitution of resource A for resource B is best defined as:
a. MPP_a/MPP_b.
b. $MPP_a/P_a \div MPP_b/P_b$.
c. P_a/P_b.
d. slope of the contract curve.

(d) _____ 9. An efficient allocation of resources among uses is one in which:
  a. the total product of each resource is maximized.
  b. the greatest possible output of each product is obtained.
  c. the marginal physical product of each resource is the same in all of its uses.
  d. the marginal rate of technical substitution of any one resource for another is the same in all their uses.

(b) _____ 10. Along the expansion path of a firm:
  a. the marginal rate of technical substitution between the resources may change.
  b. the marginal rate of technical substitution between the resources will remain constant.
  c. the level of production remains constant.
  d. the marginal rate of transformation must decrease.

(d) _____ 11. To obtain the greatest possible output from a given cost outlay, a firm should allocate the outlay among variable resources such that:
  a. the dollar expenditure on each is the same.
  b. the total product attributable to any one resource is the same as that attributable to any other resource.
  c. the marginal physical product of any one resource should be equal to that of each other resource.
  d. the marginal physical product per dollar's worth of any one resource should be the same as that of each other resource and diminishing returns should occur for each.

(d) _____ 12. Suppose that a firm uses two resources, A and B, to produce a certain product, X. If all possible ratios of A to B are considered, diminishing returns to A will occur:
  a. in Stage II, only.
  b. in Stage I, only.
  c. in Stage III, only.
  d. in Stage II for certain, and possibly in Stage I, also.

(b) _____ 13. In the road salt case, Cincinnati's adjustment was the most sensible economically because:
 a. Cincinnati is better governed than Chicago or McKeesport.
 b. Cincinnati bought less salt and more sand with the same budget level and produced the same safety level as before.
 c. no city should accept a reduction in safety at any cost, and therefore, Chicago was sensible in purchasing the same amount of road salts no matter how high the price rose.
 d. McKeesport failed to hire a public opinion polling firm to determine the level of safety that residents wanted and therefore, how much salt the residents would have wanted the city to purchase.

(a) _____ 14. In a total product diagram, the symmetry between Stage I of the one input and Stage III of the other is logical because:
 a. the total product of the one when more and more of it is applied to a constant amount of the other is the same as the average product of the other when the one increases.
 b. Stage II is the only relevant stage of production for both inputs.
 c. the law of diminishing returns holds only when both inputs are varied.
 d. none of the above

(a) _____ 15. The introduction of fructose as an alternative to sugar caused the isoquant map for the production of Coke fountain syrup to change because:
 a. technological change caused the marginal physical product of fructose to increase.
 b. the price of Coke did not change.
 c. the average cost of Coke had already changed.
 d. using fructose in syrup lowers production costs for syrup.

(b) ____ 16. One principle of economics that applies to the road salt application and the Coca-Cola application alike is:
   a. top management is just as bad in big corporations as in big cities.
   b. economic agents are rational and usually buy less of inputs whose prices increase relatively.
   c. it is difficult for large and complex organizations to adjust to new circumstances promptly.
   d. the two applications have nothing in common.

(c) ____ 17. Which of the following was not a factor leading Coca-Cola to adjust its rates of use of different sweeteners in Coke prior to the drastic change in its flavor in 1985?
   a. changes in relative prices among sweeteners
   b. experimentation with the effects on Coke's flavor of using various sweeteners in different proportions
   c. a change in the demand for Coke
   d. an increase in the supply of fructose

CHAPTER 10

COSTS OF PRODUCTION

Chapter Outline

Basic Cost Concepts
   The Alternative Cost (Opportunity Cost) Principle
   Explicit and Implicit Costs
   Cost, Resource Prices, and Efficiency
The Short-Run and Long-Run Viewpoints
   The Short Run
   The Long Run
Short-Run Cost Curves
   Total Cost Curves
   Per Unit Cost Curves
   Relationship of MC to AC and to AVC
   Most Efficient Rate of Output
Long-Run Cost Curves
   Long-Run Total Costs
   Long-Run Average Costs
   Economies of Size
   Diseconomies of Size
   Most Efficient Size of Plant
   Long-Run Marginal Cost
   Relationships between LMC and SMC

Applications

Costs of Obtaining a Higher Education
Cost Minimization by a Multiple-Unit Firm
Economies of Size in the Beer Industry

Chapter Objectives

We present the fundamental cost theory principles in this chapter. These include the opportunity or alternative cost principle, short-run and long-run viewpoints, the transition from
the principles of production to costs of production, and the
complete set of long-run and short-run cost curves. These are
as important to microeconomic analysis as the multiplication
tables are to arithmetic. They lay the foundations for supply
concepts and for the analysis of outputs and pricing in Part
Four of the book.

© 1988 The Dryden Press

Suggestions for Teaching

The greatest challenge for the instructor in this chapter is that of avoiding a discussion that is dry, dull, and mechanical. There is much of a rote nature to learn. The answer to the challenge lies in using many everyday examples of the alternative cost principle and of explicit and implicit costs. The higher education application provides some of both. In discussing short-run costs, examples of firms that produce even though incurring losses can be culled easily from The Wall Street Journal or any financial publication and there is no better way to get across the distinction between variable cost and total cost concepts. The beer industry application puts life into the issue of economies and diseconomies of size.

We are aware that the term "economies of scale" is usually used where we use "economies of size," but we believe the latter is more accurate. Economies of scale require a linear expansion path for the firm which in turn implies a homogeneous production function. Most expansion paths and production functions will not fulfill these requirements. So we use the more general term that puts no such restrictions on either.

Students often confuse the reasons for the U-shape of the short-run average cost curve with those for the U-shape of the long-run average cost curve. It is generally worthwhile to spend some time on these, spelling out carefully the uniqueness of each set of curves.

There are several common errors that our students make in drawing cost curves and that we teach them to guard against. They try to make SAC curves tangent to LAC curves at points other than their minimum points. Their LMC and SMC curves are often drawn through the tangency points of SAC and LAC curves when the tangency points are not minimum points. Their marginal cost curves often do not cut the corresponding average cost curves at the minimum points of the latter. The only answer that we can suggest to these and similar difficulties is repeated drill.

Are you still making certain that students know the meanings of all running glossary terms?

Problems and Questions for Discussion

1. It has been said that a military draft for the armed forces is necessary because the United States economy cannot afford to pay high enough wage rates to obtain a sufficient number of volunteers. What is the economic cost of a draftee when the draft is used?

2. In ordinary accounting procedures, the interest on bonds issued by a corporation is considered to be costs of production but dividends paid to stockholders are not. Discuss this procedure in terms of economic cost concepts.

3. For each of the following situations, indicate whether short-run or long-run planning is involved, giving the reasons for your answer:
   a. The ACE service station decides that it must increase the frequency of gasoline orders to the bulk distributor because of increased sales.
   b. The ACE service station decides to expand its underground storage capacity.
   c. Honest John Associates, Inc., Certified Public Accountants, installs computerized, in place of manual, accounting techniques.
   d. The Rickety Aviation Company adds an airplane to its charter service fleet.

4. Draw a typical short-run total cost curve for a firm. From this curve, derive each of the following:
   a. the average fixed cost curve
   b. the average variable cost curve
   c. the average cost curve
   d. the marginal cost curve

5. With an isoquant-isocost diagram explain a firm's least-cost resource combination. Now draw the appropriate cost curves of the firm and explain the relationship between the cost curves and what you show on the isoquant-isocost diagram.

6. Show and explain, for a firm, the relationship between its:
   a. long-run total cost curve and its various possible short-run total cost curves.
   b. long-run average cost curve and its various possible short-run average cost curves.
   c. long-run average cost curve, one of its short-run average cost curves, and the corresponding long-run and short-run marginal cost curves.

7. Prove that the long-run average cost curve is horizontal if the production function is linearly homogeneous.

8. Explain the U-shape ordinarily attributable to:
   a. a short-run average cost curve.
   b. a long-run average cost curve.

© 1988 The Dryden Press

9. "Shakeouts" have occurred in many U.S. industries during this century, but not all of these have followed the pattern of the beer industry in which a large number of smaller firms has been replaced by a smaller number of larger firms. In the meat-packing industry, for example, the trend has been just the opposite, from a small number of large firms located in the Chicago stockyards to a larger number now decentralized around the country. Go to your library and try to ascertain why this decentralized trend in the meat-packing industry occurred and why it happened when it did, and then conceptualize your results within the framework of the planning curves such as those shown in Figure 10.14 for the beer industry. (Hint: One of the factors you should consider is the effect on meat packing of the rise in motor trucking and the decline of railroads.)

10. In 1980, General Motors announced cuts in its production of cars owing to "sluggish demand." Several plants were closed and 2,100 workers were idled. Based on this information, would you judge that GM was moving from one point to another along its existing marginal cost curve or that its marginal cost curve had shifted? Explain.

11. Selling groceries involves many smaller firms in most larger cities. Speculate on the reasons that derive from the cost or supply side (ignoring demand variables). Start by considering whether or not most grocery stores would have major sources of economies of size.

12. Discuss and illustrate the logical relationships between marginal physical product and marginal cost curves, and between average product and average variable cost curves.

13. In 1986, the U.S. Department of Transportation believed that the national 55-mile-per-hour speed limit saved between 2,000 and 4,000 lives per year. To enforce it, the Department threatened to cut off highway construction funds to Arizona and Vermont, where over half the motorists exceeded that limit. (Damon Darline, "Does 55-MPH Speed Limit Save Lives? More Drivers Are Doubtful," The Wall Street Journal, April 28, 1986.) The law was changed in 1987.
   a. Assume that the speed limit saved 4,000 lives per year. What was its opportunity cost? Explain.
   b. How would an economist determine whether or not the speed limit should be maintained or abolished?

© 1988 The Dryden Press

14. What determines the upper limit on the number of firms in an industry where each firm has economies of size and operates to minimize average cost? What determines the lower limit on the number of firms in an industry where each firm has diseconomies of size and operates to minimize average cost? Under what conditions would the upper and lower limits coincide?

15. Diagram and explain the effects on total, average, and marginal cost curves of the changes in isoquants or expansion paths in the following problems for discussion in Chapter 9 of the <u>Instructor's Manual</u>:
    a. using the "supertomato" to produce Campbell's soups and other tomato products in Problem 13; and
    b. the expiration of tax credits for residential solar energy collectors in Problem 14.

16. In text Figure 10.14, draw the marginal cost curve for 1947-62 that is consistent with the shape of the $LAC_{1947-62}$ curve.

Solutions to Problems and Questions for Discussion

1. The cost to the economy is the highest-valued opportunity that is lost, which usually exceeds budgeted costs due to the low wage rate paid to conscripts. The view that the United States can not afford to pay wage rates sufficiently high to attract enough volunteers confuses budgeted costs with opportunity costs.

2. Each payment is part of the cost of capital. Interest is the return necessary to induce lenders to buy the corporation's bonds; dividends are part of the returns necessary to induce stockholders to buy the corporation's stock. The opportunity cost to bondholders and stockholders of investing in any corporation is the returns that they could obtain from buying securities of similar risk of some other corporation.

3. a. Short-run. The firm is increasing output without changing the size of its present plant.
   b. Long-run. The firm is changing the size of its plant.
   c. Short-run. The firm is substituting capital for labor but not adjusting fixed resources such as land, buildings, heavy machinery, and management that are variable in the long run only.
   d. Long-run. The firm is changing the size of its plant.

4. See appendix to the text chapter.

© 1988 The Dryden Press

5. See point F in text Figure 10.6. At the least-cost combi-
    nation $MRTS_{ab} = p_a/p_b$. In Figure 10.6 the firm is on its
    LAC curve to the right of the minimum point.

6. a. Review the discussion of text Figure 10.12(a). The
        short-run total cost curve of any given plant size lies
        above the long-run total cost curve at all output rates
        except the rate at which they are tangent.
    b. Review the discussion of text Figure 10.8. The long-
        run average cost curve is the envelope of all possible
        short-run average cost curves. At each output rate,
        the LAC curve consists of the point on the SAC curve
        that produces the designated output at the lowest pos-
        sible cost.
    c. Review the discussion of text Figure 10.12(b). Long-
        run average cost is tangent to short-run average cost
        at the output rate at which long-run marginal cost
        intersects short-run marginal cost. The slope of the
        STC curve is the short-run marginal cost for that size
        of plant and the slope of the LTC curve is the long-
        run marginal cost. Thus, SMC is less than LMC for all
        output rates less than the rate at which STC and LTC
        are tangent, and SMC exceeds LMC at output rates larger
        than the rate at which STC and LTC are tangent.

7. In the case of a linearly homogeneous production function,
    doubling all inputs in the long run leads to a doubling of
    output. If input prices are constant as inputs are doubled,
    then total costs will double. If output doubles as total
    costs double, unit costs will remain constant. Thus, long-
    run average and marginal cost curves are horizontal.

8. a. Increasing and diminishing returns to the complex of
        variable resources.
    b. Increasing and decreasing returns to size; i.e., econ-
        omies.

9. In the 1880s, the meat-packing industry went through a shakeout much like that we described for beer. Previously, livestock was shipped from Chicago to eastern markets for slaughter and distribution. But the cattle had to be fed and watered during the journey, some died, and 60 percent of the surviving weight was inedible. Huge economies loomed if beef could be slaughtered and dressed in high volume at one location and then shipped, but refrigeration was necessary to prevent disease. In 1875, Gustavus Swift invented the refrigerated railroad car which drastically cut shipping costs, increased shipments, and revolutionized the industry. Soon meat packers in Chicago grew relative to their rivals in Boston and New York, with the Swift and Armour companies dominating the dressed beef industry. (Mary Yeager Kujovich, "The Refrigerator Car and the Growth of the American Dressed Beef Industry," Business History Review 64 [Winter, 1970]:460-482.)

   The rise of trucks and the decline of the railroad caused a shakeout of the opposite kind. Rail shipment was slow owing to the delays of sorting cars and changing trains in huge railroad yards. Trucks were quicker and more direct. Thus, the industry decentralized geographically. The planning curves in text Figure 10.14 would be modified to show the SAC for smaller meat-packing plants with lower average costs (including the costs of shipment) than the larger Chicago plants that they replaced.

10. Closing or opening plants is a long-run adjustment that involves moving to a new SAC curve with its corresponding SMC curve.

11. Most supermarkets seem to have a maximum size, probably because larger sizes generate diseconomies of various kinds. Fewer, larger stores would force shoppers to drive farther and require more land for bigger parking lots. Larger stores increase shopping times for consumers as they move from aisle to aisle, require more staff to reduce pilferage, and may present more complex inventory problems.

© 1988 The Dryden Press

12. Review the discussion of text Figure 10.3. The average variable cost curve is a sort of monetized mirror image of the average product curve for variable resources. As the average product of variable resources increases (decreases), average variable cost decreases (increases). When average product is at a maximum, average variable cost is at a minimum. By the same reasoning, marginal cost is a sort of monetized mirror image of the marginal product curve for variable resources. As marginal product increases (decreases), marginal cost decreases (increases). When marginal product of variable resources equals average product at maximum average product, marginal cost equals average variable cost at minimum average variable cost.

13. a. The productive time lost by motorists and truckers on trips where faster driving could have been done plus the costs of enforcement.
    b. We would compare the value of time sacrificed and the costs of enforcement to the value of lives saved plus the extra wear and tear on cars from faster driving. The value of the gasoline saved is trivial—less than one percent of all U.S. gasoline consumption or the equivalent of raising radial tire pressure by about two pounds. The value of a life is calculated by the government for various regulatory purposes and by economists who serve as expert witnesses in wrongful death cases.

    We would also attempt to separate the effect of slower driving from other forces likely to have similar effects that occurred simultaneously. Since the 55-mile speed limit was adopted in 1973, recreational driving declined because of higher gasoline prices and energy shortages, cars became safer, drinking ages were raised in many states, and other statutes required the use of seat belts and infant safety seats. It is unlikely that all the reduction in traffic fatalities is due to the lower speed limit. Indeed, the relationship may approach zero: one economist found that what counts is the variance of speed in a stream of traffic, not its average. This is not a conclusive argument for raising the speed limit, however, for we do not know the effect a higher speed limit would have on the speed variance. (Charles A. Lave, "Speeding, Coordination, and the 55 MPH Limit," American Economic Review 75 [December 1985]:1159-1164.)

14. The upper limit is determined by the size of the market in relation to the plant size at which economies are exhausted. The lower limit is determined by the size of the market in relation to the plant size at which diseconomies occur. The upper limit and lower limit coincide only if a single plant size yields minimum average cost. This requires that all firms have the same U-shaped average cost curve. (Douglas Needham, The Economics of Industrial Structure, Conduct and Performance, New York: St. Martin's Press, 1978:152.)

15. a. The cost curves shift down. You may wish to use the sequence of steps we outlined in Problem 5 of text Chapter 10.
    b. Some families who would have selected solar energy units with tax credits will switch to other forms of energy. This raises the cost of heating so the cost curves shift up.

16. As shown in the following diagram, the marginal cost curve is below average cost when average cost is decreasing and above average cost when it is rising. Marginal cost and average cost are equal over the range of output rates where average cost is at a minimum.

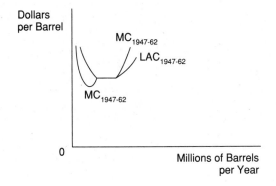

True-False Questions

(T) _____ 1. One of the costs of owning an automobile is the interest that one could have earned on the money that is invested in the automobile.

(F) _____ 2. One of the benefits of state-supported universities is that they provide educational services at lower economic costs to the society than do comparable private universities.

(F) ____ 3. With grants from the federal government, the economic costs of housing in a given community can be substantially reduced.

(T) ____ 4. Although accounting procedures show that the profits of a corporation are generally used to pay dividends to stockholders, average dividends are really a cost of production.

(F) ____ 5. The labor used by a farmer in the operation of a farm is not a cost of production since it need not be purchased or hired by the farmer.

(F) ____ 6. The long run for a business is any time period exceeding one year.

(T) ____ 7. A time period such that all resources used by a firm, except one, are variable can legitimately be called a short-run period.

(T) ____ 8. The total variable cost curve and the total cost of a firm have exactly the same shape; the total curve simply lies at a higher level.

(F) ____ 9. At any given level of output for a firm, the slope of the total variable cost curve measures average variable cost.

(T) ____ 10. Given the total variable cost curve and the total cost curve at any given level of output, the slope of either curve measures marginal cost.

(T) ____ 11. Minimum average cost occurs at the output level at which a straight line from the origin is just tangent to the total cost curve.

(T) ____ 12. The upward-sloping part of a short-run average cost curve results from the operation of the law of diminishing returns.

(F) ____ 13. The upward-sloping part of a long-run average cost curve results from the operation of the law of diminishing returns.

(T) ____ 14. The most efficient size of plant for a firm is one for which the short-run average cost curve is tangent to the long-run average cost curve at the minimum point of the short-run average cost curve.

(F) ____ 15. The most efficient rate of output for a given plant size is that at which the short-run average cost curve for the plant is tangent to the long-run average cost curve.

(F) ____ 16. To understand the relationship between average cost and marginal cost, it is helpful to think of average cost leading marginal cost up or down.

(F) ____ 17. A firm obtains the lowest cost for a given level of output by building the size of plant for which that output is the most efficient rate of output.

(F) ____ 18. The most important economies of size for a firm are those obtained from quantity discounts in the purchase of resources.

(T) ____ 19. If a firm is operating at an output level at which its short-run average cost curve is tangent to its long-run average cost curve, its short-run marginal cost curve will intersect its long-run marginal cost curve at the same output level.

(F) ____ 20. In order for a firm's long-run average cost curve to be U-shaped, the spacing of its isoquants, representing equal increments in product, must be first farther and farther apart, then closer and closer together as we move out along the firm's expansion path.

(T) ____ 21. The structure of the beer industry changed in response to changes on the cost side.

(F) ____ 22. Such concepts as average cost and marginal cost curves for the firm are theoretical constructions that have little bearing on the actual decisions made by real-world firms.

(F) ____ 23. Only long-run marginal cost curves were relevant for calculations in the brewing industry that pertained to whether or not new plants should be built.

(F) ____ 24. For a firm, LMC = SMC at the same rate of output where LMC = SAC.

(F) ____ 25. A multiple-unit firm would minimize total costs by equalizing average costs among plants.

© 1988 The Dryden Press

(F) ____ 26. Available evidence suggests that the largest brewers took advantage of rising concentration in the early 1980s to price monopolistically.

(T) ____ 27. The success of microbreweries is relatively difficult for economists to assess because some owners might view them as hobbies as well as profit-making activities.

Multiple-Choice Questions

(c) ____ 1.

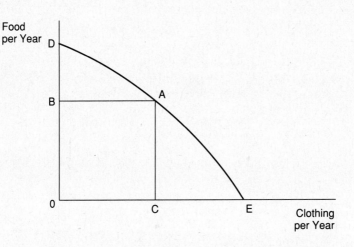

In the preceding diagram, the cost of a unit of clothing is measured by:
a. BD.
b. BD/BA.
c. the slope of a tangent to DE at point A.
d. AC/CE.

© 1988 The Dryden Press

(a) _____ 2. The statement, "There ain't no such thing as a
free lunch,"
   a. means every lunch has economic costs in the
      sense that some value of alternative goods
      must be sacrificed to obtain it.
   b. is clearly wrong since all of us have at
      some time or another been guests of others for
      lunch so that there were no economic costs
      involved.
   c. means each of us must always pay money for our
      lunches.
   d. means free school lunches are being eliminated
      in the process of fighting inflation.

(e) _____ 3. The economic costs of producing an automobile are
measured by:
   a. the price of the automobile.
   b. what it costs to import a similar automobile.
   c. the expenditures of the firm on labor and
      materials as shown in accounting records.
   d. the implicit costs incurred by the firm.
   e. the value of alternative products that the
      resources used in making the automobile could
      have produced.

(d) _____ 4. If a family purchases a house outright with no
loans, mortgages, or payments involved:
   a. there are no implicit costs associated with
      owning the house.
   b. the monthly utility bills are implicit costs.
   c. the taxes and insurance costs are implicit
      costs.
   d. the forgone interest on investment in the
      house is an implicit cost.

(c) _____ 5. In the long run for a firm:
   a. we are all dead.
   b. there will always be one or more fixed
      resources.
   c. all resources are variable.
   d. the planning period must be at least one year.

(b) _____ 6. Which of the following is not a long-run adjustment for a firm?
   a. the installation of a new computer
   b. an expansion of its sales force
   c. the acquisition of additional land area
   d. the purchase of a Learjet

© 1988 The Dryden Press

(b) _____ 7. If a firm increases its short-run output:
  a. total variable costs and total costs will both increase but by different amounts.
  b. total variable costs and total costs will both increase by the same amount.
  c. total variable costs and total costs may either increase or decrease, but the amount of change will be the same for each.
  d. total variable costs and total fixed costs will both increase.

(d) _____ 8. A firm using a complex of resources in proportions such that diminishing returns occur for each resource:
  a. is producing an output level at which average costs are falling with increases in output.
  b. is producing an output level at which average costs are rising with increases in output.
  c. is producing an output level at which average costs are constant with increases in output.
  d. may have rising, falling, or constant average costs for increases in output.

(a) _____ 9. Diminishing returns to a firm's complex of variable resources used with a given size of plant will result in:
  a. rising short-run marginal costs.
  b. falling short-run marginal costs.
  c. falling short-run average costs.
  d. minimum short-run marginal costs.

(d) _____ 10. As a firm's short-run output is increased:
  a. short-run average costs lead short-run marginal costs.
  b. fixed costs rise.
  c. average fixed costs are constant.
  d. short-run marginal costs lead short-run average costs.

(b) _____ 11. The decreasing portion of a firm's long-run average cost curve results from:
  a. large reductions in resource prices as the firm expands its size of plant.
  b. increasing efficiency due to division and specialization of labor and to possibilities of using mass production technology.
  c. increasing returns to variable resources.
  d. increasing difficulties of coordination and control.

 © 1988 The Dryden Press

(c) ____ 12. To produce a given output level most efficiently, the firm should use:
   a. the most efficient size of plant at the most efficient rate of output.
   b. the size of plant that will produce that output at its most efficient rate of output.
   c. the size of plant for which the short-run average cost is tangent to the long-run average cost curve at that output.
   d. the size of plant for which the short-run marginal cost curve equals the long-run marginal cost curve.

(a) ____ 13. For a firm encountering constant returns to scale:
   a. the long-run total cost curve will be linear and upward-sloping from the origin.
   b. total short-run variable costs will be increasing at a constant rate.
   c. the short-run average cost curve will be horizontal.
   d. the short-run marginal cost curve will be horizontal.

(b) ____ 14. The long-run average cost curve of a firm is:
   a. a line joining the minimum points of the short-run average cost curves of all possible plant sizes that the firm might use.
   b. a line tangent to the short-run average cost curves of all possible plant sizes that the firm might use.
   c. a line tangent to the short-run marginal cost curves of all possible plant sizes that the firm might use.
   d. the vertical summation of the short-run total fixed cost curves for all possible plant sizes that the firm might use.

(c) ____ 15. Which of the following factors was among the most important causes of the restructuring of the beer industry since Prohibition?
   a. Higher railroad and truck rates that made it more expensive than ever to ship heavy products such as beer.
   b. Preferences of beer consumers for bottles.
   c. Technological improvements that markedly advanced the speed of the closing line.
   d. Rising per barrel construction costs for new brewing plants.

(a) ____ 16. The upward-sloping portion of the average variable cost curve is related logically to the:
a. downward-sloping portion of the firm's average product curve.
b. the demand curve.
c. the contract curve.
d. Stage I of the variable input of production.

(b) ____ 17. The upward-sloping shapes of the short-run cost
curves depend ultimately on:
a. the prices of inputs.
b. the law of diminishing returns.
c. diseconomies of size.
d. economies of size.

(c) ____ 18. The upward-sloping shapes of the long-run cost
curves depend ultimately on:
a. the prices of inputs.
b. the law of diminishing returns.
c. diseconomies of size.
d. economies of size.

(b) ____ 19. Which of the following is a diseconomy of size?
a. Grocery stores that get bigger have to provide
more parking as well as shelf space.
b. Very big companies have "left-hand, right-
hand" problems of internal communication and
control.
c. Bigger airports with more flights per hour
cause extra traffic problems on the ground
that delay many passenger flights.
d. all of the above

(d) ____ 20. Which of the following economic forces had nothing
to do with the change in the number and size of
breweries since the 1940s?
a. preferences of consumers
b. technological change
c. changes in the cost of transporting beer
d. monopolistic pricing among brewers

(b) ____ 21. If mergers among brewers had achieved monopoly
rather than cost savings, which of the following
would not have occurred?
a. higher prices to consumers
b. relatively large output increases by the
biggest brewers
c. a smaller variety of brands and packages
d. a decrease in total output

© 1988 The Dryden Press

(d) ____ 22. Which of the following factors explains why it is difficult for economists to predict whether micro-breweries are profitable?
   a. Bigger breweries keep better accounting records.
   b. The best people in the industry always gravitate to the largest firms.
   c. At least a decade is necessary to know whether any industry is profitable.
   d. It is impossible to predict how large a loss a hobbyist would be willing to incur to stay in business.

PART FOUR

PRICES AND OUTPUT LEVELS OF GOODS AND SERVICES

In this part of the book, we develop the principles governing the pricing and outputs of goods and services—or of anything produced and sold for that matter. Part Four integrates the materials of Part Two on consumer choice and demand and Part Three on production and costs.

It is important in this set of chapters for students to obtain a clear grasp of selling market structures. In each of the three chapters we use the same general format. First, we define the type of market. Second, we emphasize the behavior of firms common to all three types of markets. Then we point up the differences in pricing and output results among the markets in the short run and in the long run. Finally, we present applications to show the real-world operation of firms and markets in each type of market. We believe that the repetitive format of the chapters enhances student learning of pricing and output fundamentals.

CHAPTER 11

PRICING AND OUTPUT UNDER PURE COMPETITION

Chapter Outline

The Very Short Run
    Rationing among Consumers
    Rationing over Time
    Sunk Costs
The Short Run
    The Firm
    The Market
The Long Run
    The Firm: Size of Plant Adjustments
    The Firm and the Market
The Welfare Effects of Pure Competition
    The Very Short Run
    The Short Run
    The Long Run

Applications

Jitneys
Taxicabs
Christina Onassis Is Scrapping Some of Her Ships

Chapter Objectives

The purely competitive market structure enables students to
view economic activity in a relatively simple form. Within its
framework the principles of profit maximization and loss minimization can be clearly developed; the effects of changes in
demand or costs on profits and losses can be demonstrated; and
the role of profits and losses in guiding and directing economic activity can be studied.

Suggestions for Teaching

It should be emphasized to students that the study of pure competition is not the sum and substance of microeconomic theory—
it is a convenient and logical starting point. It in no way
commits one to a defense of pure competition as the most desirable of all possible market structures.

© 1988 The Dryden Press

We are sometimes taken to task by our peers for concentrating on "pure" instead of "perfect competition." We believe this is nit-picking. Our use of the pure competition concept is a matter of personal preference, not one of substance. Students seem to be a little more comfortable with it intuitively since it allows for less than perfect instantaneous knowledge and adjustments. But please feel free to adjust as you see fit.

Students cannot be overdrilled on the principles of profit maximization. We go through them numerically, in terms of total cost and total revenue curves, and in terms of per unit cost and revenue curves. And some still fail to understand. Short-run loss minimization and the shutdown point are well illustrated by the Onassis shipping application. We end our discussion of the short run with a listing of the necessary and sufficient conditions for short-run equilibrium for the firm and for a market.

We try to make clear that profits for a firm mean a higher than average return on investment for the firm's owners and that this provides the incentive for entry into any profit-making market in the long run. We also list the necessary and sufficient conditions for long-run equilibrium for both a firm and a market.

The Onassis shipping fleet application also provides an example of the impact of losses over time in reducing the productive capacity of a firm as well as on the composition of that productive capacity. It illustrates the importance of the concept of exit (as the counterpart of entry) of resources from a market in response to decreasing demand and losses.

The summary of welfare effects of purely competitive market structures is not presented as a complete and definitive summary. At this juncture it is intended as an introduction only, to get students thinking in welfare terms. It will help them greatly when they get to Chapter 18.

The jitney and taxicab applications demonstrate some of the political and regulatory hazards awaiting a good many industries that would otherwise have purely competitive characteristics.

Complete mastery of the materials of this chapter will make the complexities of the next two much less troublesome.

Problems and Questions for Discussion

1. After the 1974 wheat crop was harvested, there was much discussion of large sales to the Soviet Union and the price of wheat rose sharply. Shortly thereafter, the U.S. government placed an embargo on such sales and the price dropped precipitously. However, after another month, it had increased somewhat. How would you explain these price changes? Illustrate your answer with diagrams.

2. Does it make sense to you for a building contractor to hang on to a new but empty house in order to recover costs of construction? Explain your answer.

3. A coal mine in Kentucky has been producing for many years, and it has become increasingly more expensive to mine a ton of coal from it. Under what circumstances would you advise that the mine be shut down? Illustrate your answer with a diagram.

4. Mr. and Mrs. Blondini operate a small vegetable market in San Antonio. Their accountant told them they made a profit of $10,000 last year; but their son, who is majoring in economics at the University of Texas, told them they made nothing. How would you seek to explain these conflicting statements?

5. The firms in a purely competitive industry are making profits. If they can get together and successfully block entry into the industry, show and explain the size-of-plant adjustment that any one of the firms would make.

6. Explain why it is that economic profits provide an economic incentive for additional firms to enter an industry.

7. The production function of a firm that uses resources A and B to produce X is linearly homogeneous. Explain:
   a. the marginal rate of technical substitution of A for B.
   b. the economic and uneconomic stages of production for each resource.
   c. output maximization by the firm, given the prices of the resources and the cost outlay of the firm.
   d. the firm's short-run total cost curve, assuming that a given quantity of resource B represents its plant size and A represents its variable resources, assuming pure competition in resource purchases.
   e. short-run profit maximization by the firm, assuming pure competition in resource purchasing and in product selling.
   f. the firm's long-run total cost curve, assuming pure competition in resource purchasing.
   g. long-run profit maximization by the firm, assuming pure competition in resource purchasing and in product selling.

8. The demand and supply curves in a purely competitive industry, X, are: $x_d = -500p + 2500$ and $x_s = 250p + 250$.
   a. Determine the short-run profit-maximizing output level for a firm with a cost function: $c = 0.05x^2 - 2x + 100$.
   b. Calculate the total profits that the firm can make.
   c. Derive the firm's short-run supply curve for X.

9. Go to your local city hall or law library (or perhaps the reference desk of your college or university library) and ask to see the municipal code for your city. Turn to the pages on taxicabs and check out the provisions of these ordinances to determine the degree to which they restrict entry. Is there a limit on the total number of licenses that may be issued, as in the New York case? Is there an arrangement whereby existing licensees have a right of first refusal on new licenses, in preference to new firms, should the city ever decide to allow more cabs on the streets? Are rates set by the city council? Are there any provisions of these ordinances that would allow a more competitive arrangement such as is found in Washington, D.C.? (Do you think that would be more likely if the city council members in your city took cabs more often and drove their own cars less?) What would you estimate the net effect of these ordinances to be on (a) the level of taxi rates, (b) the extent of competition, and (c) the quality of taxi service?

10. Draw a diagram similar to text Figure 11.5 and show on it each of the adjustments Christina Onassis made to save her firm. In each case explain and show which curves shift, in which directions, and when the action she took involved a movement along a curve rather than a shift. Distinguish carefully between the short-run and the long-run adjustments that she made and how the diagrammatic effects of these decisions differ.

11. In August 1981, the government of Libya demanded that all foreign oil companies operating in Libya buy more oil at Libya's price of $41 per barrel, while OPEC's price was $35 and Saudi Arabia's was $32. Libya's sales were down by half from the previous year, but it refused to cut price. (Youssef M. Ibrahim, "Libya Urges Foreign Oil Firms to Purchase More of Its Crude, but Doesn't Reduce Price," The Wall Street Journal, August 6, 1981.) Diagram and explain Libya's producer's surplus when it sells oil at $35 rather than $41.

12. In 1984, higher corn prices caused hog farmers to reduce herds, raising live hog prices to meat packers like Wilson and Rath by perhaps 25 percent. The nation has over 100 plants that kill over 2,000,000 hogs per year, but they are economical only if their expensive machinery is kept running constantly. (Marj Charlier, "Hog Shortage Is Expected to Wreak Havoc among Ailing Pork Packers This Summer," The Wall Street Journal, April 23, 1984.) If plants must be kept running to be economical, a decline in demand will lead to a reduction in the number of plants. Draw the plant marginal and average cost curves that are consistent with this result and explain your answer.

Solutions to Problems and Questions for Discussion

1. In each instance, market participants changed their anticipations about future actions of the United States that would affect the equilibrium price. Anticipation that the United States would allow more grain sales to the Soviet Union caused the anticipated demand curve to shift to the right and the equilibrium price to rise. Anticipation that the United States would place an effective embargo on wheat sales caused the anticipated demand curve to shift to the left and the equilibrium price to fall. The state of anticipations is one of the ceteris paribus conditions that applies to each state of demand, so changes in anticipations cause the position of the demand curve to change.

2.   Review the discussion of sunk costs on pages 318-319. Once the house is completed, the costs of construction are sunk and are irrelevant to deciding when to sell. The question of whether to sell it or hold it depends solely upon his expectations about whether the price he will get at a later date exceeds the price he can get now by more than the opportunity cost of using the proceeds from the sale during the interim.

3.   Review the discussion of text Figure 11.5. The mine should shut down if the price of coal is less than p_0, which is equal to minimum AVC.

4.   Accountants view profits as the difference between total receipts and total accounting costs over the relevant period. The economist-to-be son appears to be taking into account the value of the resources they have invested in the store as well as the implicit costs of their labor if they had worked for some employer in a similar capacity at a salary. He appears to have concluded that his parents made no profit because their opportunity cost equaled or exceeded the difference between total receipts and total costs.

5.   Review the discussion of text Figure 11.8. To maximize profits, each firm should choose an output rate for which long-run marginal cost equals marginal revenue. Each firm would then choose the size of plant that produces that rate of output at the least possible average cost. At the selected output rate, SAC will be tangent to LAC and SMC will intersect LMC.

6.   Entry occurs in industries where firms are earning economic profits. This is because the rate of return to investors on resources in those industries exceeds the average rate of return that they could earn elsewhere.

7. a. $MRTS_{ab} = MPP_a/MPP_b$ = slope of an isoquant at any particular point.

b. Consider first the uneconomic stages. To the left of
the left ridge line is Stage I for A and Stage III for
B. To the right of the ridge line is Stage III for A
and Stage I for B. Both resources have a common Stage
II between the ridge lines, representing the economic
combinations.

c. Maximum output is represented by the isoquant that is
tangent to the determined isocost.

d. Obtain the total product curve for A at the fixed
amount of B. Next, convert it into the total variable
cost curve as is done in the text. Now add the fixed
cost—the cost of B—at each output to obtain the total cost curve.

e. Juxtapose a linear upward-sloping-to-the-right total
revenue curve with the total cost curve and find the
output at which it lies the farthest vertical distance
above the total cost curve. Convert both curves into
per unit terms just below the total curves diagram.

f. Draw a family of isocost curves on the isoquant diagram.
At the tangency points read off the product quantities
from each isoquant and the associated total cost outlay
from each isocost. Use this information to plot the
long-run total cost curve.

g. Convert the long-run TC into LAC terms. Then draw
the appropriate LMC curve. Draw the firm's dd and MR
curves and select the output at which LMC = MR.

8. a. Solve the demand and supply equations simultaneously
to obtain: $x = 1,000$, $p = \$3$. MR = \$3, also.
MC is the first derivative of the total cost equation.
Setting the MC equation equal to \$3, solve for x.
The profit-maximizing quantity is thus 50 units.

b. TR = \$3 X 50 = \$150. TC = $125 - 100 + 100 = \$125$.
Total profit = \$25.

c. $MC = 0.1x - 2$. Find MC at various values for x and
plot the MC curve.

© 1988 The Dryden Press

9. One or more restrictions are common, but it is rare to find
    all of them.
    a. We would expect rates to be higher in cities that have
        most of these restrictions. Rates are also affected,
        however, by factors that influence the cost of service,
        such as city size and density.
    b. Restrictions on new entry reduce competition.
    c. Quality of service is more complex because of its many
        dimensions. Restrictions on the number of operating
        cabs tend to increase the times that passengers have to
        wait until a cab arrives, which is one important dimen-
        sion of quality. Other dimensions, such as cab clean-
        liness, are difficult to specify and to enforce. Some
        cities establish maximum rates to prevent "gouging,"
        but these regulations are also difficult to enforce.

10. The short-run adjustments can be characterized by text
    Figure 11.5. Assume that the long-run charter rate repre-
    sents market price at each level of demand. As demand
    declined, Onassis tied up ships for which minimum AVC ex-
    ceeded the new long-term charter rate. She made long-term
    contracts if the charter rate exceeded a ship's minimum
    AVC but was less than the ship's SAC.

    Onassis's long-run adjustments can be characterized by
    either text Figures 11.10, 11.11, or 11.12 (i) by changing
    the underlying assumption of increasing demand to decreasing
    demand, and (ii) by choosing between increasing, constant,
    or decreasing costs (we would choose increasing costs).
    Ships for which minimum AVC exceeded the long-term charter
    rate were either scrapped or replaced by smaller vessels.
    By so doing, Onassis reduced the firm's plant to a size
    consistent with the new level of demand and the associated
    equilibrium long-run charter rate.

11. Presumably, Libya's MC curve rises as oil is lifted at
    faster rates, so producer's surplus is greater if oil can
    be sold at $41.

© 1988 The Dryden Press

12. The MC and AVC curves in the following diagram are consistent with the stated facts. MC is constant over a broad
range of output rates and then rises rapidly, although
different plants have different levels of AVC and thus MC.
Both plants AVC and AVC' can operate at p_1 with demand d_1d_1
= MR_1. But a reduction in demand to d_2d_2 = MR_2 (the dot-
ted line) and p_2 causes plants with average variable cost
in excess of AVC to exit the industry. (George J. Stigler,
The Theory of Price, 3d ed. [New York: Macmillan, 1966]:
141-44.)

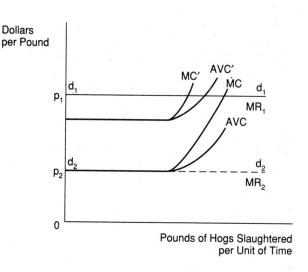

Dollars per Pound

Pounds of Hogs Slaughtered per Unit of Time

True-False Questions

(F) _____ 1. If there are many sellers of a homogeneous product, the elasticity of the demand curve facing any
one seller will be the same at any given price as
that of the market demand curve.

(T) _____ 2. In the very short run, costs of production play
no part in the determination of the equilibrium
price.

(T) _____ 3. Speculation serves to even out the level of consumption and to decrease the variations in price
of a product during the period over which its
supply is fixed.

(T) ____ 4. Since one firm in a purely competitive market can-not affect the market price of the product, move-ments <u>along</u> the market demand curve will <u>shift</u> the position of the demand curve facing the firm.

(F) ____ 5. The profit-maximization postulate provides the logical basis for the analysis of individual firm behavior because this is the only objective that business firms pursue.

(F) ____ 6. In order to maximize short-run profits, the firm must produce and sell the output at which its total receipts are maximized.

(F) ____ 7. In order to maximize short-run profits, the firm must produce and sell the output at which its total costs are minimized.

(T) ____ 8. To say that profits are maximized at the output at which marginal cost equals marginal revenue is to say that they are maximized at the output at which total revenue and total costs are increas-ing at the same rate.

(F) ____ 9. The short-run supply curve of the firm is that part of its average variable cost curve lying to the right of and above minimum average variable cost.

(F) ____ 10. If a firm receives a price for its product greater than average variable costs, it is always possible for profits to be made.

(T) ____ 11. If the price of a firm's product is less than its minimum average variable cost, it should reduce its output to zero to minimize losses.

(F) ____ 12. In a constant cost industry, an increase in de-mand has no effect on the short-run price of the product.

(F) ____ 13. Profits are maximized by a firm at the output level at which total costs are equal to total receipts.

(T) ____ 14. If a firm is making substantial profits and mar-ginal revenue exceeds marginal cost at the output level it is producing, profits can be increased by increasing output.

(F) ____ 15. If a firm is in a no-profit output position with an optimum size of plant operated at the optimum rate of output, it should get out of the industry.

(T) ____ 16. The short-run impact on price of a change in demand is the same regardless of whether the industry is one of increasing, decreasing, or constant costs.

(T) ____ 17. Long-run differences between increasing, decreasing, and constant cost industries turn on the impact of entering firms on the prices of resources used in producing the product.

(T) ____ 18. In a private enterprise economy, profits and losses provide the incentive for productive capacity to follow consumer demands.

(T) ____ 19. When an industry is in long-run equilibrium, the resources used in producing the product are generating a contribution to consumer welfare as great as they could generate in any other use.

(F) ____ 20. If short-run marginal cost of a product is equal to product price, both variable and fixed resources used by the firm must be making their maximum contributions to consumer welfare.

(F) ____ 21. The principal attraction of jitneys in the 1914-20 era was that they essentially duplicated the lines of service offered by trolleys.

(F) ____ 22. There was always an excess supply of jitneys during the 1914-20 era because jitney drivers were notorious for ignoring their own opportunity costs during times of recession.

(F) ____ 23. The trolley companies miscalculated in their failure to oppose the taxicab operators just as they had the jitney operators, because taxis provided exactly the type of door-to-door services that had made jitneys so attractive.

(T) ____ 24. The ocean shipping industry is quite close to being purely competitive because no single firm owns more than a few percent of the total tonnage.

(F) ____ 25. The difference between the short-run and the long-run adjustments to a decline in demand by the Onassis firm was one of degree rather than kind.

(T) ____ 26. In the short run, ships in the Onassis fleet for which long-term charter rates were less than average cost but greater than minimum average variable cost were leased for long-term charter.

(T) ____ 27. In the short run, ships in the Onassis fleet for which long-term charter rates were less than minimum average variable cost were tied up.

Multiple-Choice Questions

(b) ____ 1. If a firm in a purely competitive industry in-creases price above the equilibrium level:
   a. it will lose most of its customers.
   b. it will lose all of its customers.
   c. it must advertise to avoid losing customers.
   d. it must lower its costs to make a profit.

(a) ____ 2. The essence of the very short-run economic problem is the:
   a. rationing of a good for the period over which its quantity cannot be changed.
   b. recovery of the firm's variable costs.
   c. determination of when the firm should shut down.
   d. equating of marginal revenue and marginal costs by the firm.

(b) ____ 3. Speculative activity:
   a. usually has a destabilizing effect on price.
   b. usually has a stabilizing effect on price.
   c. increases the elasticity of demand.
   d. decreases the elasticity of demand.

(d) ____ 4. For a purely competitive firm, the marginal reve-nue curve:
   a. increases as output is increased.
   b. decreases as output is increased.
   c. coincides with the total revenue curve.
   d. coincides with the demand curve facing the firm.

(d) ____ 5. In the short run, a firm maximizes profits or minimizes losses by producing an output at which:
    a. total revenue exceeds total cost.
    b. total revenue equals total cost.
    c. marginal revenue exceeds marginal cost.
    d. marginal revenue equals marginal cost.

(c) ____ 6. To minimize losses, a firm should shut down if the price is less than:
    a. average cost.
    b. marginal cost.
    c. average variable cost.
    d. total cost.

(b) ____ 7. The output level at which a firm's marginal cost equals marginal revenue is also the one at which:
    a. marginal cost equals minimum average cost.
    b. the slope of the total revenue curve equals the slope of the total cost curve.
    c. total revenue is maximum.
    d. total revenue equals total cost.

(a) ____ 8. For a firm to be in long-run equilibrium, it is necessary that:
    a. long-run marginal cost equals short-run marginal cost equals marginal revenue, and that short-run average cost equals long-run average cost but average costs need not be equal to marginal revenue.
    b. it uses a most efficient size of plant at the most efficient rate of output.
    c. long-run marginal cost equals short-run marginal cost equals marginal revenue equals short-run average cost equals long-run average cost.
    d. both (b) and (c)

© 1988 The Dryden Press

(d) ____ 9. For a purely competitive <u>industry</u> to be in equilibrium, it is necessary for each firm in the
industry that:
  a. long-run marginal cost equals short-run
     marginal cost equals marginal revenue, and
     that short-run average cost equals long-run
     average cost but need not be equal to mar-
     ginal revenue.
  b. it uses a most efficient size of plant at the
     most efficient rate of output.
  c. long-run marginal cost equals short-run mar-
     ginal cost equals marginal revenue equals
     short-run average cost equals long-run aver-
     age cost.
  d. both (b) and (c)

(c) ____ 10. The primary cause of long-run increasing costs
for an industry is:
  a. inflation.
  b. labor unions.
  c. increases in resource prices resulting from
     the entry of new firms.
  d. the law of diminishing returns.

(a) ____ 11. The short-run effects of an increase in demand
for a product are:
  a. the same for a constant cost industry, a
     decreasing-cost industry, and an increasing-
     cost industry.
  b. higher prices in an increasing-cost industry
     than in a constant cost industry.
  c. lower prices in a decreasing-cost industry
     than in a constant cost industry.
  d. both (b) and (c)

(c) ____ 12. Which of the following is <u>not</u> a reason why Christina Onassis found it uneconomical to liquidate
her fleet in the short run?
  a. It probably took time to find vacant shipyards
     to lay up the ships and tear them apart.
  b. She was committed to contracts to buy more
     ships which would have been expensive for her
     to breach.
  c. Tearing apart the ships made owners of the
     firm unhappy.
  d. It was more profitable to keep part of the
     firm intact in the short run.

(b) ____ 13. The long-run industry output effect of an increase
in demand will be greatest for:
a. an increasing-cost industry.
b. a decreasing-cost industry.
c. a constant-cost industry.
d. periods of inflation.

(c) ____ 14. In the very short run when conditions of pure
competition prevail, consumer welfare is maximized
when:
a. price controls and rationing are put into
effect.
b. income is equally divided among all consumers.
c. prices are such that there are no surpluses or
shortages and for each consumer the marginal
rate of substitution between any two goods is
the same.
d. the marginal rate of substitution between
luxury goods and necessities is greater for
rich people than for poor people.

(a) ____ 15. When the short-run marginal cost of a product is
the same for a firm as the price of the product it
produces:
a. the contributions of the variable resources
used by the firm to consumer welfare are as
great as they would be in alternative uses.
b. consumer welfare would be increased by a
decrease in the product price.
c. consumer welfare would be increased by an
increase in output.
d. the firm should shift its marginal cost curve
downward.

(b) ____ 16. In the long run, the price system in a purely
competitive economy:
a. creates much instability.
b. leads toward maximization of consumer welfare.
c. results in inefficient utilization of resources by firms.
d. encourages advertising by individual firms
to enlarge their market shares.

© 1988 The Dryden Press

(a) ____ 17. Which of the following types of local ordinances would <u>not</u> have raised the average costs of jitney driving and thus not had the tendency of restricting jitneys from the local transportation market directly or indirectly?
  a. forcing jitneys to take passengers to their homes if requested to do so
  b. requiring that all jitney drivers do so as a full-time occupation
  c. forcing jitneys to pay a royalty tax on their total revenues to the trolley companies
  d. forcing jitneys to get licenses before soliciting business in downtown central business districts.

(c) ____ 18. In 1982, a steel company in the United States was considering shutting down one of its plants but decided not to because the shutdown costs would have exceeded the costs of continuing to operate. Which of the following would <u>not</u> have been a cost associated with shutting the plant down?
  a. paying termination benefits to each employee in accordance with the provisions of labor union contracts
  b. environmental requirements of the U.S. government that required certain portions of the land on which the plant was located would be returned to its "natural" condition
  c. plant managers were afraid it would never become profitable again
  d. all of the above

(c) ____ 19. Which of the following would <u>not</u> be a logical long-run response by Onassis to the decline in demand for oil tankers?
  a. scrapping some ships
  b. replacing some large ships with smaller vessels
  c. tying up a large fraction of her fleet in ports for an indefinite duration
  d. diversifying into nonshipping activities

(d) ____ 20. Which of the following was <u>not</u> a reason why jit-
               neys competed effectively with trolleys until
               entry restrictions were imposed?
               a. Jitneys provided flexible routes and service
                   along and away from trolley lines that con-
                   sumers wanted.
               b. There was an inexhaustible supply of part-time
                   or unemployed jitney owners whose implicit
                   wage was relatively low.
               c. The flat-fare price of the trolley companies
                   gave the jitneys an advantage for relatively
                   short trips.
               d. The rate of return on investment in trolley
                   lines was relatively high.

CHAPTER 12

PRICING AND OUTPUT UNDER PURE MONOPOLY

Chapter Outline

Costs and Revenues under Monopoly
   Costs of Production
   Revenues
The Short Run
   Profit Maximization: Total Curves
   Profit Maximization: Per Unit Curves
   Two Common Misconceptions
   Short-Run Supply
The Long Run
   Barriers to Entry
   Size of Plant Adjustments
Price Discrimination
   Third-Degree Price Discrimination
   First-Degree Price Discrimination
   Second-Degree Price Discrimination
The Welfare Effects of Pure Monopoly
   Short-Run Output Restriction
   Long-Run Output Restriction
   Inefficiency of the Firm
   Sales Promotion Activities
Regulation of Monopoly
   Price Regulation
   Taxation

Applications

Finding the Right Monopoly Price
Price Discrimination by Medical Laboratories and Physicians

Chapter Objectives

In this chapter we show students the effects on output and
price when a market has only one seller. The demand curve facing the firm is downward-sloping rather than infinitely elastic.
The marginal revenue curve lies below the demand curve rather
than coinciding with it. In maximizing profits, a monopolist
restricts output below and charges a higher price than the one
at which marginal cost equals price. Further, a monopolist may
practice price discrimination, so we extend the principles of
profit maximization to the cases of first-, second-, and third-
degree price discrimination. Additionally, when profits are

161   © 1988 The Dryden Press

made in the long run, the monopolist blocks entry into the industry, restricting the output expansion which profits would otherwise motivate. Monopoly distorts the allocation of an economy's production capacity.

Suggestions for Teaching

We emphasize first of all that the rules for profit maximization are the same for a monopolist as they are for a pure competitor. The response of a monopolist to exogenous market and cost variables is essentially the same as the response of a pure competitor. The monopolist is not necessarily a "bad" guy nor is the pure competitor necessarily a "good" guy. After all, both seek to maximize profits.

Next we point up the difference between the two market structures, noting carefully that these lie on the demand side rather than on the cost side. We give special attention to the relation between the demand curve facing a monopolist and the marginal revenue curve. We take students carefully through the two appendices to the chapter. Again, we go through the principles of profit maximization with numbers, total revenue and total cost diagrams, and per unit revenue and cost diagrams, specifying the conditions for both short- and long-run equilibrium. But the application on finding the right monopoly price warns that the monopolist's task is not always easy—nor is there any guarantee of profits because of a monopoly position.

The major problem in third-degree price discrimination cases is that of locating the firm's overall marginal revenue curve. Once this is done, the pieces fall into place rather easily. The application on medical laboratories and physicians explains a very common and famous case of price discrimination.

The output restriction issue enables us to begin orienting students toward the welfare implications of resource allocation among different uses. It becomes apparent that consumers value resources more in monopolized profit-making uses than in other uses where they may be stuck, and that long-run production capacity in monopolized markets tends to be too small relative to that in competitive markets.

Problems and Questions for Discussion

1. Explain carefully and completely why it is that the marginal revenue curve of a monopolist lies below the demand curve faced by the firm.

© 1988 The Dryden Press

2. a. Draw a downward-sloping straight-line demand curve for widgets and assume that the seller of the widgets is a monopolist. Identify the output level at which the price elasticity of demand equals one.
    b. Just below the demand diagram, draw the corresponding total revenue diagram with its output axis directly below and identical to the output axis of the demand diagram. Identify the output level at which total revenue is maximum.
    c. On the demand diagram, draw the marginal revenue curve. Identify the output level at which it is zero.
    d. Explain why the output levels identified in (a), (b), and (c) are all the same.

3. Compare and contrast short-run profit maximization by a pure monopolist with that of a pure competitor; i.e., illustrate each and point out both the similarities and the differences between them.

4. Why will a monopolist not produce an output level at which its marginal cost equals the product price? Illustrate your answer with a diagram.

5. a. Show with a diagram and explain the long-run equilibrium position of a monopolist.
    b. Now show and explain the long-run effects on price, output, and profits of an improvement in techniques of production.
    c. Redraw the diagram for (a) and, instead of (b), show and explain the effects on price, profits, and output of an increase in demand for the product.
    d. How would the effects of (b) differ if the industry were one of pure competition?
    e. How would the effects of (c) differ if the industry were one of pure competition?
    f. Would you expect a higher level of consumer welfare under (b) or under (d)? Why? under (c) or (e)? Why?

6. Can you provide any reasons why a taxicab company would want an exclusive franchise in a city? Explain. Can you provide any reasons why an exclusive franchise should be granted by the city government? Explain.

© 1988 The Dryden Press

7. Suppose that a state regulatory commission requires an electric utility firm in a city to charge no more than:
   a. average costs of production for its product. Show with a diagram and explain the effects on the quantity demanded compared with the quantity supplied.
   b. marginal costs of production for its product. Show with a diagram and explain the effects on the quantity demanded compared with the quantity supplied.

8. The City of Kismet places an annual license fee on the High Dive swimming pool that serves the youngsters of that town. The High Dive management tells the city commission that it must, as a consequence, raise its prices. Advise the management on whether it is right or wrong, providing adequate reasons for your answer.

9. Assume that the demand curve facing a monopolist is:

$$x = 25 - 5p,$$

and the cost function is:

$$c = 0.5x^2 - 2x + 100.$$

   a. Derive the marginal revenue equation.
   b. Determine the profit-maximizing or loss-minimizing output level.

10. Suppose you are Henry Kissinger's agent and it is your responsibility to book Kissinger into speaking engagements throughout the world. Sketch out your best guess as to the nature of the demand curve for Kissinger's services and its elasticity. Draw and explain the marginal revenue curve. Will the demand curve become more or less elastic in the long run? What assumptions did you make about the number of close substitutes for Kissinger's services?

11. Some people believe that real estate agents, theatrical agents, and agents for movie stars or recording artists are little short of leeches who do little to earn their substantial brokerage fees. After reading the article about lecture bureaus from Fortune, what services do you (as an economist) think these people perform in exchange for their fees? Do you think that movie stars, recording artists, and other famous people would hire such agents if the personalities themselves were equally adroit at estimating demand functions?

12. Some economists have argued that the market for a durable good, such as automobiles or refrigerators, could never be monopolized. Explain why this argument is probably true or false.

13. A monopolist has two basic choices in attempting to maximize profits: (a) to raise prices to the profit-maximizing level, then wait for other firms to realize it and attempt to enter the industry; or (b) to set the price a little above marginal cost, to make profits only slightly above the competitive level and thereby deter entry. If you were the monopolist, what factors would lead you to choose either strategy (a) or (b)? Explain.

14. Assume a competitive industry is converted to a monopoly by one firm buying out the others and by the government limiting entry. Explain why the conversion would cause price to rise but not indefinitely.

15. In 1983, a U.S. Government study found that 900 rural counties had a doctor "shortage." This was expected to fall by 58 percent in 1994 when the nation would have 640,000 physicians and a "surplus" of about 90,000. (From The Wall Street Journal: Mark V. Pauly, "The Doctor Drawbridge," November 8, 1985; and Becci M. Breining, "Blessings of a Doctor 'Surplus'," November 29, 1983.)
    a. How would an economist evaluate claims of a doctor "shortage" or "surplus"?
    b. How would the rising supply of physicians affect successful third-degree price discrimination?

16. Explain the purpose of each of the following "restrictions" on the purchase of airline tickets at discount fares that were common among airlines in 1986:
    a. purchase the ticket seven, fourteen, twenty-one, or thirty days in advance of travel depending on the discount
    b. stay at least one Saturday night at the destination
    c. travel on a Tuesday or Wednesday
    d. cancellation fees for discount tickets that increase with the size of the discount, but no cancellation fees for tickets purchased at the regular nondiscount fares

17. Under the U.S. Constitution, Congress adopts a bill by sim-
    ple majority vote. The president may reject the bill in
    its entirety, in which case Congress may enact the bill over
    his veto by a two-thirds vote. The president, unlike gov-
    ernors of 42 states, does not have a "line item" veto where-
    by he can reject parts of a bill and accept others. Presi-
    dents and Congresses learn each other's preferences for ex-
    penditures in the course of hundreds of dealings each year.
    In an appropriation bill, Congress can advance its interests
    by adding spending for programs that the president does not
    want to those that he does want. In 1985, Congress refused
    President Reagan's request for a line item veto on money
    bills. (Laurie McGinley, "Reagan to Seek a Law Allowing
    Him to Veto Items in Money Bills," The Wall Street Journal,
    January 5, 1984.)
    a. Explain the "all-or-nothing" offers that Congress
       (the seller) gives the president (the buyer) as price
       discrimination. Would you characterize it as first-,
       second-, or third-degree?
    b. Show the area of consumer's surplus that the president
       could capture with the item veto.

18. Some prescription drugs, such as antibiotics or cortisone,
    are sold by veterinarians for animal consumption at lower
    prices than they are sold by pharmacies for human consump-
    tion.
    a. Is this price discrimination? Explain.
    b. If so, which degree? Explain.

Solutions to Problems and Questions for Discussion

1. Except for the one-unit sales level, marginal revenue will
   be less than price as long as the monopolist charges the
   same price for all units sold. He must lower price to
   increase sales by one unit. As a result, total revenue
   increases by the price of the additional unit but declines
   by the sum of the price decline for each of the previous
   units. Marginal revenue is the net of the two amounts.

2. a. Midway down the demand curve.
   b. Same as (a).
   c. MR equals zero when elasticity equals unity.
   d. Using the geometric measure of elasticity, $\varepsilon = 1$ where
      MT = OM, or midway down the curve. Since MR = $p - p/\varepsilon$,
      MR equals zero when ε equals unity, and MR is zero when
      TR is at a maximum.

3. As in text Figure 11.4, the purely competitive firm maximizes profit where SMC equals MR, with MR equal to market price. In text Figure 12.3, the monopolist maximizes profit where SMC equals MR, with MR less than market price.

4. Review the discussion of text Figure 12.13. The purely competitive industry produces output rate X and sells it at price p. If the productive capacity of the competitive industry were taken over by a monopolist, the monopolist would maximize profit at output rate X_1 and charge price p_1. If the monopolist were to sell at the competitive industry's price and output rate, it would lose profit on each additional unit sold between X_1 and X because SS(MC) exceeds MR.

5. a. See text Figure 12.6 and discussion. LMC = SMC = MR, and size of plant is such that SAC = LAC at the profit-maximizing output.
   b. The set of cost curves shifts downward. Size of plant is adjusted so that the new LMC = SMC = MR, and SAC = LAC at the higher profit-maximizing output and the lower price.
   c. DD and MR shift to the right. LMC = MR at a higher output level. Size of plant is increased to the point at which LMC = SMC = MR and SAC = LAC. Price changes, up or down or none at all, depend on the comparative changes of DD and possible economies of size, if any.
   d. New firms would enter until profits are eroded away.
   e. New firms would enter until profits are eroded away.
   f. Under (d) and (e). Consumers pay only what it costs to produce the goods. There is no output restriction. Firms use most efficient plant sizes at most efficient rates of output.

6. A firm would seek the profits that a monopoly offers. The city might prefer a monopoly in spite of the welfare losses it causes for taxi consumers if it could capture through taxes or other devices a share of the resulting monopoly gains.

© 1988 The Dryden Press

7. a. Review the discussion of text Figure 12.14. Draw in
        the regulated price associated with the intersection of
        AC and DD; label that price p_2 and the associated out-
        put x_2. At the price p_2, the monopolist would choose
        to supply the quantity x_3 at which the horizontal line
        from p_2 intersects MC. At p_2 the quantity demanded x_2
        exceeds the quantity supplied x_3, which causes a short-
        age.
    b. This is the solution depicted in Figure 12.14. The
        regulated price p_1 is set where MC intersects DD at A,
        and the monopolist produces output rate x_2.

8. Review the discussion of text Figure 12.16. A lump-sum
    license fee does not change marginal cost and therefore does
    not change price; provided, however, that the fee does not
    reduce the monopolist's profits so much that he earns less
    than the competitive rate of return on the resources that
    he has invested. A lump-sum license fee that large would
    cause the firm to shut down.

9. a. Rearrange the demand equation to read $p = 5 - 0.2x$.
        $TR = xp = 5x - 0.2x^2$. $MR = 5 - 0.4x$.
    b. $MC = 0.1x - 2$. Since profits are maximized at the out-
        put at which $MC = MR$, solve $5 - 0.4x = 0.1x - 2$. Out-
        put $x = 14$.

10. All we can say without further study is that we would ex-
    pect the demand curve for Kissinger's services to be greater
    and less elastic than that of most other excabinet secre-
    taries. His marginal revenue curve is less than his demand
    curve at all prices except the highest, but we expect that
    Kissinger can engage in some price discrimination. His de-
    mand curve will become more elastic over time as more former
    government officials enter the lecture business. Even Kis-
    singer has substitutes.

11. Agents and brokers must offer services that are productive.
    Why else would sellers and buyers employ them?

12. The supply of used durable goods is so large and so dif-
    fusely held that monopolization of the market for new re-
    frigerators or cars would be very costly. New and used
    durables are substitutes: when the prices of new cars go
    up, the prices of used cars usually follow.

13. It would depend on entry costs. If these costs were high,
    we would attempt to maximize profit by following strategy
    (a). If entry costs were low we would choose strategy (b).

14. Price should jump to the monopoly level following conversion as the monopolist attempts to equate MR and MC. Thereafter, price should change only if demand or cost conditions change. An immediate additional use would decrease profits.

15. a. A shortage would not exist unless there is a price ceiling. A surplus would not persist in the absence of a minimum price control or price floor.
    b. The more suppliers, the more difficult it becomes even for established surgeons to maintain discriminatory fee structures.

16. The purpose is third-degree discrimination. Business travelers often have a less elastic demand than vacationers and others. Each restriction is intended to avoid giving price cuts to business people.
    a. Business people often travel on short notice, so discounts are given only to vacationers and others who can plan trips well in advance.
    b. Business travelers usually want to spend the weekend home, so the Saturday night restriction excludes many of them.
    c. Business people travel most on Sunday evening, Monday, and Fridays, so discounts for only Tuesday or Wednesday flights effectively exclude many of them.
    d. Business travelers often cancel or change their plans, so penalties discourage them from booking discount flights and then cancelling on short notice.

17. a. The purpose is first-degree discrimination. Congress tailors the bill by adding as many provisions that the president does not want as it believes he will tolerate. Thus, Congress captures as much of the president's surplus as it can.
    b. The area of consumer's surplus that the Congress and president vie over is indicated by triangle ABp_0 in text Figure 12.11.

18. a. It is discrimination only if the marginal costs of production and distribution differ between the two markets. Costs of selling and insuring for product liability are probably lower for animal than for human consumption, so it is not clear that the lower price to veterinarians is discriminatory.
    b. If costs were identical, then it would be third-degree discrimination. The lower price for animal consumption is consistent with the lower value that most people place on the lives of their animals relative to their own lives or those of relatives and friends.

True-False Questions

(F) ____ 1. Pure monopoly is a very common market structure in the United States, even outside the public utility field.

(T) ____ 2. The profits made by a monopolist—if profits are made—create incentives in the economic system that tend to destroy the monopoly position.

(F) ____ 3. A good example of monopoly is provided by the General Motors Corporation.

(F) ____ 4. The marginal revenue curve of a monopolist is usually downward-sloping to the right and coincides with the demand curve facing the firm.

(T) ____ 5. A nondiscriminating monopolist with no costs of production and desiring to maximize profits should set the price and output at the level at which price elasticity of demand equals one and marginal revenue equals zero.

(F) ____ 6. Monopolists always make profits in the short run.

(F) ____ 7. In the long run, monopolists ordinarily will build optimum size plants and operate them at optimum rates of output.

(F) ____ 8. Most nondiscriminating monopolists face inelastic demand curves in the neighborhood of their profit-maximizing prices.

(T) ____ 9. There is no difference on the cost side between a purely competitive seller and a monopolistic seller; the difference between them is in the conditions of demand that they face.

(T) ____ 10. For a monopolistic firm to be in long-run equilibrium, it is necessary that short-run marginal costs equal long-run marginal costs and that short-run average costs equal long-run average costs; but it is not necessary that price equals marginal cost and marginal revenue or that price equals average cost.

(T) ____ 11. For third-degree price discrimination to be profitable, the price elasticities of demand among the markets for which discrimination is to occur must be different at each possible price level.

© 1988 The Dryden Press

(F) ____ 12. A third-degree price-discriminating monopolist will charge highest prices in those markets in which price elasticity of demand is greatest.

(F) ____ 13. At any given output level for a firm, marginal revenue equals price minus the ratio of demand elasticity to price.

(T) ____ 14. The primary cause of short-run output restriction by a monopolist is that marginal revenue is less than price.

(T) ____ 15. One of the economic "sins" of monopoly is that when a monopolist is maximizing profits, the value of the variable resources used in the production of the monopolist's product is greater for consumers than in the production of alternative goods sold under conditions of pure competition.

(T) ____ 16. An excise tax levied on the product of a monopolist will cause the monopolist to reduce output and increase price.

(F) ____ 17. A lump-sum tax or a tax on a monopolist's profits will cause the monopolist to reduce output and increase price.

(T) ____ 18. Monopoly in a private enterprise economic system tends to result in outputs relatively too large in the competitive sectors of the economy and relatively too small in the monopolized sectors.

(T) ____ 19. If a regulatory agency sets a maximum price on a monopolist's output that is below the profit-maximizing price but above the level at which marginal revenue equals marginal cost, the monopolist will increase output and sales.

(T) ____ 20. Ella Fitzgerald, Milton Friedman, Elton John, Henry Kissinger, Linda Ronstadt, and Frank Sinatra all have monopoly power in the sale of their services.

(F) ____ 21. To some extent, each of the personalities in Harry Walker's lecture bureau were substitutes for each other and therefore would logically face horizontal demand (and marginal revenue) curves just as a purely competitive firm would.

(T) ____ 22. A monopoly of land would be almost impossible to achieve.

(T) ____ 23. A seller who can price discriminate in the first degree essentially is able to convert his demand (average revenue) curve into a marginal revenue curve.

(T) ____ 24. "Buy one for $25 and get the second one for one cent" is essentially second-degree price discrimination.

(F) ____ 25. The physicians and medical laboratories in the chapter application were essentially practicing price discrimination in the first degree.

Multiple-Choice Questions

(a) ____ 1. Which of the following is a good example of pure monopoly?
   a. the local gas company
   b. U.S. Gypsum Corporation
   c. Exxon
   d. General Motors Corporation

(c) ____ 2. Which of the following are necessarily different for a monopolistic firm and a purely competitive firm?
   a. the marginal cost curve
   b. the short-run average cost curve
   c. the demand curve facing the firm
   d. the long-run average cost curve

Questions 3 and 4 are based on the following diagram:

© 1988 The Dryden Press

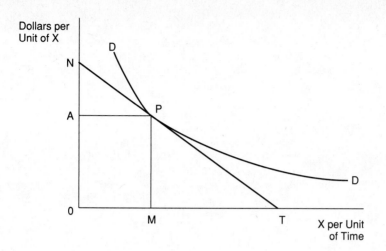

Dollars per Unit of X

X per Unit of Time

(c) ____ 3. Marginal revenue at output level OM is measured by:
   a. MP.
   b. MT/OM.
   c. MP — AN.
   d. NP.

(d) ____ 4. Price elasticity of demand at output level OM is measured by:
   a. PT/PN.
   b. MP/NA.
   c. MT/OM.
   d. all of the above.

(c) ____ 5. In order to maximize short-run profits, a nondiscriminating monopolist should produce the output at which:
   a. marginal cost equals marginal revenue equals price.
   b. marginal cost equals average cost.
   c. marginal cost equals marginal revenue, but marginal revenue is less than price.
   d. total cost equals total revenue.

(c) ____ 6. A monopolist selling an output at which demand is elastic:
   a. should increase sales enough to get on the inelastic part of the demand curve.
   b. will want to decrease sales and get on the inelastic part of the demand curve.
   c. will have a positive marginal revenue.
   d. will have a negative marginal revenue.

(b) ____ 7. In the long run, a profit-maximizing monopolist will build:
   a. a smaller than most efficient size of plant for which short-run marginal cost equals marginal revenue.
   b. the size of plant with a short-run average cost curve tangent to the long-run average cost curve at the profit-maximizing output.
   c. a larger than most efficient size of plant for which short-run marginal cost equals marginal revenue.
   d. a most efficient size of plant in order to minimize costs.

(a) ____ 8. A nondiscriminating monopolistic firm as compared with a purely competitive firm will restrict output because:
   a. the monopolist's marginal revenue is less than product price.
   b. the monopolist's marginal costs tend to be greater.
   c. the monopolist is unable to change the size of plant as easily as the pure competitor.
   d. of the relative inability of the monopolist to obtain resources.

(b) ____ 9. A third-degree price-discriminating monopolist should divide sales among markets such that:
   a. average cost is less than the price in each market.
   b. marginal revenue is the same in each market.
   c. price is the same in each market.
   d. the elasticity of demand is the same in each market.

(b) ____ 10. When third-degree price discrimination occurs, the price:
   a. tends to be the same in all markets.
   b. will be lowest in the market in which elasticity of demand is greatest.
   c. will be highest in the market in which elasticity of demand is greatest.
   d. in each market will be that at which elasticity equals one.

(d) ____ 11. One economic "evil" of monopoly is that the:
   a. monopolist seeks to make unfair profits.
   b. monopolist overbuilds plant and equipment.
   c. monopolist faces an inelastic demand.
   d. monopolist's profit-maximizing output is less than that which would contribute most to consumer welfare.

(a) ____ 12. A lump-sum tax on a monopolist's profits usually will:
   a. not affect the profit-maximizing output and price.
   b. decrease both the output and the price at which profits are maximized.
   c. increase both the output and the price at which profits are maximized.
   d. decrease the output and raise the price at which profits are maximized.

(a) ____ 13. A specific tax on a monopolist's product will:
   a. induce the monopolist to raise the price and lower the output level.
   b. be borne entirely by the monopolist.
   c. be valuable in offsetting the adverse effects of monopoly on economic welfare.
   d. prevent the monopolist from making profits.

(d) ____ 14. Suppose that a monopolist has fixed costs only. No variable costs are involved in the production of his product and his output level can be whatever he chooses it to be. To maximize profits he should select an output level such that:
   a. demand will be inelastic.
   b. marginal revenue will be positive.
   c. demand will be elastic.
   d. demand will be of unitary elasticity.

(d) ____ 15. Which of the following suppliers would not face a downward-sloping demand curve for their services?
   a. Jimmy Carter
   b. Leftwich and Eckert
   c. Bruce Springsteen
   d. our local filling station
   .

(a) ____ 16. Which of the following conditions might make you doubt that the medical laboratories described in the article in the text were actually price discriminators?
   a. Greater distances and more transport costs were involved in picking up blood samples from Medicare patients than private patients.
   b. Private patients were treated by specialists whereas Medicare patients were usually treated by general practitioners.
   c. Medicare patients were usually hospitalized in public hospitals whereas private patients were usually in private hospitals.
   d. none of the above

(b) ____ 17. Which of the following is probably third-degree price discrimination?
   a. All telephone customers are charged lower prices after 5:00 p.m.
   b. People who shop at grocery stores during weekdays are given twice as many trading stamps per dollar of purchase as people who shop evenings or weekends.
   c. Men who shop in a department store and buy two suits at the regular price for a total purchase of at least $400 are given "free" a $35 pair of slacks.
   d. all of the above

(a) ____ 18. Which of the following could be a valid reason why prices are higher at grocery stores in "inner city" areas relative to suburban areas even though the store chains do not practice price discrimination?
   a. Insurance rates are higher in inner city areas owing to greater risks of theft and fire.
   b. Suburban consumers have higher incomes.
   c. Suburban consumers have fewer alternatives for grocery purchase owing to lower population density.
   d. none of the above

(c) _____ 19. Which of the answers in question 17 appears to be second-degree price discrimination?
a.   answer a
b.   answer b
c.   answer c
d.   answers a and c

CHAPTER 13

PRICING AND OUTPUT UNDER IMPERFECT COMPETITION

Chapter Outline

Special Characteristics of Imperfect Competition
Collusion versus Independent Action in Oligopoly
   Perfect Collusion
   Imperfect Collusion
   Independent Action
   Classification Limitations
The Short Run
   Monopolistic Competition
   Oligopoly: Perfect Collusion
   Oligopoly: Imperfect Collusion
   Oligopoly: Independent Action
The Long Run
   Entry into a Market
   Adjustments with Entry Restricted
   Adjustments with Entry Open
Nonprice Competition
   Advertising
   Differences in Quality and Design
The Welfare Effects of Imperfect Competition
   Output Restriction
   Efficiency of Individual Firms
   Cartelization Wastes
   Sales Promotion Effects
   Range of Products

Applications

OPEC: A Cartel?
Agricultural Marketing Orders
Restraints on Advertising Eyeglass Prices

Chapter Objectives

Imperfect competition includes the enormous range of market
structures between the two polar extremes of pure competition and
pure monopoly. This diversity is accounted for by variations in
conditions of demand rather than conditions of supply. We divide
these diversities into two principal subparts: the theory of
oligopoly and the theory of monopolistic competition.

© 1988 The Dryden Press

Oligopolistic markets include a wide variety of structural arrangements. We sample these arrangements to convey to students their common characteristics, including (1) interdependence among sellers in a market, (2) incentives for collusion among sellers, (3) incentives for a single firm to break away from a collusive arrangement, (4) presence of entry barriers, and (5) nonprice competition. We do not try to present "the" theory of oligopoly since none exists and none is likely to be developed, given the diversity among such markets.

The theory of monopolistic competition tells us little analytically that is not contained in the theory of pure competition—and it is not as easy to use. It does provide students more practice in using the theory of the firm and somewhat more insight. Its main value is in description rather than in analysis.

Suggestions for Teaching

First, we describe the sources of diversity that account for the range of imperfectly competitive market structures. These sources are the number of sellers, interdependencies among them, product differentiation, entry conditions, and the nature of competition. Second, we drill students on the short-run and long-run profit-maximizing solutions utilizing the same analytical framework as in Chapters 10, 11, and 12. We again emphasize the important motivations provided firms by profits and losses, and entry and exit. Third, we analyze the welfare implications of certain features of imperfect competition: output restrictions, firm efficiency, cartelization, sales promotion, and product differentiation.

Oligopoly is not a unique market structure like pure competition and pure monopoly were. Students find it useful to view oligopoly on a continuum from pure monopoly on the one hand, shading off into pure competition (and monopolistic competition) on the other hand. Interdependence among sellers—a new concept to students—encourages attempts at collusion.

The OPEC application illustrates a weak market-sharing arrangement that seems to attract keen student interest. Depending upon what OPEC is doing, the subject may be newsworthy when your class is given. The agricultural marketing order application shows additional nuances of collusive arrangements. It also illustrates how imperfect cartelization can be even when government attempts to discourage rivalry.

We omit the classical duopoly cases. These are generally recognized as intellectual games that at most illustrate oligopolistic interdependence. In our opinion, they add little content to the analysis of oligopolistic markets. We also omit game theory on the same grounds. However, anyone who disagrees can easily insert either or both into the analytical pattern that we develop.

Oligopolistic theory is rich in diagrammatic possibilities. We take advantage of them to increase student familiarity with graphic techniques—the centralized cartel, market-sharing cartels, the kinked demand curve, idle firms in a cartel, price leadership by a dominant firm, and the like. One can easily include reaction curves and other types of diagrams. At the same time, we like to keep in mind that the majority of students in intermediate price theory are not economics graduate students.

We have very little new to suggest for teaching monopolistic competition. We point up the small elements of monopoly that arise from the slight downward slope of the demand curve facing the firm, a marginal revenue curve that lies below the demand curve, the possibility of impeded entry into a market, and limited sales promotion activities. The application on advertising in the health services professions indicates that suppression of advertising may also serve to suppress competition.

Problems and Questions for Discussion

1. Why do price wars erupt from time to time in oligopolistic industries but never do so in purely competitive industries?

2. a. Explain in terms of demand elasticities why individual firms have an incentive to break away from a cartel arrangement.
    b. In view of your answer to part (a), why would firms want to form a cartel in the first place? (Perhaps the OPEC countries provide an example.)

3. a. What are the major factors that prevent newcomers from breaking into the manufacture and sale of automobiles?
    b. If you were interested in making this industry more competitive, what advice would you give the government with respect to its policies toward it?

4. Would you be in favor of having all automobile repair stations in your city licensed by the city government? Why or why not?

5. Why do the firms in many oligopolistic industries use sales promotion activities rather than price cuts to enlarge their markets?

6. Suppose that a pair of duopolists collude to maximize their joint profits. They are able to discriminate in the sale of their product between Market I and Market II. Their average costs differ with firm A's lying substantially higher than firm B's. Determine:
   a. the appropriate total output.
   b. the sales and price in each market.
   c. the allocation of production quotas to each firm.
   d. the average costs of each firm.

7. Assess OPEC's effectiveness as a quasi-cartel based on the last month of clippings about oil pricing and supplies from one of the large daily newspapers.

8. In what sense is OPEC a market-sharing collusive arrangement and in what sense is it not? Explain.

9. Crude oil is not homogeneous. "Light" grades are cheaper to refine relative to their per barrel yield of products (gasoline, heating oil, and aviation fuel). OPEC uses Saudi Arabia's "Arab light" oil for its "benchmark" price that is usually mentioned in news stories, but then establishes price "differentials" for other grades. Light grades in 1983-84 sold at premiums of $3 to $10 per barrel more than heavy grades.

   In Problem 12 of the Instructor's Manual Chapter 9, we saw that refineries adjusted by converting to processes that increase the yield of refined products from lower-priced heavy crudes. But they converted to heavy crudes faster than supplies increased. The demand for heavier crudes increased relative to lighter grades. The refinery investments are reversible only at a substantial cost.

   Most of the light crudes are produced in OPEC countries (especially Nigeria), although the quality of oil varies among OPEC members and some produce medium as well as light grades. Light crudes are also common in Britain, Norway, and Mexico. Heavy crudes are mainly found outside of OPEC, in Alaska, California, Canada, South America, and many other countries. (William Epstein and Joseph Barnea, "Heavy Crude Is OPEC's Achilles Heel," The Wall Street Journal, January 18, 1985.)

   Explain how these developments complicated OPEC's task of reaching agreement on prices and quotas in 1984-85.

© 1988 The Dryden Press

10. If the Canadian egg cartel yields a total welfare loss to consumers that exceeds the total welfare gain to growers, why do not consumers join together to pay growers to increase output to where price equals marginal cost? Can you think of any other method of getting rid of this cartel that is consistent with democratic political processes? Explain.

11. Milk production within the European Economic Community is cartelized. To reduce the surplus at the chosen price, each milk-producing country within the EEC is assigned a total quota that it in turn must divide among its milk producers. The United Kingdom introduced a preliminary quota scheme in 1984. (William de Salis, "Quotas and the Landowner," Country Landowner 36 [July 7, 1984], 8.) Evaluate each of the following rules for whether it increases or decreases the cost to Britain of producing its total milk quota.
   a. The quota allocated to an owner applies to all the land within the EEC that he owns. Quota is freely transferable between parcels within the owner's total holding.
   b. Quota is allocated to individual landowners and can not be transferred to other producers apart from selling the land.
   c. Quota can not be leased between landowners in whole or in part unless the land itself is leased.

12. An association of colleges has established "guidelines" for recruiting freshmen that discourage each of the following: (i) switching between schools by students already enrolled; (ii) advertising in student publications that work to the disadvantage of some schools (such as a Florida university's ad in student newspapers in the Boston area during a bad winter); (iii) giving students early notice of guaranteed admission and financial aid packages with deadlines for acceptance before the student is likely to have heard from competitors; and (iv) giving some students grants based strictly on merit without regard to financial "need."
   a. Who benefits from these rules? Explain.
   b. Would you expect them to be effective in limiting competition among colleges? Explain.

13. In 1980, five physicians in a small Texas town, the town's only physicians, were accused by the U.S. Federal Trade Commission of threatening to boycott a hospital that planned to give hospital privileges to a sixth doctor on terms the five did not like. The FTC alleged that the five tried to discourage the hospital from making this contract more on competitive grounds than on the sixth doctor's qualifications. The five doctors threatened to refuse to provide emergency room service or to refer patients to the new doctor if the hospital guaranteed him a minimum annual income. ("Five Texas Doctors Accused of Trying to Bar Competition," The Wall Street Journal, August 8, 1980.) Which market structure do you think best fits the market for physicians in this small town? Explain.

14. How do convenience stores such as Li'l General, Seven-Eleven, and Honk-N-Holler differentiate their products? Consider one such store and explain what you would expect the nature of the demand curve facing it to be. (Let the quantity axis simply show units of food.)

15. Explain and illustrate the position of an individual firm in monopolistic competition when the firm and the industry are in long-run equilibrium with entry into the industry open.

16. Explain and illustrate the position of an individual firm in long-run equilibrium in an industry of monopolistic competition when entry into the industry is blocked.

17. What is your reaction to governmentally enforced price-fixing by hair cutting establishments in a given city (or county) based on the argument that this will enable them to earn sufficient income to maintain clean and sanitary shops?

18. Would you favor or oppose a law that prohibits attorneys from advertising? Why or why not?

19. Using your library's indexes to newspapers and periodical literature for the past several years, analyze the structure, recent activities, and effectiveness of one of the following cartels:
    a. international ocean shipping conferences, one of which is established for each major route——such as the United States/East, South Africa, and Inter-American freight conferences——and given antitrust immunity by the U.S. Federal Maritime Commission
    b. International Air Transport Association
    c. International Cocoa Agreement
    d. International Coffee Organization
    e. International Natural Rubber Agreement
    f. International Sugar Agreement
    g. International Tin Council

20. A partial list of the occupations and professions subject to licensing in one state includes dentists, physicians, optometrists, opticians, pharmacists, veterinarians, accountants, architects, attorneys, barbers, civil engineers, building contractors, cosmetologists, funeral directors and embalmers, structural pest control contractors, ship brokers, furniture and bedding inspectors, registered nurses, vocational nurses, dry cleaners, chiropodists, chiropractors, social workers, marriage and family counselors, cemetery operators, operators of seeing-eye dog schools, private investigators and adjusters, shorthand court reporters, collection agents, and landscape architects.
    a. Check the business and professions laws for your state and make a similar list. Are there any substantial differences from the one given here?
    b. Select a half-dozen occupations at random from your list. In which market structure does each seem to fit best? Explain why in each case.
    c. For the same half-dozen occupations, on the basis of economic analysis, why do you think the state legislature requires licensing? Do you agree or disagree with the practice? Defend your position.
    d. Do these laws prohibit advertising of prices? Do they contain sanctions against advertising?
    e. Is each profession governed by a board made up primarily of practitioners or consumers?

Solutions to Problems and Questions for Discussion

1. In pure competition, no firm can influence market price.
   Market price in long-run equilibrium is equal to each firm's
   minimum long-run average cost and can not go lower without
   causing some firms to exit the industry. In oligopoly, an
   individual firm can influence market price. Price leadership by a dominant firm or attempts at collusion may raise
   market price above each firm's minimum long-run average
   cost. When these arrangements break down, however, firms
   acting independently may start cutting price competitively,
   sometimes with disastrous results.

2. a. Review the discussion of text Figure 13.2. A firm
      that cuts price secretly while the cartel maintains its
      price will have a more elastic demand curve than the
      market demand curve in price ranges around the cartel
      price. Thus, its demand curve is dd, and its marginal
      revenue is higher at x_a than the cartel's at output
      level X. By increasing output, the price-cutting firm
      attracts business from the cartel and increases its
      profits.
   b. The cartel's purpose is to decrease the elasticity of
      demand facing individual firms to that of the market
      demand, reducing their incentives to charge prices below
      the industry profit-maximizing level.

3. a. The entry rate is low because the costs of constructing
      an optimally sized plant are very large and because of
      consumer loyalty to existing brands.
   b. Remove artificial barriers to imports, such as the "vol-
      untary" quotas on Japanese automobiles.

4. We would not. Licensing restricts entry. Restricting entry
   tends to raise price and makes the industry less responsive
   to consumer demands.

5. Promotional campaigns attempt to push the firm's demand
   curve to the right and make it less elastic. The purpose is
   to increase sales without inciting competitive price cutting. Rivals may eventually begin sales promotion campaigns
   of their own, but the innovating firm may earn extra profits in the meantime.

6. a. The marginal cost curves for the two firms are summed horizontally as in text Figure 10.13, and the marginal revenues for the two markets are summed horizontally as in text Figure 12.10. The total output is determined where the total marginal cost curve intersects the total marginal revenue curve—such as output rate x in Figure 12.10.

    b. To maximize profits, Figure 12.10 shows that the total output is divided between the two markets so that their marginal revenues equal each other and equal total marginal revenue r.

    c. As indicated in Figure 10.13, quotas should be divided between the two firms so that their marginal costs are equal.

    d. For each firm's output quota, average cost equals the height of the average cost curve above the X-axis.

7. The following factors are important in this assessment:
    a. whether spot prices have been rising or falling
    b. whether there have been reports of secret price cutting, especially by Saudi Arabia
    c. whether there have been reports of growing conflict between the short-run and long-run maximizers
    d. whether the Iran-Iraq war has been resolved or worsened
    e. whether Britain, Mexico, and other non-OPEC producers have been holding down output in support of OPEC

8. OPEC members attempt to agree on market shares, but they do not achieve the monopoly price and output. They disagree over which price will achieve maximum profits for the group. Their marginal costs differ and they have not devised arrangements whereby low marginal costs producers can compensate high marginal costs producers for cutting back. Overproduction and secret price cutting are common because OPEC lacks a centralized enforcement mechanism. Thus, OPEC remains unstable.

9. Producers of light crudes wanted the prices of heavy crudes raised. Most of the heavy crude production was outside OPEC, so all OPEC could do was cut the price of its light-crude substitutes. This is why such light-crude producers as Britain, Mexico, and Nigeria (an OPEC member) led the price cutting in 1984-85 against each other to regain sales lost to heavy-crude producers. Over the long run, as refineries invest in more facilities to process heavy crudes, OPEC's future looks even more uncertain.

© 1988 The Dryden Press

10. The total welfare loss to consumers may exceed the total
    gain to producers, but the per family loss to consumers
    is only about $10 per year while the per farm gain to pro-
    ducers is about $14,500. The per family costs of lobbying
    to eliminate the cartel far exceed the per family welfare
    loss, while the opposite is true for producers. So, the
    cartel survives, although growers have to spend about half
    their monopoly gains in lobbying governmental officials
    for support. Borcherding and Dorosh argue that probably the
    most effective way to eliminate the cartel is to buy back
    the quotas with public funds, although in the long run this
    tends to encourage the formation of additional cartels.

11.   a. This rule lets the owner fill his quota on his
               most productive (least-cost) parcels. It reduces
               the cost of producing Britain's total quota.
     b. and c. These rules make the transfer of quotas from
               higher-cost farms to lower-cost farms more expen-
               sive and therefore make such transfers less
               likely. They raise the cost of producing Brit-
               ain's total quota.

12. a. The schools of the association expect the rules to en-
        able them to attract and hold more students than would
        be possible without them. Students with good grades
        who may not qualify for financial aid according to the
        financial-aid guidelines that colleges collusively use
        may benefit.
    b. Not really. Individual institutions have incentives
        to violate these agreements secretly. Many schools now
        are offering at least some scholarships based on merit
        alone.

13. Oligopoly, because of the small number of sellers.

14. Products are differentiated by location, hours of services,
    and the range of products carried relative to conventional
    grocery stores. Less elastic than for conventional stores
    because of product differentiation.

15. Review the discussion of text Figure 13.11. Entry shifts
    the demand curves faced by individual firms downward and
    their cost curves upward. These shifts cause profits to
    fall toward zero.

16. Review the discussion of text Figure 13.10. Blocked entry
    generates profits at the output at which SMC equals LMC
    equals mr, and at which SAC equals LAC.

17. Consumers prefer stores that are clean to those that are filthy, especially if both charge the same prices. Consumers will choose on this basis provided the information about which stores are clean can be ascertained at relatively low cost. Government inspection of premises and sanitary regulations serve a useful purpose when such information is expensive and time-consuming for consumers to uncover. These requirements, however, can be imposed without limiting the number of licensed sellers. Arguments that licenses must be restricted to generate sufficient income to keep the premises clean are usually attempts to justify cartelization and higher-than-competitive prices.

18. We would oppose it. We can not think of any reason why consumers would be harmed by advertising. We believe the claim that advertising "demeans" the legal profession is a device for limiting competition similar to that in the eyeglasses application.

19. Depends on facts discovered.

20. Depends on facts discovered.

True-False Questions

(F) _____ 1. Over the years, economists have developed a general theory of oligopoly that can be used to explain and predict oligopolistic pricing and output in most cases.

(T) _____ 2. One of the problems in oligopoly analysis is the difficulty of predicting with accuracy how rivals will react to market activities of any one firm in an industry and how the reactions of others will affect the market of any one firm.

(F) _____ 3. Differentiated oligopoly means that the firms in an industry sell different kinds of products that actually are not very good substitutes.

(T) _____ 4. A centralized cartel faces the market demand curve for the product and ideally (for the firms in the market) would act as a pure monopoly.

(F) _____ 5. Output quotas assigned cartel members should be such that average costs of each firm are the same if cartel total costs for any industry output level are to be minimized.

© 1988 The Dryden Press

(T) ____ 6. The industry short-run marginal cost curve for a centralized cartel is the horizontal summation of the individual firm short-run marginal cost curves.

(T) ____ 7. The potential demand curve facing any one firm that contemplates breaking away from a cartel is more elastic at the cartel price level than the market demand curve.

(F) ____ 8. The demand curve facing Ford Motor Company for its output would have about the same elasticity as the market demand curve for automobiles.

(T) ____ 9. The low-cost firm in an industry is in a unique position to be a price leader.

(F) ____ 10. The demand curve facing the dominant firm in the dominant firm model has about the same elasticity at each price level as the market demand curve.

(T) ____ 11. In the dominant firm model, the dominant firm and each small firm produce output levels at which their respective marginal costs equal their respective marginal revenues.

(F) ____ 12. A kink in the demand curve facing a firm will be mirrored at a lower level by the marginal revenue curve.

(T) ____ 13. Entry barriers to many industries exist because they are supported by governmental units.

(F) ____ 14. Ordinarily, there will be no relationship between barriers to entry and the existence of collusion in an oligopolistic industry.

(F) ____ 15. Most of the advertising done by firms in an oligopolistic industry is intended to enlarge individual firm sales by shifting the industry demand curve for the product to the right.

(T) ____ 16. Advertising is often used successfully to differentiate the products of the sellers in an industry, even though these products all have identical physical characteristics.

(T) ____ 17. A major welfare loss resulting from an oligopolistic market structure is a waste of resources in sales promotion rivalry.

(F) _____ 18. OPEC always wants higher prices because it knows that there are relatively few good substitutes for petroleum in the consuming countries.

(T) _____ 19. Saudi Arabia wants to hold prices down because it knows that demand elasticity for its output tends to be larger the higher the price.

(T) _____ 20. A group of firms that becomes a successful cartel will generally charge a price that lies in the elastic area of the industry demand curve.

(F) _____ 21. An agricultural marketing order permits collusion without generating welfare losses for consumers.

(F) _____ 22. The agricultural marketing orders for California-Arizona citrus are effective because they block entry.

(T) _____ 23. The quotas imposed on Canadian egg producers caused egg prices in Canada to rise.

(T) _____ 24. The main difference between markets of pure competition and monopolistic competition is the existence of product differentiation in the latter.

(T) _____ 25. Product differentiation among the firms in an industry make it difficult, if not impossible, to construct a clear industry demand curve.

(F) _____ 26. In the short run, the firms in a monopolistically competitive industry will usually charge the same price.

(F) _____ 27. In an industry of monopolistic competition, much rivalry for market shares usually exists among firms.

(T) _____ 28. Blocked entry into an industry of monopolistic competition usually requires the support of the government.

(F) _____ 29. If entry into a monopolistically competitive industry is blocked, the firm will have an incentive to build a less than optimum size of plant.

© 1988 The Dryden Press

(F) ____ 30. Firms in an industry of monopolistic competition, when entry is open and long-run equilibrium exists, will build larger than optimum plant sizes and operate them at greater than optimum rates of output.

(T) ____ 31. In long-run equilibrium, industries of monopolistic competition are usually alleged to have excess capacity and zero profits.

(T) ____ 32. For a firm to be in long-run equilibrium in monopolistic competition, long-run marginal cost equals short-run marginal cost equals marginal revenue; and these are less than price which equals average costs.

(T) ____ 33. Although monopolistic competitors may engage in advertising to expand their respective markets, the advertising is not retaliatory as it frequently is in oligopoly.

(T) ____ 34. Some sales promotion wastes are likely to occur in monopolistic competition as sales promotion efforts of some firms are offset by those of others.

(T) ____ 35. Sellers in a monopolistically competitive market have an incentive to use governmental regulation to convert their industry from a more competitive to a less competitive arrangement.

(T) ____ 36. Sellers in a monopolistically competitive market will tend to advertise unless there are legal prohibitions on this form of behavior.

Multiple-Choice Questions

(c) ____ 1. The demand curve facing an oligopolist is usually:
   a. well defined and easily determined.
   b. rather inelastic in the neighborhood of market price.
   c. difficult to locate with precision since its position and shape depend on the behavior of rivals.
   d. of unitary elasticity.

© 1988 The Dryden Press

(a) _____ 2. The distinguishing feature of an oligopolistic market structure is:
   a. the interdependence among sellers.
   b. the independence of each seller.
   c. product differentiation.
   d. a kinked demand curve.

(c) _____ 3. In most oligopolistic industries, a strong incentive exists to:
   a. raise the product price.
   b. make the demand curve facing the firm as elastic as possible.
   c. join together to maximize industry profits.
   d. join together to better serve the public.

(d) _____ 4. In order to minimize costs in a central cartel arrangement for any given output level:
   a. quotas should be assigned so that average costs are the same for each firm.
   b. all firms should charge the same price.
   c. there should be as much product differentiation as possible.
   d. quotas should be assigned so that marginal costs are the same for each firm.

(c) _____ 5. If one firm in a cartel arrangement breaks away and pursues independent pricing policies:
   a. it violates the Sherman Act.
   b. it faces a demand curve of approximately the same elasticity as the market demand curve for the product in the neighborhood of the market price.
   c. it faces a demand curve more elastic than the market demand curve in the neighborhood of the market price.
   d. it will not be able to maximize profits.

(a) _____ 6. Market-sharing cartels approximate the monopoly price and output of a product:
   a. only under rather unusual circumstances such as equal sharing of the market and identical cost curves.
   b. in almost all cases when they exist.
   c. if they have effective price leaders.
   d. by engaging in sales promotion activities.

(b) _____ 7. Price leadership provides:
   a. an effective way to maximize industry profits.
   b. a means of acting collusively on prices with-
      out overtly violating the antitrust laws.
   c. a direct means of dividing up the market among
      the firms in the industry.
   d. a strong incentive for chiseling on the part
      of individual firms.

(c) _____ 8. In the dominant firm price leadership model, each
      small firm is assumed to:
   a. set its own price for its output.
   b. sell at minimum average costs.
   c. face a perfectly elastic demand curve.
   d. face the market demand curve.

(b) _____ 9. In the dominant firm model, the dominant firm:
   a. faces the market demand.
   b. faces a quantity demanded at each price level
      equal to what the total market will take less
      what the small firms want to sell.
   c. faces a demand curve less elastic than the
      market demand curve at each price.
   d. chooses a price independently of the actions
      of small firms.

(b) _____ 10. In the kinked demand curve case, an increase in
      costs of production (an upward shift in the cost
      curves):
   a. will increase the price charged by the firm if
      the marginal cost curve continues to cut the
      discontinuous segment of the marginal revenue
      curve.
   b. will not increase the price charged by the
      firm if the marginal cost curve continues to
      cut the discontinuous segment of the marginal
      revenue curve.
   c. will not affect total profits if marginal cost
      equals marginal revenue in the discontinuous
      segment of the marginal revenue curve.
   d. generally causes an increase in demand.

(c) _____ 11. In many oligopolistic industries, barriers to
      entry:
   a. are relatively insignificant.
   b. exist only in the short run.
   c. are effected by and enforced by governmental
      units.
   d. are a major deterrent to profit maximization.

© 1988 The Dryden Press

(b) _____ 12. Natural barriers to entry are those:
   a. imposed by the government.
   b. stemming from market size and, for the in-
      dividual firm, the size of plant necessary
      to take advantage of economies of size.
   c. resulting from predatory pricing.
   d. resulting from monopolization of resources
      necessary to produce a product.

(b) _____ 13. Most advertising done by firms in a typical oligopolistic industry:
   a. is intended to provide consumers with infor-
      mation that will enable them to purchase more
      intelligently.
   b. is intended to expand the market share of the
      advertising firm.
   c. is intended to aid the firm by expanding the
      total market demand for the product.
   d. shifts demand in highly predictable amounts.

(a) _____ 14. Changes in the design and quality of product by
   the firms in an oligopolistic industry:
   a. may result in significant product improvement.
   b. shift demand in highly predictable amounts.
   c. are relatively costless to consumers.
   d. should be carried to the point at which their
      total costs equal the total amount of revenue
      that they generate.

(d) _____ 15. Which of the following is most likely to be a
   positive welfare effect of oligopolistic market
   structures?
   a. lower prices and larger outputs than would
      prevail under pure competition
   b. efficiency of operation in the sense of opti-
      mum sizes of plant operated at optimum rates
      of output
   c. consumer benefits from sales promotion ac-
      tivities
   d. wider range of product qualities than exist
      in pure competition and pure monopoly

(d) _____ 16. Which of the following is a relatively unimpor-
   tant factor that oligopolists can safely ignore?
   a. market entry
   b. government regulations
   c. changes in price, advertising, and brands
      introduced by rivals
   d. the kinked demand curve

(d) ____ 17. Which of the following goals generally has eluded
OPEC?
a. It has been able to agree on quotas but not a
means for enforcing them.
b. It has been able to agree on prices occasion-
ally, but not on a means for preventing secret
price cutting.
c. It has been able to agree on the need for
coordinated action among the group members but
not on the level of price that maximizes the
group's profits.
d. all of the above

(a) ____ 18. Which of the following will reduce the stability
of a cartel?
a. a rising number of buyers
b. a group of buyers composed of a few large
ones as opposed to many small ones
c. a fixed number of buyers, all of whom are
repeat customers
d. a group of buyers that colludes against the
cartel

(d) ____ 19. Which of the following is not a consequence of the
marketing orders that regulate Canadian eggs?
a. welfare losses to consumers
b. lost economies of size to producers
c. an income transfer from consumers to producers
d. net benefits to consumers

(b) ____ 20. Which of the following is not a consequence of the
marketing orders that regulate California-Arizona
citrus?
a. higher fresh fruit prices to consumers
b. higher prices of frozen citrus products
c. minimizing production costs for the industry
as a whole
d. an expansion in the number of acres planted

(c) ____ 21. In monopolistic competition, profit maximization
requires that:
a. price equals average costs.
b. price equals marginal costs.
c. marginal revenue equals marginal costs.
d. marginal costs equal average costs.

(b) _____ 22. In an industry of monopolistic competition, we find:
   a. many firms selling identical products.
   b. many firms selling differentiated products.
   c. few firms selling identical products.
   d. few firms selling differentiated products.

(c) _____ 23. Monopolistic competition is characterized by:
   a. price wars.
   b. rivalry among sellers.
   c. independence among sellers.
   d. collusion.

(d) _____ 24. The marginal revenue curve of a monopolistic competitor ordinarily:
   a. is horizontal.
   b. coincides with the demand curve facing the firm.
   c. coincides with the market demand curve.
   d. lies below the demand curve, which tends to be highly elastic, and slopes downward to the right.

(b) _____ 25. Long-run profit maximization under monopolistic competition ordinarily results in:
   a. most efficient plant sizes operated at optimum rates of output.
   b. less than most efficient plant sizes operated at less than most efficient rates of output.
   c. greater than most efficient plant sizes operated at greater than most efficient rates of output.
   d. less than optimum plant sizes operated at optimum rates of output.

(c) _____ 26. Entry into industries of monopolistic competition:
   a. is often blocked by the relatively small size of the market as compared with a relatively large size of plant required by individual firms to achieve economies of size.
   b. is usually blocked by governmental actions.
   c. is usually open.
   d. both (a) and (b)

(d) _____ 27. It is frequently argued that in monopolistic competition, in the long run there will be:
   a. product shortages.
   b. product surpluses.
   c. a shortage of plant capacity.
   d. excess plant capacity.

© 1988 The Dryden Press

(a) ____ 28. In the long run, firms in monopolistic competition:
   a. make zero profits.
   b. may make positive profits if entry is open.
   c. may incur losses.
   d. try to block entry.

(a) ____ 29. Advertising in monopolistic competition is used primarily to:
   a. enlarge the market of the advertiser.
   b. shift the market demand curve to the right.
   c. offset advertising of rivals.
   d. counteract losses.

(b) ____ 30. As a result of product differentiation, the demand curve facing a firm is made:
   a. more elastic.
   b. less elastic.
   c. less stable over time.
   d. more difficult to define.

(c) ____ 31. The market demand curve for a differentiated product is difficult to portray diagrammatically because:
   a. different firms have different market shares.
   b. of the unpredictability of consumers.
   c. units of product among sellers are not homogeneous.
   d. of cost differences among sellers.

PART FIVE

THE DETERMINATION OF AND THE FUNCTIONS OF RESOURCE PRICES

Unfortunately, the theory of resource pricing, employment, and
allocation gets slighted in most intermediate-level microeconomics courses. In our view, it is at least as important as the
theory of pricing output of goods and services. In fact either
one is incomplete without the other. Moreover, issues of public
policy involve labor and capital resources at least as often as
they involve such consumer goods as toasters, milk, and refrigerators.

From the outset, students must be thoroughly familiar with the
theory of production. Whereas most of Parts Two, Three, and Four
were oriented toward markets and prices of goods and services,
Part Five is concentrated on the markets for resources. Buying
market structures are as important as selling market structures.
In Chapter 14 we develop the theory of resource pricing and
employment for the various structural conditions in product and
resource markets. This body of theory has so many useful applications that we devote Chapter 15 entirely to applications.
In Chapter 16 we examine the principles governing the allocation
of resources among different employments, and in Chapter 17 we
develop the principles determining income distribution.

CHAPTER 14

PRICING AND EMPLOYMENT OF RESOURCES: THEORY

Chapter Outline

Resource Market Structures
Resource Purchases and Costs of Production
   Least-Cost Resource Combinations
   Marginal Physical Products, Marginal Costs, and Profit
     Maximization
Pricing and Employment of a Variable Resource: Pure Competition
  in Purchasing
   The Demand Curve of the Firm: One Resource Variable
   The Demand Curve of the Firm: Several Resources Variable
   The Market Demand Curve
   The Market Supply Curve
   Resource Pricing and the Level of Employment
   Monopolistic Exploitation of a Resource
Pricing and Employment of a Variable Resource: Monopsony
   Resource Supply Curves and Marginal Resource Costs
   Pricing and Employment of a Single Variable Resource
   Simultaneous Employment of Several Variable Resources
   Conditions Giving Rise to Monopsony
   Monopsonistic Exploitation of a Resource
   Measures to Counteract Monopsony
   The Concept of Mobility
General Profit-Maximizing Conditions: All Market Structures
Economic Rent

Chapter Objectives

The principles of resource pricing and employment are essentially demand and supply principles, so we must construct resource demand and supply curves. Resource demand curves are built on the principles of production. First, we show how a firm's demand curve for a resource is generated; then we move to the market demand curve for it. The market supply curve, the resource price, the supply curve for the firm, and firm and market levels of employment follow in that order. We then modify these results to take into account the possibility of monopsony in the resource market, and show general profit-maximizing conditions for all market structures. Finally, we discuss the concept of economic rent.

© 1988 The Dryden Press

Suggestions for Teaching

We find it useful to review least-cost combinations of resources before constructing a firm's demand curve for a resource. Then we move to the simplest possible case—the firm's demand curve for a resource that is the only variable resource it uses. We have yet to find a more effective device for constructing it than the material in our first discussion question below.

Students tend to confuse resource quantities with product quantities and resource prices with product prices. The answer to the confusion lies in drill and repetition. Some homework based on numerical and graphic examples may be helpful. This is why we use letters at the end of the alphabet to denote products and those at the beginning to represent resources.

The use of indifference curve techniques to construct individual labor supply curves provides an opportunity both to review those techniques and to apply them in a new context. Instructors fortunate enough to have uniformly high quality students can go one step further, changing the horizontal axis to measure units of work directly and showing indifference curves that slope upward to the right.

We emphasize that a monopolist's demand curve for a resource is in most respects the same as a pure competitor's, except that in computing a monopolist's marginal revenue product curve for a resource, the additional fact that marginal revenue decreases as the firm increases product output must be taken into account. In obtaining the market demand curve for a resource, the most difficult point to get across is that if all users of the resource are monopolists there will be no external effects from a resource price change. We stress—and repeat—that the effects of increasing industry output are <u>already</u> taken into account in the firm's product marginal revenue curve.

For monopsony in resource purchases we follow the same pattern of analysis. First we consider the simple case in which the firm uses only one variable resource. Then we analyze the case in which the firm uses several variable resources.

After defining monopsony, we show the relationship between the supply curve of a resource to a firm and the marginal resource cost curve of that resource. Then we demonstrate profit maximization by a firm with respect to a resource purchased monopsonistically. We explain how monopsony can be counteracted. Our students often become intrigued with the possibility of offsetting monopsony by the imposition of a minimum price on the resource. We spend considerable time discussing the difficulties involved in determining and implementing the "correct" minimum prices where a number of separate monopsonistic situations occur in an economy.

Problems and Questions for Discussion

Questions 1-3 are based on the diagram below:

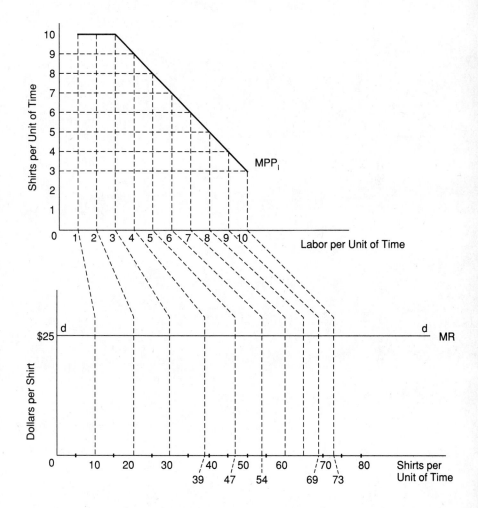

© 1988 The Dryden Press

1. a. Use the information on the diagram to derive and plot
        the marginal revenue product curve for labor in the man-
        ufacture and sale of shirts by the firm. Assume that
        labor is the only variable resource used. Note the to-
        tal output levels associated with each possible level
        of employment.
    b. If the price of labor is $100 per day, how much should
        the firm employ to maximize profits? Explain.
    c. If the price of labor is $175 per day, how much should
        the firm employ? Explain.
    d. Explain the firm's demand curve for labor.

2. What differences do you perceive in the concepts of mar-
    ginal revenue product of a resource and the value of mar-
    ginal product of a resource?

3. Explain the reasons for the downward slope of the marginal
    revenue product curve for a resource.

4. Suppose a firm uses three variable resources—labor, power
    saws, and hand saws.
    a. Explain how these resources are likely to be related
        to one another.
    b. What will be the effect of an increase in the number
        of power saws used on the marginal revenue product of
        labor? on the marginal revenue product of hand saws?
    c. Draw and explain the firm's marginal revenue product
        and demand curves for power saws.

5. What effect will an increase in the price of T-shirts have
    on the marginal revenue product curve of firms for sewing
    machines in that industry? Explain and illustrate with a
    diagram.

6. In order to compute the demand curve for a resource, is
    it necessary that all of the firms using the resource be
    in the same industry? Explain.

7. Explain and illustrate with diagrams the so-called "exter-
    nal" effects of an increase in price of resource A.

8. Suppose that the firms employing common labor sell products under conditions of pure competition.
   a. Explain and illustrate the equilibrium wage rate and level of employment. What can be said regarding each firm's marginal revenue product for labor with respect to the price of labor?
   b. Congress now passes a minimum wage law and the pre-scribed minimum hourly wage rate is below the equilibrium level of (a) above. What will be the effects of the law?
   c. Congress now raises the level of the minimum hourly wage rate above the equilibrium level of (a). What kinds of adjustments will each firm make? Why?
   d. With respect to (c) above, explain the effects of the minimum wage on the market as a whole. What do you think about the merits of a minimum wage rate for labor purchased under purely competitive conditions?

9. Economic rent is said to be a short-run phenomenon. What do you think about this belief?

10. To test the proposition that the supply-of-labor curves for most individuals bend backward at some wage, spend an hour in the government documents room of your college or university library and see what has happened to the length of the average work week in this country since the early part of this century.

11. Explain the consequences for a competitive firm of fulfill-ing the conditions of text Equation 14.4 but not Equation 14.6.

12. Explain the sense in which lower-skilled, less-trained, less-productive workers compete with higher-skilled, better-trained, more-productive workers.

13. In Europe, political pressure makes it expensive for over-staffed firms either to lay off workers or go out of busi-ness. Some governments, for example, have enacted laws re-quiring firms to make lump-sum payments to redundant workers who become unemployed. ("The New Economy," Time, May 20, 1983, p. 65.)
   a. Rewrite text Equation 14.6 to fit these facts.
   b. Explain the short-run consequences of these governmental policies.
   c. Explain the long-run consequences.

© 1988 The Dryden Press

14. For a firm that uses two resources, A and B, to produce a product X:

$$MPP_a/MRC_a = MPP_b/MRC_b = 1/MC_x = 1/MR_x$$

   a. Is the firm a monopolist or a pure competitor in the sale of its product?
   b. Is the firm a monopsonist or a pure competitor in the purchase of resources A and B? Explain.

15. Explain the difference, if any, between the marginal revenue product and the value of marginal product of a resource under:
   a. pure competition.
   b. pure monopoly.

16. Suppose that both monopolistic sellers and purely competitive sellers use resource A, and that there are enough users so that pure competition exists in the purchase of A.
   a. Explain the demand curve for A of one of the monopolistic sellers of product.
   b. Explain the demand curve for A of one of the purely competitive sellers of product.
   c. Explain the market demand curve for A.
   d. Given the market supply curve of A, explain its equilibrium price.
   e. What can you say about the allocation of A between a competitive seller and a monopolistic seller of product?

17. A portion of the supply curve for resource A to a firm is as follows:

Price of A	Quantity
$5	10
6	11
7	12
8	13

Compute and plot the marginal resource cost curve for A.

18. A manufacturer-seller of steel ingots is a monopolist in the domestic market and a pure competitor in the foreign market.
   a. Explain the determination of the profit-maximizing output, the price(s) at which it sells, and the quantities sold in each market.
   b. Suppose that for all possible sales levels in the foreign market, the average cost is above the demand curve. What should be done about sales in this market? Explain and illustrate.
   c. Referring to part (a) above, designating the output of ingots as X, and supposing that he purchases monopsonistically two resources A and B to produce the product, explain the determination of the appropriate quantities and prices of resources A and B.

19. Discuss the pros and cons of collective bargaining as a means of offsetting various monopsony situations that may occur across the economy.

Solutions to Problems and Questions for Discussion

1. a.

Labor per Unit of Time	MRP of Labor
1	$250
2	250
3	250
4	225
5	200
6	175
7	150
8	125
9	100
10	75

   b. Nine units of labor per day. $MRP_1 = MRC_1$.
   c. Six units of labor per day. $MRP_1 = MRC_1$.
   d. In the short run, when the only variable resource is labor, the firm's demand curve for labor is its marginal revenue product curve for labor.

2. Review the discussion of text Equations 14.7 and 14.8. Marginal revenue product equals marginal physical product multiplied by marginal revenue. It measures the worth of a unit of the resource to the firm. Value of marginal product equals marginal physical product multiplied by product price. It measures the value of a unit of the resource to consumers.

3. Marginal physical product of labor declines as more units

3. Marginal physical product of labor declines as more units
    of labor are employed. Marginal revenue product equals mar-
    ginal physical product multiplied by marginal revenue. For
    a purely competitive firm, marginal revenue equals product
    price and is constant, so the marginal revenue product curve
    is downward-sloping because marginal physical product falls
    as more units of labor are employed. For a monopolist, mar-
    ginal revenue declines more rapidly than product price as
    output increases. Thus, a monopolist's marginal revenue
    product curve declines because both marginal physical prod-
    uct <u>and</u> marginal revenue are declining.

4. a. Power and hand saws are substitutes. Labor is comple-
        mentary to each.
    b. More power saws cause the marginal revenue product of
        labor to shift to the right and the marginal revenue
        product of hand saws to shift to the left.
    c. Review the discussion of text Figure 14.3. The mar-
        ginal revenue product of power saws is downward-sloping
        to the right. The demand curve for power saws when
        the quantity of labor is variable will be more elastic
        than a marginal revenue product curve for power saws.

5. Review the discussion of text Equation 14.9. The higher
    price of T-shirts implies a higher marginal revenue for T-
    shirts. The higher the marginal revenue for a given mar-
    ginal physical product curve for sewing machines, the high-
    er the marginal revenue product curve for sewing machines.

6. No. The market demand curve for a resource reflects the
    external effects of a simultaneous change in output by <u>all</u>
    firms that use the resource as its price changes. Whether
    all these firms are in the same industry is irrelevant.

7. Review the discussion of text Figure 14.4.

8. a. The market supply curve of labor slopes upward to the
        right and an equilibrium wage rate and level of employ-
        ment are established where it intersects the market
        demand curve for labor. The market demand curve is the
        horizontal summation of the quantities that each firm
        will take at various wage rates after the firm has made
        an equilibrium adjustment to each wage rate. Each firm
        chooses to hire the quantity of labor where its marginal
        revenue product equals the equilibrium wage rate.
    b. The legal minimum wage rate has zero effect on employ-
        ment when it is less than the market equilibrium wage
        rate.
    c. When the legal minimum wage rate exceeds the market
        equilibrium wage rate, firms reduce the quantities of
        labor hired. Each firm's marginal revenue product curve
        slopes downward to the right, so the quantity of labor
        it hires falls until its marginal revenue product equals
        the legal minimum wage rate.
    d. The total quantity of labor demanded declines in each
        industry where the legal minimum wage rate exceeds the
        equilibrium rate. Workers who can no longer obtain jobs
        at the higher wage rate either queue for jobs in these
        industries or search for jobs in industries that are not
        covered by the legal minimum wage rate.

9. We agree. Economic rents are the returns to fixed re-
    sources after variable resources have been paid. The longer
    the period under consideration, the fewer the firm's fixed
    resources. High rents stimulate entry by resources from
    other industries, and the mobility of these resources will
    be greater the longer the run.

10. The average work week has declined.

11. It would minimize production costs for a given output
    rate but would not necessarily purchase the quantities of
    resources to produce the output rate that would maximize
    profits.

12. The less-skilled workers take a lower wage.

13. a. Firms are encouraged to hire at least some redundant workers. Thus,

$$MPP_c/p_c > MPP_1/p_1 = 1/MC_x < 1/MR_x.$$

The firm does not use a least-cost resource combination. Its marginal cost is p_1/MPP_1, and its marginal cost will exceed marginal revenue from the sale of its product.
   b. Firms would not maximize profits and may earn losses.
   c. Fewer new firms would enter these industries.

14. a. We can't tell from the information available. The firm is a monopolist if MR_x is less than p_x, and it is a pure competitor if they are equal.
   b. Again, we can't tell. The firm is a monopsonist if MRC_a exceeds p_a and if MRC_b exceeds p_b, and it is a pure competitor if each pair is equal.

15. a. and b. Review the discussion of text Equations 14.7 and 14.8, and the reasons for the differences between columns (7) and (8) in text Table 14.1.

16. a. The monopolist's demand curve is its marginal revenue product curve. As shown in text Table 14.1(b), the monopolist's MRP_a at each price is less than its VMP_a.
   b. The purely competitive seller's demand curve is its marginal revenue product curve. As shown in Table 14.1 (a), its MRP_a at each price equals its VMP_a.
   c. The market demand curve will be the sum of the quantities purchased by each individual buyer of A at each price of A after external effects of product price changes have been taken into account.
   d. The equilibrium price is determined where the market supply curve and the market demand curve intersect.
   e. Each firm adjusts the quantity of the resource that it employs so that its marginal revenue product equals the equilibrium market price of the resource. For the purely competitive seller, marginal revenue product equals value of marginal product, so the price for the resource that it pays reflects the value of the products that it adds to the economy's output. For the monopolist, marginal revenue product is less than value of marginal product, so it stops short of employing the resource at the level at which the price it pays reflects the value of the products that it adds to the economy's output. Society values more output by the monopolist relative to outputs of other things. Nevertheless, the resource is paid the same price by firms in each market situation.

17.

Price of A	Quantity	Marginal Resource Cost
$5	10	
6	11	$16
7	12	18
8	13	20

Plotting price against quantity yields a portion of the supply curve. Plotting marginal resource cost against quantity
yields a portion of the marginal resource cost curve.

18. a. The following diagram is based on text Figure 12.10 for
   third-degree discrimination assuming no communication
   between markets. Foreign DD and MR are horizontal at
   the foreign price p_f, and the summed marginal revenue is
   MR_T (the kinked solid lines). Total output is x, determined where MC intersects MR_T. It sells x_d at p_d at
   home and the difference between x and x_d at p_f abroad.

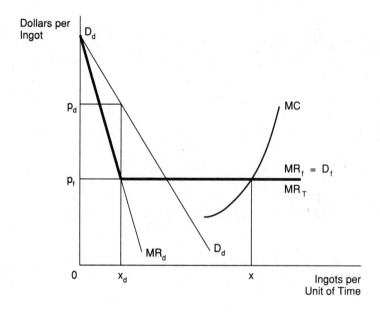

   b. Aside from the marginal conditions, what matters is
   whether total revenue exceeds total cost for both markets combined, not whether average cost exceeds price
   in either market.

   c. The monopsonist maximizes profits in accordance with
   text Equation 14.6 where MR_T from the figure above is
   substituted for MR_x. It pays each resource a price that
   reflects its monopsony, but it manufactures the output
   x that was determined in part (a).

© 1988 The Dryden Press

19. Review the discussion of text Figure 14.9. The exact wage rate that offsets the monopsony completely is difficult to determine. A minimum price between p_a and p_{a1} will counteract part of the monopsony but will leave some exploitation intact. A wage rate between p_{a1} and v will eliminate exploitation, but at the expense of some unemployment. Would you expect union negotiators to cease wage bargaining at the level at which exploitation is just offset? We wouldn't.

True-False Questions

(T) _____ 1. When a firm is using resources in a least-cost combination, the marginal cost of the product is equal to the price of any one of the resources that it uses divided by the marginal physical product of that resource.

(T) _____ 2. If a firm is using three resources—labor (1), machines (m), and electricity (e)—and is maximizing its profits, then:

$$MPP_1/MRC_1 = MPP_m/MRC_m = MPP_e/MRC_e$$

(F) _____ 3. Conceptually, the marginal revenue product and the value of marginal product of a resource are the same.

(T) _____ 4. The marginal revenue product curve is the firm's demand curve for a resource if that resource is the only variable resource used by the firm.

(T) _____ 5. A decrease in the price of lumber will tend to cause an increase in the demand for nails.

(F) _____ 6. A decrease in the price of concrete to paving contractors will tend to increase the demand for asphalt.

(T) _____ 7. An increase in the price of fuel oil will tend to increase the demand for coal.

(T) _____ 8. A firm's demand curve for one of several variable resources will be more elastic than the marginal revenue product curve of that resource.

(F) _____ 9. To obtain the market demand curve for a resource, we sum horizontally the marginal revenue product curves of the resource for the firms that use it.

© 1988 The Dryden Press

(T) ____ 10. An increase in the price of product X will increase the value of marginal product of resource
A which is used in the production of X.

(F) ____ 11. An increase in the price that a single firm must
pay for labor will usually be offset by increases
in efficiency on the part of the firm.

(T) ____ 12. A firm tends to employ that quantity of a resource at which the marginal revenue product of
the resource equals the marginal resource cost.

(F) ____ 13. A firm that employs resources in the correct
proportions will also be employing them in the
correct absolute amounts.

(T) ____ 14. A firm that employs resources in the correct
absolute amounts will also be employing them in
the correct proportions.

(T) ____ 15. Economic rent is a short-run phenomenon.

(F) ____ 16. Every person's labor supply curve bends back on
itself at some wage rate level.

(T) ____ 17. Economic rent of a resource unit is that portion
of its price (or wage rate) in excess of its
opportunity cost.

(F) ____ 18. A monopolistic seller of product faces a downward-
sloping resource supply curve.

(T) ____ 19. A firm's marginal revenue product curve of a
resource lies below its value of marginal product
curve of the resource.

(T) ____ 20. There is no essential difference between the
demand curve for a resource of a monopolistic firm
and that of a purely competitive firm.

(T) ____ 21. In obtaining the market demand curve for a resource used only by monopolists, there are no external effects to take into account; therefore,
the market demand curve is a horizontal summation
of individual firm demand curves.

(F) ____ 22. Monopolistic exploitation of a resource means that
monopolistic sellers of product pay less for units
of a given resource than purely competitive firms
that purchase the same resource.

(F) ____ 23. When a monopolist is maximizing profits, the value of marginal product for any one variable resource that it uses will be equal to the price of the resource.

(T) ____ 24. Marginal revenue product of a resource measures the value of a unit of resource to the firm that uses it, while value of marginal product measures the value of a unit of the resource to the consuming public.

(T) ____ 25. Monopolistic exploitation of a resource by a firm is measured by the difference between its value of marginal product and its marginal revenue product when the firm is maximizing its profits.

(T) ____ 26. Monopsony in resource buying occurs when the buyer faces a non-horizontal resource supply curve.

(T) ____ 27. For a monopsonist, marginal resource cost is usually greater than the resource price.

(F) ____ 28. Usually low-paid workers, like grape pickers, are exploited monopsonistically while high-paid workers, like TV entertainers, are not.

(T) ____ 29. The mobility of units of a resource tend to be restricted when there are only a few users of that kind of resource.

(T) ____ 30. Monopsonistic exploitation of a resource implies that a unit of the resource is worth more to the purchasing firm than the firm pays for it.

(T) ____ 31. The marginal cost of a unit of product produced by a monopsonist that uses resources A and B is equal to:
$$MRC_a/MPP_a = MRC_b/MPP_b.$$

(T) ____ 32. If an appropriate minimum price can be established for a resource that is purchased monopsonistically, the monopsony power of the purchaser may be completely offset.

(T) ____ 33. Measures that increase resource mobility—particularly education through the college or university level—tend to be effective in counteracting monopsony.

Multiple-Choice Questions

Questions 1 and 2 are based on diagram below.

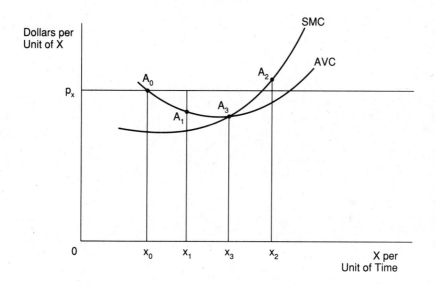

(b) _____ 1. The firm will <u>not</u> be using a least-cost combination of variable resources if:
a. its output level is x_1 and its average variable costs are x_1A_1.
b. its output level is x_2 and its average variable costs are x_2A_2.
c. its output level is x_3 and its average variable costs are x_3A_3.
d. its output level is x_0 and its average variable costs are x_0A_0.

(a) _____ 2. If the firm uses two variable resources, A and B,
then at output level x_3:
a. $MPP_a/MRC_a = MPP_b/MRC_b > 1/P_x$.
b. $MPP_a/MRC_a = MPP_b/MRC_b < 1/P_x$.
c. $MPP_a/MRC_a > MPP_b/MRC_b = 1/P_x$.
d. $MPP_a/MRC_a = MPP_b/MRC_b = 1/P_x$.

(d) ____ 3. If the marginal revenue product of a resource is less than its price:
   a. the firm is incurring losses.
   b. the firm is making profits.
   c. its employment level should be increased.
   d. its employment level should be decreased.

(d) ____ 4. If a decrease in the price of resource A causes a shift to the right in the marginal physical product of resource B, then:
   a. B must be a substitute for A.
   b. the demand curve for B will shift to the left.
   c. the demand curve for A will shift to the right.
   d. B must be complementary to A.

(c) ____ 5. The values of marginal product and the marginal revenue product of a resource to a purely competitive firm are:
   a. identical in dollars and in concept.
   b. identical in concept.
   c. identical in dollars but not in concept.
   d. different in both dollars and concept.

(c) ____ 6. The values to society of a unit of resource A used in producing product X are measured by:
   a. its marginal physical product.
   b. the price of X.
   c. its marginal physical product multiplied by the price of X.
   d. its marginal physical product divided by its price.

(c) ____ 7. A firm's demand curve for labor, when labor is one of several variable resources used, is:
   a. the marginal revenue product curve for labor.
   b. the value of marginal product curve for labor.
   c. more elastic than the marginal revenue product curve for labor.
   d. less elastic than the value of marginal product curve for labor.

(a) ____ 8. For a firm that makes cardboard boxes, a decrease in the price of cardboard will:
  a. shift the marginal revenue product for labor to the right.
  b. shift the marginal revenue product for labor to the left.
  c. be unlikely to change the quantity of cardboard demanded.
  d. increase the firm's demand for cardboard.

(a) ____ 9. The market demand curve for unskilled labor is made up of:
  a. the summation of the quantities that each firm will take at various possible wage rates when each firm in the market has made an equilibrium adjustment to each wage rate.
  b. the summation of the demand curves for labor of each firm in the market.
  c. the quantities of labor that all firms in the market will take at each possible wage rate, holding constant the quantities of all other resources used.
  d. all of the above.

(b) ____ 10. If a union succeeds in obtaining a wage rate for its members that is higher than the equilibrium level:
  a. the level of employment is not likely to be affected.
  b. employers will not be willing to hire as much labor as before and unemployment will result.
  c. the total wage bill will usually increase.
  d. all union members will find themselves better off.

(b) ____ 11. Under conditions of pure competition in product sales and resource purchases, resource units are:
  a. paid less than they are worth to the society.
  b. paid what they are worth to the society.
  c. paid more than they are worth to business firms.
  d. paid less than they are worth to business firms.

(a) ____ 12. If a firm uses resources A and B in the correct absolute amounts for profit maximization, then:
  a. $MPP_a/MRC_a = MPP_b/MRC_b$.
  b. $MPP_a = MPP_b$.
  c. $MRP_a = MRP_b$.
  d. all of the above

© 1988 The Dryden Press

(d) _____ 13. In the following diagram, total economic rent is
              equal to:
              a. xa · ox.
              b. xb · ox.
              c. bc · ox.
              d. ac · ox.

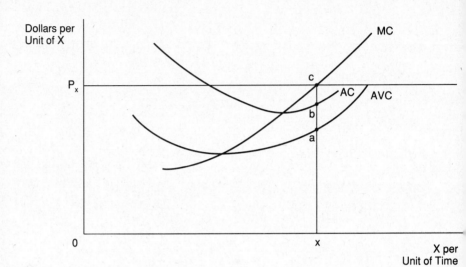

(c) _____ 14. Economic rent is:
              a. what is paid for land that can be used in the
                 growing of various alternative crops.
              b. what one pays to hire a piece of equipment,
                 such as an automobile.
              c. the residual left for a firm's fixed resources
                 after the variable resources have been paid
                 their alternative costs.
              d. the same as economic profits.

(b) _____ 15. A monopolist's demand curve for a variable re-
              source when that resource is the only variable
              resource used is the monopolist's:
              a. marginal revenue curve.
              b. marginal revenue product curve.
              c. value of marginal product curve.
              d. none of the above

(b) ____ 16. To maximize profits, a monopolist that buys resource A competitively must employ an amount at
which its:
a. value of marginal product equals its marginal
resource cost.
b. marginal revenue product equals its marginal
resource cost.
c. value of marginal product equals its price.
d. marginal physical product equals its price.

(a) ____ 17. For a monopolist using several variable resources,
all of which are purchased competitively, the
firm's demand curve for one resource:
a. can be determined only by taking into account
the internal or firm effects of a change in
its price.
b. is the value of marginal product curve for the
resource.
c. is the marginal revenue product curve of the
resource.
d. can be determined only by taking into account
the external or market effects of a change in
its price.

(c) ____ 18. Monopolistic exploitation of labor occurs because:
a. monopolists are less concerned about public
welfare than are pure competitors.
b. unions find monopolists more difficult to deal
with than pure competitors.
c. the marginal revenue product of labor is less
than its value of marginal product.
d. the supply curve of labor slopes upward to the
right.

(a) ____ 19. If all the users of resource A are pure monopolists in the sale of product, the market demand
curve for the resource is:
a. the horizontal summation of individual firm
demand curves for the resource.
b. indeterminate because each monopolist is in a
different industry.
c. the horizontal summation of individual firm
marginal revenue product curves.
d. the horizontal summation of individual firm
value of marginal product curves.

(a) ____ 20. The marginal resource cost curve of a monopsonist:
a. lies above the resource supply curve if
the latter is upward-sloping to the right.
b. coincides with the resource supply curve
if the latter is upward-sloping to the right.
c. lies above a horizontal resource supply
curve.
d. lies below a horizontal resource supply
curve.

(b) ____ 21. Monopsony occurs:
a. throughout most markets for unskilled labor.
b. as a result of resource immobility among
potential employers.
c. wherever firms face downward-sloping demand
curves for their outputs.
d. whenever marginal revenue product of a resource is not equal to marginal resource
cost.

(d) ____ 22. The price paid for a resource that is purchased
monopsonistically is usually:
a. greater than its marginal resource cost.
b. equal to its marginal resource cost.
c. equal to its marginal revenue product.
d. less than its marginal revenue product.

(b) ____ 23. One of the problems created by monopsony is that
it:
a. reduces the pay received by unskilled workers.
b. induces the employer to hire less than the
socially desirable quantity of the resource.
c. usually results in monopoly in product sales.
d. separates the marginal revenue product curve
from the value of marginal product curve.

(c) ____ 24. Which of the following sets of profit-maximizing
conditions applies to <u>all</u> types of selling markets
and all types of buying markets?
a. $MPP_a/P_a = MPP_b/P_b = 1/P_x$
b. $MPP_a/P_a = MPP_b/P_b = 1/MR_x$
c. $MPP_a/MRC_a = MPP_b/MRC_b = 1/MR_x$
d. $MPP_a/MRC_a = MPP_b/MRC_b = 1/P_x$

(b) _____ 25. In order for a union to offset labor monopsony, it must be able to obtain a wage rate from the employer equal to:
a. the value of marginal product, where the value of marginal product curve intersects the labor supply curve.
b. the marginal revenue product, where the marginal revenue product intersects the labor supply curve.
c. the value of marginal product, where the value of marginal product curve intersects the marginal resource cost curve.
d. the marginal revenue product, where the marginal revenue product curve intersects the marginal resource cost curve.

Questions 26-29 are based on the diagram below.

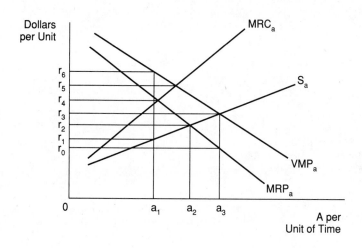

(a) _____ 26. Profits are maximized at:
a. output a_1 and price r_1.
b. output a_1 and price r_4.
c. output a_2 and price r_2.
d. output a_3 and price r_3.

(b) _____ 27. Monopolistic exploitation is measured by:
a. $r_1 r_4$.
b. $r_4 r_6$.
c. $r_1 r_6$.
d. $r_0 r_3$.

© 1988 The Dryden Press

(a) ___ 28. Monopsonistic exploitation is measured by:
   a. r_1r_4.
   b. r_4r_6.
   c. r_1r_6.
   d. r_0r_3.

(b) ___ 29. The appropriate minimum price to offset monopsony with no adverse employment effects is:
   a. r_0.
   b. r_2.
   c. r_3.
   d. r_4.

(a) ___ 30. If monopoly occurs in the sale of its product, a firm tends to pay units of any resource that it uses:
   a. what they are worth in alternative employments.
   b. what they are worth to society.
   c. less than they are worth to the firm.
   d. amounts equal to the value of marginal product of the resource.

CHAPTER 15

PRICING AND EMPLOYMENT OF RESOURCES: APPLICATIONS

Chapter Outline

The Effects of Complementary Capital on Farm Labor Wages
Job Competition from Undocumented Aliens
Monopsony in Professional Baseball
    The Reserve Clause
    The Extent of Exploitation
    Baseball's Defense of the Reserve Clause
    Competition Replaces Monopsony
Straits, the Suez Canal, and Economic Rent from Ocean Shipping
Monopoly Rents from Quotas on Hong Kong Textiles

Chapter Objectives

Applications of the theory of resource pricing and employment,
as with the theory itself, often get short shrift in intermediate
price theory courses. The organization of Chapter 15 attempts to
reduce this defect. Students know that understanding markets for
final products is important to them as consumers, but they also
realize that understanding markets for resources is important to
them as producers. Most of them are part-time suppliers of labor
during college, and all will be full-time suppliers after gradu-
ation.

As with Chapter 4, Chapter 15 is devoted exclusively to applications. Each of the five essays develops one of the main theoretical principles found in Chapter 14 with a topical subject drawn
from newspapers or everyday events.

Suggestions for Teaching

Many students find it difficult to apply the theory they have
learned. As with other activities, application usually gets
easier with practice. Most economists have developed confidence
in the analytical power of economic theory by applying it with
satisfactory results to real-world problems that they encounter.
Through practice, undergraduates will develop their own confidence. These materials were designed to make applications easier
by showing students exactly how to proceed. Our students tell
us that they enjoy these applications as much or more than any
in the book.

223   © 1988 The Dryden Press

The essay on the short-handled hoe shows the relation between complementary and substitute resources. It drives home once more one of the most central concepts in economic theory: the difference between movements along a curve and a shift in the curve itself. Students commit this error just as often in analyzing markets for resources as in analyzing markets for final products.

The essay on alien workers applies straightforward supply-and-demand analysis to one of the most complex policy dilemmas of the 1980s. It illustrates how the mobility of labor causes an event in one labor market to affect other markets. It shows the power of basic price theory principles.

Most students view baseball as a sport, so conceptualizing it as an industry unlocks new ways for thinking about labor markets. Monopsony lowered the wage rates ball players received, and eliminating the monopsony raised them. We ask our students whether they have considered the possibility that the employers with whom they will interview for jobs in their senior year are likely to collude on whom to hire and how much to pay. After thinking about it, they realize that employers are usually too numerous, diverse, and diffuse for collusion to work. We point out, however, that some states have allowed tacit "no raiding" agreements in such professions as accountancy and law.

We have also found that it is relatively easy to get students to think about economic rent and rent-seeking activity. We define economic rent as the residual payment to a resource that cannot be changed in quantity. The Suez Canal application shows that rents have an upper limit even for unique natural resources in a crucial part of the world. The Hong Kong textiles essay explains monopoly arrangements that affect millions of American consumers. Rent seeking can also be seen in competition for sugar import quotas, cable television franchises, certificates for airline routes in the era before deregulation, and taxicab licenses in most cities to name only a few examples. Use examples of monopoly rents generated by public policy in your college community and nearby cities whenever possible.

Problems and Questions for Discussion

1. The wage rates of migratory workers in the California vineyards are comparatively low.
   a. How would you explain this phenomenon?
   b. What would be the effect of laws that restricted further immigration among workers likely to take such jobs? Explain.

2. Assume that the United States relaxes the rules that limit the number of immigrants from Mexico. Draw a supply and demand diagram to indicate and explain the areas corresponding to each of the following effects:
   a. the loss to domestic workers
   b. the gain to the extra immigrant workers admitted
   c. the elimination of the deadweight losses owing to removal of the restriction

3. Labor unions that secure wage rates above market-clearing levels must ration excess supplies in some manner. Explain, using appropriate diagrams, each of the following actions that various unions have used from time to time:
   a. admitted only persons from families of existing members to membership
   b. "sold" memberships through high initiation fees
   c. created hiring halls and placed members in jobs on a first-come-first-served daily basis
   d. granted jobs to members on the basis of seniority

4. Suppose a state begins certifying the qualifications of nursery salespersons who have passed tests and served specified apprenticeships. The tests pertain to plant species, diseases, and suitability for gardens. About 44 percent of those who take the tests fail them; those who pass get identifying name tags and shoulder patches. The program is being imitated by other states. "What Do Those Nursery Patches Mean? Certified Nurserymen," Sunset, June 1980, 204-205.)
   a. Diagram and explain the effects you would expect the program to have in the labor market for salespersons in nurseries and in the retail market for nursery plants.
   b. Can you identify any deadweight loss in your market diagram? Explain.

5. In 1982, it was argued that the boom times for Washington, D.C. lawyers were over. Their law firms handle clients' problems with the government and some engage in lobbying-type activities. The recession of 1981-82 dampened business of such clients and the climate of deregulation may have reduced disputes of business firms with the government. Consequently, growth of law firms ceased; layoffs occurred for junior attorneys; and attorneys' average incomes declined. (Stephen Wermiel, "Washington Lawyers Seeing Signs that the Boom Times Have Passed," The Wall Street Journal, March 18, 1982.) Draw a diagram for attorneys' services and show the effects of such changes on hourly compensation and on total hours worked. Which curves shift? Why?

© 1988 The Dryden Press

6. Look upon employers as "wage discriminators" analogous to sellers of products who are price discriminators.
   a. Give a real example or a hypothetical case of second-degree and third-degree wage discrimination that is analogous to second-degree and third-degree price discrimination.
   b. What conditions would be necessary for wage discrimination in each instance to be successful?

7. In the third paragraph of the text article about alien workers, the author said that aliens are "often exploited." Using the economic analysis developed in Chapter 14, does alien labor appear to fit the case of monopolistic exploitation? Of monopsonistic exploitation? Explain.

8. In some states the major accounting firms have had "no raiding" agreements whereby they avoid competing for each other's employees. Some states have had rules or "codes of ethical conduct" that discourage raiding, although it usually is not prohibited.
   a. What would you expect to be the effects of such agreements or provisions, if enforced, on the level of wage rates and the mobility of accountants between firms? Explain.
   b. Which firms would tend to benefit from these rules? Which ones would tend to be harmed? Explain.
   c. Would you expect such rules to be more easily enforced in a large, urbanized state or in a small, rural state? Explain.

9. In the early 1980s, imported steel amounted to about 20
    percent of the U.S. steel market. About 15 percent of the
    steel sold in the United States was purchased by the auto-
    mobile industry. About half of that was bought by General
    Motors, entirely from American steel producers. In 1982, GM
    announced that it would no longer order steel on a plant-by-
    plant basis from among a group of a dozen or so producers at
    their published list prices or discounts from those lists.
    To cut operating costs, it would buy steel from whichever
    producer bid the least. Steel producers already were making
    low profits owing to declining auto sales and foreign com-
    petition, and GM's announcement was expected to reduce prof-
    its further. It was expected that the number of GM's steel
    suppliers would drop by one-half, and that GM would gain
    favorable long-term advantages from the lowest bidders.
    (Amal Nag, "GM Is Adopting Bidding System for Buying Steel,"
    The Wall Street Journal, March 23, 1982.)
    a. Would you expect for GM to have monopsony power over
        American steel producers? Explain.
    b. Would you expect that GM "bought American" purely out
        of national loyalty? Explain.

10. Initially, in enacting textile import quotas, the United
    States placed quotas only on imported garments made of
    cotton. (David Birnbaum, "How Hong Kong Beat the Textile
    Quotas," The Wall Street Journal, January 5, 1987.)
    a. What adjustments to this rule by profit-maximizing Hong
        Kong textile producers would you have predicted? Ex-
        plain.
    b. What changes in the U.S. quota regulations would have
        been required to cope with the adjustments by Hong Kong
        producers that you described in part a? Explain.

11. The U.S. quota policy raised the price of imported garments
    into a more elastic region of the market demand curve for
    garments. (David Birnbaum, "How Hong Kong Beat the Textile
    Quotas," The Wall Street Journal, January 5, 1987.)
    a. What adjustment to the higher price elasticity by
        profit-maximizing textile producers would you have pre-
        dicted?
    b. What changes in U.S. quota regulations would have been
        required to cope with the adjustments by producers that
        you described in part a? Explain.

12. Explain the differences in rent-seeking behavior between each of the following situations versus Hong Kong textile quotas:
    a. diving crews competing to locate treasure-laden Spanish galleons in the Caribbean
    b. people queuing at airports to get a free airline ticket distributed as a promotional device
    c. scientists competing to make a discovery that is expected to lead to a Nobel prize

13. Review the materials on the New York City taxicab market described in text Chapter 11. City regulations limit the total number of licenses to 11,787 and divide them into two categories: 4,969 that must be owned by individuals, and 6,818 that must be owned by fleets of more than one vehicle. Labor unions have raised the operating costs of the fleet companies above those for nonunionized individual operators. In 1982, individual medallions sold for about $10,000 more than the fleet medallions.

    During the 1970s, about 4,000 of the fleet medallions were transferred to what are called mini-fleets—two taxicabs owned and operated by a corporation with two stockholders. Often these transactions were arranged by brokers without the two shareholders even having met. Brokers also arranged for bank loans and filed the corporate paperwork with city authorities. ("New York City Looks at Taxi Regulation," Regulation, March/April 1982, 11-13, 36.) All medallion taxicabs charge the same fares that are set by the city. Do New York taxi consumers derive any benefits from mini-fleet corporations and medallion brokers? Explain.

14. Explain the difference between the rents captured by the Egyptian Suez Canal authority and the rents captured by owners of New York City taxicab medallions (described in Chapter 11) when their medallions are sold for more than they paid for them.

15. In April 1987, the price of a seat on the New York Stock
    Exchange (NYSE) reached $1,000,000 for the first time. The
    price had been as low as $40,000 in 1977. One must own or
    lease a seat to trade in the securities listed on the NYSE.
    The number of seats has been fixed at 1,366 since 1953, and
    about 100 change hands in the average year. (Michael A.
    Hiltzik, "Cost of NYSE Membership Is Going Up," Los Angeles
    Times, May 2, 1987.)
    a. What determines whether the price of a seat rises or
        falls? Explain.
    b. Should the price of a NYSE seat be described as an eco-
        nomic rent or a monopoly rent? Explain.
    c. In 1975, the NYSE abolished its schedule of fixed com-
        missions that members were required to charge when se-
        curities were bought and sold in favor of a competitive,
        unregulated regime. What would have been the effect
        of this change on the price of a NYSE seat? Explain.
    d. In 1987, about one-third of owners leased their seats to
        other traders. (Annual rentals were 12 to 18 percent
        of the seat's price.) What should have happened to the
        values of seats when the NYSE abolished the rule that
        prohibited leasing?

16. "For Sale: 71 Bed...Hospital; $10,000 a Licensed Bed," read
    an advertisement (Los Angeles Times, May 20, 1981). State
    and federal regulations in the 1970s restricted the supply
    of hospital beds to reduce billings to governmental insur-
    ance programs. Many smaller hospitals were purchased by na-
    tional chains that could capture economies of size through
    more efficient billing, purchasing, and inventory proce-
    dures. (Barbara Bry, "Bidding War for Hospitals: Patients
    Pick Up Bill," Los Angeles Times, April 12, 1981.)
    a. What economic term would you use to describe the per bed
        buyout prices of hospitals referred to above? Explain.
    b. What economic and demographic factors would cause per
        bed buyout prices to be high in some locations and lower
        in others? Explain.
    c. What characteristics of the hospital itself would case
        per bed buyout prices to be higher?
    d. In the mid-1980s, the U.S. Government reduced the pay-
        ments made to hospitals for Medicare patients. Hospi-
        talization and surgery procedures that used to be re-
        imbursed at full costs were paid according to a pre-de-
        termined schedule of maximum prices. Hospitals were
        forced to cut average costs by laying off staff and con-
        tracting out some services that outside suppliers could
        perform more efficiently (e.g., laundry). By 1987 the
        industry was undergoing a shakeout and some hospitals
        were in financial danger. Explain the effect of these
        forces on the per bed values mentioned earlier.

17. Inflation during the 1970s increased the popularity of "collectibles," and the prices of some rare wines exceeded $1,000 per bottle. In 1980, a New York State regulation prevented anyone from selling liquor without a license, including collectors. This prevented Christie's, a major Park Avenue auctioneer of antiques and fine art, from auctioning wines owned by individual collectors or their heirs. Enforcement of the regulation was urged by liquor stores. (Daniel Hertzberg, "Christie's Intent to Auction Wine Seems to be Souring," The Wall Street Journal, December 29, 1980.)
    a. Explain who benefits in New York if this regulation is enforced.
    b. Explain who benefits outside New York if this regulation is enforced.

18. Typically, dentists operate one-dentist offices, but they employ differing numbers of auxiliary personnel: hygienists who clean teeth (designated hereinafter by L_1), chairside assistants (L_2), and clerical workers (L_3). Some states restrict the number of hygienists and chairside assistants that may be used in conjunction with dentists and other resources. Almost none restricts clerical workers. Assume that a dentist's output, x, is measured by the number of patients treated per week.
    a. Rewrite Equation 14.3 for the three resources in states that impose effective restrictions on the use of auxiliary personnel. (i) How do the restrictions change the utilization of each resource? (ii) What is the effect of the restrictions on MC_x? Explain.
    b. Some states are permissive, imposing weak restrictions on the number of hygienists and chairside assistants. Others are very restrictive. Would costs of production be minimized more often by dentists in states with permissive regulations or in states with restrictive regulations? Explain.
    c. Assume that the procedures for establishing the rules and restrictions on dental practice in each state are dominated by dentists. Why would dentists benefit by restricting the use of hygienists and chairside assistants but not clerical workers? Explain.

19. Go to the newspaper and periodical literature indexes in your library and write a short essay explaining quota arrangements for importation of automobiles, beef, shoes, steel, or sugar, or for the production of U.S. tobacco leaf. Explain how and when the program came about, diagram its resource allocation effects on the price and quantity available of the good, and analyze who benefits and who loses from it in the short run and long run.

© 1988 The Dryden Press

Solutions to Problems and Questions for Discussion

1. a. Such workers have relatively low levels of training and the supply of them is relatively large.
   b. Restricting supply would tend to increase the wage rate of workers who are already working in the vineyards.

2. In the following diagram, assume that removing the immigration restriction shifts supply from S_0 to S_1.
   a. w_1w_2AB.
   b. L_2BCL_1.
   c. BAC to employers and BCD to workers.

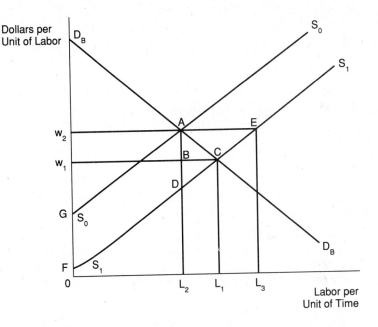

3. In the diagram for the previous question, assume that a union negotiates w_2 when the market-clearing wage rate is w_1. Now OL_2 jobs must be rationed among OL_1 workers. Actions (a), (b) and (d) are rationing devices that shift supply from S_1 to S_0. They force the L_2L_1 workers to take jobs elsewhere. Action (c) encourages L_2L_1 workers to remain idle in this industry, waiting for work to open up.

© 1988 The Dryden Press

4. a. In the previous diagram, the program attempts to
        shift supply from S_1 to S_0. We would not expect the
        program to be very successful in raising the wage
        rate above w_1, since many nurseries have experienced
        but unlicensed sales people.
    b. ACD, if the program is successful.

5. The demand for lawyers is derived in part from the amount
    and kind of legislation and regulations adopted by govern-
    ment. Fewer new laws and regulations and perhaps broader
    interpretations of existing laws and regulations caused
    the demand for these lawyers' services to decline. During
    a recession, fewer new businesses are formed and existing
    businesses tend to embark on fewer new activities. Both
    forces cause the demand for Washington lawyers to shift
    left, leading to lower wage rates, layoffs, fewer total
    hours worked, and slower promotions.

6. a. Overtime wage rates are an example of second-degree
        discrimination. All employees are offered the same
        terms, but the higher wage applies only to the extra
        hours worked. Third-degree wage discriminatio would
        require paying different wages to employees having
        the same training and doing the same work. This would
        occur where a company has plants located in two (or
        more) distinct and separated labor markets.
    b. Wage discrimination is attractive because workers can
        not resell their labor to each other. Overtime wage
        rates usually are offered to all employees and the
        hours they work are relatively easy to monitor. The
        success of third-degree wage discrimination requires
        that the employees receiving the lower wage rate not
        search for information about wage rates among their
        colleagues in the firm or in the labor market outside,
        and/or not be able to move to other labor markets.

7. Some people think that a low wage rate alone is evidence
    of exploitation, but we disagree. Of the two types of ex-
    ploitation that we think could occur, monopolistic exploi-
    tation is possible when the growers are in a successful ag-
    ricultural marketing cartel. As we argued in Chapter 14,
    they would have to pay a wage rate at least as high as farm
    workers could earn elsewhere. Paying the "alternative"
    wage rate does not eliminate monopolistic exploitation, how-
    ever. The "cartel" can still cause price to exceed margin-
    al revenue for individual producers to cause exploitation.
    Monopsonistic exploitation is possible if growers organize
    and make a single all-or-nothing wage rate offer to workers.
    This may explain why farm workers organize unions. More
    research would be necessary to reach stronger conclusions.

© 1988 The Dryden Press

8. a. If such agreements were enforced, wage rates would fall because of the consequent monopsony.
   b. All firms would tend to gain, although some would gain more relatively than others from the monopsony profits. Workers (accountants) now paid the lower monopsonistic wage rates or salaries are the losers.
   c. Probably in the small, rural state. It would be more difficult to reach and monitor collusive agreements in big cities with many firms.

9. a. GM is an important buyer of steel, but we doubt that its 7 or so percent of total sales is enough to give it monopsony power. Steel producers have too many alternatives to GM.
   b. Anyone, let alone gigantic firms subject to government regulations, might be tempted to prefer American to foreign goods if their qualities and prices (net of transport costs) were identical. Steel imports amounting to 20 percent of the market probably keep American steel prices competitive with imports.

10. a. The Hong Kong producers increased production and exports to the United States of garments made of wool, linen, silk, and synthetics that were exempt.
    b. The exemptions were eventually replaced with quotas.

11. a. Hong Kong producers relocated factories in such quota-free countries as China, Indonesia, and Malaysia.
    b. Quotas were eventually applied to these countries also, which led Hong Kong producers to open factories in Bangladesh, Mauritius, and Sri Lanka.

12. For each case, the competition is for economic rents. For Hong Kong textiles, the competition is for monopoly rents that have been created by governmental restrictions.

13. Brokers and mini-fleet corporations are rent-seeking activities that would be unnecessary in the absence of the restrictions. They reduce the cost of providing New York with a given number of cabs by increasing fleet company competition with individual operators, and therefore benefit consumers.

14. The fees received by the Suez Canal authority are economic rents. The returns to owners of New York medallions are monopoly rents since they arise from governmental restrictions on entry.

© 1988 The Dryden Press

15. a. Owners of seats earn income by charging commissions on securities they purchase or sell. Often commissions are a percentage of a transaction's value (price of the stock multiplied by the number of shares), so bull markets tend to push commission revenue up and bear markets bring them down. So does the average daily volume of shares traded.
    b. It is an economic rent. Monopoly rent requires an entry restriction. The United States places no overt restriction on the formation of new stock exchanges, and new exchanges are organized from time to time in New York and other cities. NYSE seats are limited in the same sense that memberships to the most prestigious country clubs or condominiums at the most popular locations are limited. The higher prices go, however, the more elastic demand is and the more likely substitutes will arise.
    c. Prices of seats declined when cartelized commission rates were replaced with competitive rates. Trading probably increased as commissions went down, but not enough to offset the smaller percentage of each transaction that owners of seats got.
    d. We would expect prices to have increased. The more extensive the property rights that accompany a physical resource, the more people usually are willing to pay for it.

16. a. Returns generated by restrictions on resource mobility are called monopoly rents.
    b. Hospitals in the Sunbelt and in suburban locations where potential patients had private insurance would generally have higher per bed purchase prices.
    c. Monopoly rent is the return to fixed resources after variable costs are paid, so it would be greater the lower the variable costs. Hospital characteristics that affect variable costs include the facility's size, age, equipment, and the specialities offered by its medical staff.
    d. The switch to fixed-price reimbursement cut hospital income, as did the rise in competition among hospitals. Monopoly rents declined, as did per bed values.

17. a. Auctions are popular among buyers because they lower the cost of locating and purchasing rare goods, and they are popular among sellers because they lower the costs of locating buyers. Without auctions, buyers must purchase from liquor stores or travel to auctions outside New York. Collectors or their heirs must incur the extra costs of shipping their wines to auctioneers outside New York. In New York, Christie's loses commissions on what it could have sold. New York liquor stores that sell rare wines gain because they have less competition.

   b. The supply of liquor in auctions outside New York rises, benefiting those buyers and auctioneers.

18. a. $MPP_{11}/MRC_{11} > MPP_{13}/MRC_{13} = 1/MC_x$, and
    $MPP_{12}/MRC_{12} > MPP_{13}/MRC_{13} = 1/MC_x$.

   (i) If restrictions are effective, the marginal physical products of the restricted resources (L_1 and L_2) will increase relative to that of the unrestricted resource (L_3). Hence the ratio of unrestricted to restricted resources will increase. An empirical study estimated that the rate of change of the marginal physical products of the restricted resources was positive at their present levels of employment; i.e., the marginal physical products were increasing. This indicates that dentists were operating in Stage I for the restricted resources.

   (ii) The restrictions cause MC_x to rise.

   b. The restricted resources would be underutilized relative to the unrestricted resources more in the restrictive states than in the permissive states. Empirical findings support this.

   c. Hygienists substitute for dentists for some procedures, whereas chairside assistants are complementary. Restricting hygienists increases the demand for dentists, and restricting chairside assistants reduces the number of patients per week that a dentist's office can handle. Thus, restrictions on these resources effectively allocate output shares within a cartel. (Arthur S. DeVany, Wendy L. Gramm, Thomas R. Saving, and Charles W. Smithson, "The Impact of Input Regulation: The Case of the U.S. Dental Industry," The Journal of Law and Economics 25 (1982):367-381).

19. Depends on facts discovered.

True-False Questions

(F) ____ 1. The introduction of the long-handled hoe would have caused employers of farm workers to move along the existing marginal revenue product of labor curve to a lower quantity of labor employed.

(T) ____ 2. The long-handled hoe amounted to less capital than the short-handled hoe even though the long-handled hoe was bigger and more expensive.

(F) ____ 3. The introduction of the long-handled hoe in a purely competitive farming industry would cause a shift to the left of a typical farmer's marginal revenue product curve of labor curve but not his value of marginal product of labor curve.

(F) ____ 4. In the short-handled hoe application, the marginal revenue product of labor was determined by the quantity of complementary capital available, not by the law of diminishing returns.

(T) ____ 5. In the short-handled hoe application, the quantity of complementary capital was constant along a given marginal revenue product of labor curve.

(T) ____ 6. The downward slope of the marginal revenue product of labor curve is determined by the law of diminishing returns.

(T) ____ 7. In the undocumented aliens application, blocking immigration tended to harm employers and consumers of goods produced in nonagricultural industries and benefit producers and consumers of agricultural goods.

(T) ____ 8. Apparently one of the beneficiaries of an attempt to block immigration by undocumented aliens would be domestic workers in nonagricultural industries.

(T) ____ 9. Blocking aliens from nonagricultural employment will increase unemployment among them unless they can move to jobs in agricultural industries.

(F) ____ 10. Blocking undocumented aliens from nonagricultural jobs affects nonagricultural industries only.

(T) ____ 11. The labor supply curve for alien workers can be summed horizontally with the labor supply curve for domestic workers to yield a total supply curve for the nonagricultural labor market.

(F) ____ 12. The effect of the monopsony against professional baseball players was to negate the law of diminishing returns.

(T) ____ 13. The source of the monopsony in professional baseball was collusion among the club owners rather than players lacking information about alternatives or having sufficient geographical mobility.

(F) ____ 14. The baseball players union has used strikes to combat the monopsony of the club owners since 1975.

(T) ____ 15. Economists conclude that the wage rates of baseball players have been roughly equal to their marginal revenue products since 1975.

(T) ____ 16. The reserve clause was the key to the baseball club owners' monopsony prior to 1975.

(F) ____ 17. For all its faults, the baseball reserve clause at least achieved its objective of roughly balancing the distribution of playing talent among teams in a league.

(T) ____ 18. Gerald Scully's research indicates that the portion of the economic rents of players that the owners received prior to 1975 was substantial.

(F) ____ 19. The profit-maximizing strategy of the Egyptian Suez Canal authority should be to charge ships able to use the canal the highest price that the market will bear.

(T) ____ 20. The availability of substitutes places upper limits on the economic rents that can be obtained even from unique natural resources like straits or canals.

(T) ____ 21. To maximize profits, the Egyptian Suez Canal authority as a general matter should raise transit fees when the price of crude oil declines and lower them when the price of crude oil rises.

(T) ____ 22. The welfare losses to consumers from quotas or restrictions are understated by the costs that producers incur in competing to acquire quota rights.

(T) ____ 23. A monopoly rent is a higher-than-competitive rate of return created by governmental restraints on resource mobility.

(T) ____ 24. Auctioning the textile quotas in Hong Kong would allow a more efficient use of resources because the firms that valued quota rights most (and which therefore would bid the most) could use the quotas most productively to satisfy consumer demand.

(F) ____ 25. The only effect of a monopolization scheme like the Hong Kong textile quotas is to transfer income from consumers to producers.

(F) ____ 26. The gains to producers from the Hong Kong textile scheme were precisely offset by losses to consumers.

(F) ____ 27. Restricting the importation of Hong Kong textiles made the domestic supply curve for textiles more elastic.

(F) ____ 28. Restricting the importation of Hong Kong textiles made the total supply curve of textiles (the horizontal summation of domestic supply plus imports) more elastic.

Multiple-Choice Questions

(d) ____ 1. The main reason why employers of agricultural labor would not willingly adopt the long-handled hoe without legislation is:
  a. the market was composed of too few alien workers.
  b. the market was composed of too many alien workers.
  c. it was a wasteful type of rent seeking.
  d. any one employer who switched to the longer hoe and suffered a decline in productivity would have been placed at a competitive disadvantage.

(a) ____ 2. The quantity of capital that is complementary to labor is:
   a. fixed along each marginal revenue product curve.
   b. variable along each value of marginal product curve.
   c. variable along each marginal revenue product curve.
   d. fixed in the long run.

(c) ____ 3. Using the short-handled hoe instead of the long-handled hoe would have been represented by:
   a. a rise in the productivity of capital.
   b. moving along a given marginal revenue product of labor curve.
   c. a shift to the left of the marginal revenue product of labor curve.
   d. a shift to the right of the marginal revenue product of labor curve.

(b) ____ 4. Which of the following does not affect the quantity of labor employed in the short-handled hoe application?
   a. the law of diminishing returns
   b. monopoly rents
   c. the productivity of the short-handled hoe
   d. the productivity of the long-handled hoe

(d) ____ 5. Which of the following is not a conclusion that can be drawn from the undocumented aliens application?
   a. Affecting supply in one market affects wages in other markets if labor is mobile.
   b. Restricting the supply of aliens in the non-agricultural market will raise wage rates for those workers who remain employed in the non-agricultural market.
   c. Society loses because it sacrifices a higher value of marginal product in the nonagricultural market for a lower value of marginal product in the agricultural market.
   d. The demand for aliens in the nonagricultural market declines.

© 1988 The Dryden Press

(a) _____ 6. Which of the following groups, in addition to the undocumented aliens, loses when undocumented aliens are blocked from working in the nonagricultural sector?
   a. other workers who were already employed in the agricultural sector
   b. consumers of agricultural products
   c. farmers who hire undocumented aliens
   d. government agencies that have to enforce the law

(d) _____ 7. Which of the following is <u>not</u> a valid statement about the post-1975 baseball players labor market?
   a. The reserve clause is now worthless to the owners.
   b. Players have high rents because of low opportunity costs in many cases.
   c. The owners' share of the players' economic rents appears to be falling.
   d. The antitrust immunity of the owners is still a valuable privilege.

(a) _____ 8. The observation that players with guaranteed long-term contracts were more likely to have more disability days than players with short-term contracts is not likely to be a successful form of long-run behavior for players because:
   a. club owners will take such behavior into account in the wages they offer for successive contracts if the number of disability days is abused.
   b. other club owners are not likely to observe the behavior and it probably will not be reported by sports writers, so the players can easily get away with it.
   c. such behavior is never rewarding when dealing with a monopsonist.
   d. none of the above

(a) _____ 9. The outcome of a strike such as occurred between a union of ballplayers and an association of club owners is difficult to predict because:
   a. no observer knows precisely the values that each side places on its next-best alternative, because each side keeps such information secret.
   b. it is hard to judge which side has the better lawyer doing the negotiating for it.
   c. each side is a monopoly.
   d. all of the above

(a) ____ 10. Which of the following would you expect to be exploited monopsonistically?
   a. a professional football player
   b. a bricklayer in Chicago
   c. a construction worker in Oklahoma
   d. all of the above

(c) ____ 11. In which of the following cases would you expect monopsony to occur?
   a. the employment of a baseball player by the Los Angeles Dodgers after 1975
   b. the employment of an unskilled worker by General Motors
   c. the employment of coal miners in a remote Appalachian company town
   d. the employment of a neurosurgeon by Billings Hospital in Chicago

(b) ____ 12. Which of the following would be the ideal profit-maximizing strategy for the Suez Canal authority for each ship that was physically capable of using the canal, assuming it knew the cost to time and other resources to each ship of circumnavigating Africa?
   a. charging the price for which the elasticity of market demand is one
   b. first-degree price discrimination
   c. second-degree price discrimination
   d. third-degree price discrimination

(a) ____ 13. Which of the following would not increase the profits of the Suez Canal authority?
   a. a rise in the price of crude oil
   b. a fall in the price of crude oil
   c. a rise in the demand for crude oil
   d. none of the above

(a) ____ 14. Which of the following represents the most accurate comparison between changes in the profits
of the Suez Canal authority and changes in the
profits of the Onassis shipping firm described in
Chapter 11?
a. When the profits of the one are increasing
(decreasing), generally the profits of the
other are increasing (decreasing).
b. When the profits of the one are increasing,
the profits of the other will be decreasing.
c. When one makes short-run profits, the other
makes long-run losses.
d. There is no logical connection between their
profits.

(b) ____ 15. Which of the following statements characterizes
the relation between the revenues of the Suez
Canal authority and the revenues of the Hong Kong
textile producers?
a. The Suez Canal authority earns monopoly rents
whereas the Hong Kong producers make economic
rents.
b. The Suez Canal authority earns economic rents
whereas the Hong Kong producers make economic
rents.
c. Neither makes economic rents.
d. Neither makes monopoly rents.

(c) ____ 16. The monopoly rent to the U.S. producers of textiles after the quota program is adopted can be
characterized as:
a. an increase in producers' surplus.
b. a decrease in producers' surplus.
c. the net result of an increase and a decrease
in producers' surplus.
d. precisely equal to the loss in consumer's
surplus.

(d) ____ 17. Hong Kong textile quotas will yield:
a. deadweight losses to the economy as a whole.
b. monopoly rents to producers.
c. a wealth transfer from consumers to producers.
d. all of the above

(a) ____ 18. The value of the welfare losses owing to the Hong Kong textile quotas as shown in Figure 15.11 will be understated by:

    a. the costs of resources devoted to rent-seeking to acquire the monopoly rights.

    b. triangle EAM.

    c. rectangle pp'BE.

    d. none of the above

(b) ____ 19. Assume that the New York taxicab medallion discussed in Chapter 11 sells for $50,000 but that the price includes the used taxicab to which the medallion is attached. (Sometimes medallions are sold jointly with the automobile.) If the cab without the medallion can be sold for $5,000, the value of the economic rent would be:

    a. $50,000 because the value of the used taxicab is not part of the driver's opportunity costs.

    b. $45,000 because the value of the used taxicab has an opportunity cost and thus cannot be considered part of the economic rent.

    c. $55,000 because most owners of medallions would be shrewd enough to bargain for the value of the car separately from the value of the medallion.

    d. none of the above

CHAPTER 16

RESOURCE ALLOCATION

Chapter Outline

Resource Allocation and Welfare
Resource Markets
Resource Allocation under Pure Competition
   Allocation within a Given Submarket
   Allocation among Submarkets
Conditions Preventing Efficient Allocation
   Monopoly
   Monopsony
   Nonprice Impediments
   Price Fixing

Applications

Allocating Airport Landing Slots without Prices
Creating and Exchanging Property Rights to Pollute
The Davis-Bacon Prevailing Wage Law

Chapter Objectives

In this chapter we show the functions of resource prices in allocating resources among different uses and users. It is important for students to learn that, in general, an inefficient allocation of units of a resource will lead to price differences in its various employments and that these in turn provide incentives for a reallocation that is more efficient. They should also learn that every movement of a resource unit from a lower to a higher value of marginal product use will increase national income. We point out some of the major impediments to achieving correct allocations of resources.

Suggestions for Teaching

Little new ground is broken in this chapter. For the most part, it is an extension of the theory of Chapter 14. We try to get across the very important role of resource prices in securing both full employment of resource units and an efficient allocation of them among their many uses. We find it helpful to give numerous examples of special interest groups that place roadblocks in the way of these market processes. The Davis-Bacon Act application makes the point. In addition, contrasts between nonmarket and market solutions to allocation problems,

245   © 1988 The Dryden Press

like those discussed in the applications on airport landing
slots and rights to pollute, are useful.

An important point that seems to elude many students is that
the reallocation of resource units from lower to higher value
of marginal uses increases national income. A little drill
with numbers showing the loss compared with the gain as a unit
of resource is transferred is usually worthwhile.

We prefer to wait until we sum up the course in Chapter 18 to
discuss explicitly the efficient allocation of resources among
products and the appropriate product mix for the society. However, anyone desiring to discuss resource allocation from the
welfare point of view can certainly do so conveniently at this
point.

Problems and Questions for Discussion

1. Explain the conditions that must be met if units of a giv-
    en resource are to be allocated "correctly" among its vari-
    ous uses. What does a "correct" allocation imply in terms
    of the contribution of the resource to GNP? Explain.

2. Over the last fifty years, demand for television sets has
    increased substantially relative to the demand for radios.
    Explain in terms of marginal revenue products and wage rates
    the implications of the changes in demand on the allocation
    of electronic technicians.

3. Historically, there has been a substantial wage rate dif-
    ferential for common labor used on the farm and for common
    labor used in industry. In recent years, the differential
    has been narrowing.
    a. Show with diagrams and explain what has been happening
        in these two labor markets.
    b. If common labor in industry were completely unionized
        and if the union were able to maintain wage rates above
        what they would be in the absence of unions, what would
        be the implications for labor reallocation? for GNP?

4. We often hear the slogan that any given kind of labor should
    receive equal pay for equal work. Under what circumstances,
    if any, would you argue that this slogan is wrong? Right?

© 1988 The Dryden Press

5. Suppose that among the users of resource A there is a monopolistic seller of product and a purely competitive seller of product. All users purchase the resource competitively.
   a. Would you expect the resource to be correctly allocated among users? Explain and illustrate diagrammatically with respect to these two firms.
   b. Can units of the resource be allocated in a way that will increase GNP? Explain.

6. Suppose that three interrelated markets can be identified for common labor and that wage rates are currently $10, $8, and $6 per hour, respectively, in the three markets.
   a. If a minimum wage law were enacted fixing minimum wage rates at $8 per hour in all markets, what would happen to wage rates and employment in each of the three markets?
   b. If a minimum wage rate of $10 an hour were applicable only to the first two markets, what would happen to wage rates and employment in each of the three markets?
   c. Would you consider the results of (a) and (b) above to be a "good thing"? Explain.

7. Suppose that the labor market for bricklayers is purely competitive and that the users of bricklayers sell their outputs under conditions of pure competition. Initially, bricklayers are allocated so that Pareto optimality prevails.
   a. Suppose now that some users become monopolists in the sale of product, while others remain as pure competitors. Explain and show diagrammatically the effects of the monopolization on the wage rate, the level of employment, and the allocation of bricklayers.
   b. Can the monopoly be offset by unionizing all bricklayers?
   c. Suppose that only the bricklayers working for monopolists are unionized and that they succeed in raising wage rates for union members above what they would be otherwise. What are the effects on both union and nonunion employment levels? on nonunion wage rates? on the allocation of bricklayers?

8. Suppose that some degree of monopsony in the purchase of labor occurs because there are only two users of this kind of labor. One user is relatively smaller than the other and, at any given wage rate, faces a more elastic supply curve for the labor. Workers are free to move between the users so that a common wage rate will prevail. Will labor be "correctly" allocated between the users? Why or why not? Illustrate your answer with diagrams.

9. Consider the historic North-South wage differential. Underlying the differential is a lower ratio of labor to capital in the North than in the South. It is often argued that the appropriate reallocation of resources would be a movement of labor to the North and a movement of capital to the South. What happens to reallocation incentives if, through minimum wage laws or through collective bargaining, wages in the South are brought up to the level of those in the North?

10. In the country of Nud the main agricultural crop is wheat, although corn and soybeans can be produced. There are two grades of agricultural land, A and B, with the A grade being the better. All farms are the same size and contain only A or B land—not both. There are many farms of each grade. All farms must be irrigated to make them produce. The irrigation system is owned and operated by the government. The government provides exactly w_o gallons of water per year— no more, no less. The objective of the government in allocating water is to maximize wheat output.

   a. The government gives water away to farms but there is not enough for all farms to obtain all they want. The Secretary of Agriculture insists that A grade farms should be given all they want and B grade farms should get what is left on a first-come, first-served basis. What advice would you give him/her if the national objective is to be achieved?

   b. If the water were to be priced so that the price system allocates water, how should the price and the allocation between A and B grade farms be determined? Would the allocation be "correct"? Explain. Would you advise use of the price system? Why or why not?

   c. Do you think it would ever be advisable to produce corn or soybeans as well as wheat? Explain.

11. In 1980, the Graduate Medical Education National Advisory Commission forecast a surplus of 90,000 physicians by 1990 and 140,000 by 2000. The report did not define surplus (at what wage rate?) or put forth any analytical framework for determining how many physicians the U.S. ought to have. Nevertheless, this study led in 1985 to proposals to reduce the "overcrowding of the health care field," not by reducing enrollments in regular medical schools but by restricting entry of "doctor substitutes"—osteopaths, nurse practitioners, American graduates of foreign medical schools, chiropractors, psychotherapists and acupuncturists. (Mark V. Pauly, "The Doctor Drawbridge," The Wall Street Journal, November 8, 1985.)

Draw a diagram for the physician market based on the assumption that the wage rate is at a higher-than-market-clearing level. Draw a separate diagram for the physician substitute market with a market-clearing wage rate (to keep it simple, assume that all substitutes are alike). Assume that physicians restrict the rights of physician substitutes to practice. Show the effects on wage rates and employment in each market.

12. In the early 1980s, the U.S. government estimated that nearly 900 rural counties—one-fourth of all U.S. counties —had a doctor shortage. This was expected to decline about 60 percent by the early 1990s. Owing to the "oversupply" of physicians, competition for patients in urban areas would lead more physicians to migrate to higher-paying jobs in rural areas. Among those more likely to settle in rural areas, however, are the physician substitutes mentioned in the previous questions—such as foreign medical graduates, nurse practitioners and osteopaths. A larger fraction of these professionals are trained in primary medical care, relative to graduates of American medical schools who specialize to a greater degree. (Becci M. Breining, "Blessings of a Doctor 'Surplus'," The Wall Street Journal, November 29, 1983.)

Diagram and explain how the proposal described in the previous question would affect the wage rates and the distribution of physicians between urban and rural markets.

13. The FAA's newly created market in landing and departure slots was criticized by some members of Congress as a "federal giveaway" of "windfall profits" to airlines.
   a. Explain in what sense this criticism is relevant.
   b. Explain why this "giveaway" appears to promote efficient airport resource use.

14. Review Problem 7 of text Chapter 16 concerning sugar quo-
    tas. In 1987, some members of Congress proposed auction-
    ing sugar quotas. The government would capture some of the
    "quota rents" that its policy created and thereby reduce
    the federal deficit. According to one estimate, converting
    all quota allocation schemes from administrative assignments
    to auctions could eventually yield the U.S. government $10
    billion per year. (Monica Langley, "The Idea of Auctioning
    Import Rights Appeals to Lawmakers Faced with Trade, Budget
    Gaps," The Wall Street Journal, February 6, 1987.)

    Compare the resource allocation consequences of allocating
    sugar quotas by competitive auction rather than the adminis-
    trative assignments used at the present (like those for Hong
    Kong textiles). Which method would be more likely to gen-
    erate a correct allocation of quota rights? Explain.

15. Reread the application about pollution rights in text Chap-
    ter 16 and the applications about solar light and the Dutch
    toads from text Chapter 2.
    a. Explain the basic economic problem in each case and
        their similarities.
    b. Explain the similarities and differences among the so-
        lutions that were developed for each problem. Explain
        which solutions you would expect to be more effective
        and why.

16. Diagram and explain the effects of Davis-Bacon on:
    a. the substitution by federal contractors between high-
        skilled and low-skilled labor.
    b. the substitution by federal contractors between capital
        and labor.

Solutions to Problems and Questions for Discussion

1. The resource is allocated correctly when its value of mar-
    ginal product in each employment is the same. The resource
    is making its maximum contribution to GNP, because no net
    additions to product can be obtained by transferring units
    of the resource among employments. The technical conditions
    that must be met for a correct allocation are set forth in
    the equations on p. 514 in the text.

2. Assume that the marginal revenue products of electronic technicians in television production and radio production are initially equal to each other and to the wage rate, and that the level of aggregate demand remains constant. Rising demand for televisions relative to radios means that the price of televisions increases relative to radios. Thus, the marginal revenue products of electronics technicians in the production of televisions rise relative to that for radios. Television producers can afford to pay more for electronics technicians, so they bid up the wage rate. To the degree that technicians are mobile, labor is reallocated between television and radio production until the marginal revenue products in each case are equal to the higher wage rate. Employment of technicians increases in television and decreases in radios.

3. a. Review the discussion of text Figure 16.1. Area 1 is analogous to farming with a relatively large initial supply of common labor, and Area 2 is analogous to industry with a smaller initial supply. Over time, common labor migrates from Area 1 to Area 2 and wage rates for the two areas tend toward equality.
   b. Review the discussion of text Figure 16.4. Labor reallocation does not occur. Workers who migrate from Area 1 would be unemployed in Area 2. Employers in Area 2 would not hire additional workers since an increase in the ratio of labor to capital would lower the marginal revenue product of labor below the wage rate. Labor would not be making its maximum contribution to GNP because labor's value of marginal product in industry would exceed its value of marginal product in farming.

4. Workers in free markets with identical marginal revenue products will get the same wage rates through market forces. If wage rates are controlled to compel equal pay for equal work, however, then the demand side is ignored and price is no longer free to perform its allocative function.

© 1988 The Dryden Press

5. a. No. Resource A will be allocated correctly among users when its value of marginal product in each employment is the same. Draw separate diagrams for a monopoly seller and a purely competitive seller. In equilibrium, the price of A will equal the monopolist's marginal revenue product of A and the pure competitor's value of marginal product of A (which is the same as his marginal revenue product of A). Value of marginal product of A is higher for the monopolist user, so the allocation is incorrect.

   b. Marginal revenue product of A shows the contribution that a unit of A makes to the total receipts of one firm. Value of marginal product of A measures the contribution of a unit of A to the value of the economy's output. Reallocating A from the pure competitor to the monopolist would increase net national product.

6. a. A legal minimum wage rate of $8 per hour will have zero effect on the markets where $8 and $10 are the equilibrium wage rates. It reduces employment and generates a surplus of labor in the market where the equilibrium wage rate is $6.

   b. A legal minimum wage rate of $10 per hour will have zero effect on the market where $10 is the equilibrium wage rate. It reduces employment and generates a surplus of labor in the $8 market. This labor may migrate to the $6 market, increasing supply and reducing the wage rate below $6.

   c. Not us. The workers who remain employed at higher-than-equilibrium wage rates will benefit, but making this group better off through the minimum-wage approach requires making workers who lose their present jobs worse off. Further, as unemployed workers move from jobs with high wage rates to jobs with lower wage rates, society sacrifices a higher value of marginal product for a lower one. Net national product declines.

7. a. Draw separate diagrams for a typical monopoly user and a typical purely competitive user. For the monopoly user, product marginal revenue is now less than price, so its marginal revenue product of bricklayers is less than its value of marginal product for bricklayers. The monopoly user hires the number of bricklayers for which its marginal revenue product equals the wage rate, whereas the purely competitive user hires the number for which the value of marginal product of bricklayers equals the wage rate. Therefore, conversion of firms from pure competitors to monopolists reduces the number of bricklayers hired by the monopolists. As these unemployed workers move into the purely competitive area, marginal revenue products and wage rates fall in both areas. There will be a net decline in employment since fewer workers want to work at lower wage rates.

The monopolist's marginal revenue product must be equal to the pure competitor's value of marginal product for bricklayers for the monopolist to hire bricklayers at the market price. But when bricklayers are allocated so that their values of marginal product in one use are greater than in other uses, the allocation is incorrect from the point of view of economic efficiency and welfare. A correct allocation of bricklayers from society's viewpoint requires reallocating them from the purely competitive users to the monopoly users until the values of marginal product are equal for both types of users.

   b. No. Unionization raises the wage rate and leads the monopolists and the pure competitors to hire fewer bricklayers. The monopolists adjust by hiring fewer bricklayers along their marginal revenue product curves until their marginal revenue products equal the higher wage rate. The pure competitors adjust by hiring fewer bricklayers along their value of marginal product curves until their values of marginal product equal the higher wage rate. Unionization does not remove the discrepancy between the marginal revenue products and values of marginal product for the monopolists, so the allocation of resources is still incorrect. Society would prefer for bricklayers to be transferred from the pure competitors to the monopolists, but neither the price system nor unionization accomplishes it.

   c. Unionization of the monopoly firms raises the wage rate and leads to the employment of fewer bricklayers by monopolists. Unemployed bricklayers move to the submarket of purely competitive firms, shift the supply of labor to the right, decrease the wage rate, and increase employment. Unionization does not correct the distortions generated by monopoly—that is, unequal values of marginal product among different uses. Moreover, unionization of the monopoly firms causes bricklayers to move from firms where they were earning higher marginal revenue products to firms where they are earning lower marginal revenue products.

8. Review the discussion of text Figure 16.3. The allocation of labor among buyers with differing degrees of monopsony will not be correct. An equilibrium allocation of labor will be achieved when all firms are paying the same price for the resource. But to the extent that the supply curves of the resource of different firms have differing elasticities, marginal resource costs and marginal revenue products of the resource among the different buyers will not be equal. Therefore, the resource will not be allocated to maximize its contribution to net national product.

9. Review the discussion of text Case II and Figure 16.4. The legal minimum wage rate in both areas is w_2, with the South taking the place of Area I and the North taking the place of Area II. The incentives for owners of capital in the North to migrate to the South decline. In the South, the higher minimum wage rate generates unemployment. These workers will not find it beneficial to migrate to the North, however, because employers in the North will not hire more than L_2 workers at wage rate w_2.

10. a. We would advise them to allocate water between the two grades of farms so that its value of marginal product in each grade is the same.
    b. If water were allocated by the price system, the conditions listed in the equations on text p. 514 would be met. The allocation would be correct in the sense that no reallocation of water between grades of farms would increase net national product. We would favor use of the price system because it maximizes net national product.
    c. Corn and soybeans will be produced when their demands increase relative to that of wheat. The values of marginal product of water for corn and soybeans will rise relative to the value of marginal product of water for wheat, and water will be reallocated until the conditions on text p. 514 are reestablished.

11. Restricting supply in the physician substitute market will increase the demand for physicians. This prevents the wage rate for physicians from falling as much as it would otherwise.

© 1988 The Dryden Press

12. Restricting the supply of physician substitutes reduces the competition to physicians for jobs in rural counties. Physician wage rates in rural and urban counties are higher than they would be otherwise.

13. a. The airlines did not have to buy the slots in the first place, although they did incur costs for slots to be maintained through the scheduling committees. Such criticism is relevant, however, only if the FAA had been willing to hold an auction to capture the monopoly rents for the U.S. government.
    b. Assigning exchangeable rights to airlines assures their cooperation in improving resource allocation. Airlines able to use slots most efficiently (most profitably) will be the ones that will obtain them.

14. The buyer bidding the most would have the highest expected marginal revenue product from using quota rights. With administrative allocations, it is more difficult to discover which firms would have had the highest expected marginal revenue products and therefore would have bid the most had an auction been held. Perhaps the buyers that spend the most lobbying for quota rights would also have bid the highest, but such firms may not always win the competition.

15. a. Each case involves an environmental "spillover" effect whereby one economic activity is imposing costs on other activities without compensation: one property owner's new house blocks a neighbor's solar collector; motorists kill toads; and industrial firms pollute the surrounding air.
    b. Each solution involves creating new property rights that impose duties on parties to take into account more of the consequences of their activities: limiting the size or position of the new house; altering economic growth to preserve natural habitats; and allowing firms to pollute only if they buy rights to do so.

    Establishing new property rights that allow transactions to occur inexpensively strikes us as the most effective solution because it is more likely to encourage efficient resource use in the normal course of profit-maximization activities. Solar rights will also be more effective if they are exchangeable among neighbors at low cost. The toads cannot transact, so their survival is more tenuous. It depends on the willingness of environmentalists to work for their protection and on the community to pay taxes for projects to protect toads.

16. a. Davis-Bacon restricts federal contractors from paying less for low-skilled labor. At the Davis-Bacon minimum wage rate, they prefer to hire high-skilled relative to low-skilled workers.

b. Davis-Bacon raises the price of on-site labor relative to on-site capital equipment, and so encourages substitution of capital (plus the off-site labor that produces the capital). Whether the demand for labor increases or decreases on net is not clear.

True-False Questions

(F) ____ 1. Units of a resource are correctly allocated when the marginal revenue product of the resource is the same in all of its employments.

(T) ____ 2. When units of a resource are free to move among different employments and prices are free to move up and down, the price system will tend to allocate the resource in such a way that its price will be the same in alternative employments.

(T) ____ 3. Movement of units of a resource from lower paying to higher paying uses will increase national income only if they are also moving from lower value of marginal product uses to higher value of marginal product uses.

(T) ____ 4. Movement of units of a resource from lower paying to higher paying uses could conceivably also be movements from higher value of marginal product uses to lower value of marginal product uses.

(T) ____ 5. If a resource is so allocated that its value of marginal product is the same in all of its uses, it is making its maximum contribution to national income.

(F) ____ 6. Ordinarily, the wage rate will tend to be higher in an area where the labor and capital ratio is higher than in an area where the labor-capital ratio is low.

(T) ____ 7. In competitive markets, an incorrect allocation of a given resource causes the price of the resource to differ among its uses; and these price differences tend to bring about a correction of the poor allocation.

(F) ____ 8. The historic North-South wage differential reflects a poor allocation of resources and tends
to be corrected by a movement of both labor and
capital from the North to the South.

(F) ____ 9. Monopolistic sellers of product that use resource
A tend to use too little of it as indicated by
the fact that the marginal revenue product of the
resource will exceed its price.

(T) ____ 10. If the market for resource A is competitive, the
price system will tend to allocate the resource
so that its price is the same in all uses; but, if
some firms that use it are monopolistic sellers,
it will not be allocated correctly.

(F) ____ 11. One way to correct the poor allocation of resource
A that results when some users are monopolists and
others are pure competitors is to force the monopolists to pay higher prices for it.

(F) ____ 12. Ordinarily, one would not expect unions to cause
units of the kinds of labor that they represent to
be poorly allocated.

(F) ____ 13. One of the best devices currently in use to bring
about a correct allocation of labor is the minimum wage law.

(T) ____ 14. A union that causes the wage rates of its members
to be fixed above the level that would prevail in
its absence guarantees that the kind of labor it
represents will be poorly allocated.

(F) ____ 15. A reallocation of labor from a low wage area to a
high wage area would not be expected to increase
national income since the increase in wage rates
in the area that labor is leaving would tend to be
offset by the decrease in wage rates in the area
that labor is entering.

(F) ____ 16. If there are only two users of a given resource
and both pay the same price for it, it is probably
allocated correctly.

(F) ____ 17. State licensing laws for plumbers tend to improve
the allocation of plumbers among states.

(T) ____ 18. In pure monopsony, since there is only one employer of the resource in question, an allocation problem does not exist.

(T) ____ 19. An important nonprice cause of poor allocation of labor is ignorance of alternative employment opportunities.

(T) ____ 20. Resource price fixing is likely to have adverse effects on resource allocation and may cause unemployment as well.

(F) ____ 21. The rules imposed by the FAA at congested airports before 1986 made airlines willing to give up landing slots now in exchange for landing slots in the future, provided they valued the future slots more than the current slots.

(T) ____ 22. The FAA's slot allocation system before 1986 worked to the advantage of newer, growing airlines relative to older, established airlines.

(T) ____ 23. The Davis-Bacon prevailing wage law strengthens unions because it raises the cost of nonunion wage competition.

(F) ____ 24. The Davis-Bacon law produces transfers of wealth from taxpayers to union members but there is no deadweight loss to the economy as a whole that is caused by the law.

(T) ____ 25. The Davis-Bacon Act can be circumvented by defining skill levels that federal contractors need and then setting the lowest wage rate necessary to get the number of workers that is desired on each project.

(T) ____ 26. Polluting firms have incentives to economize on scarce resources including the disposal of wastes because the property rights created by EPA are exclusive and transferable.

(F) ____ 27. Defining pollution rights to be exclusive and transferable also corrects for whatever inefficient resource use polluting firms might generate as a result of product monopoly.

 © 1988 The Dryden Press

Multiple-Choice Questions

(a) ____ 1. If bricklayers (B) are incorrectly allocated between Ripley (R) and Perkins (P), one can be sure that:

a. $VMP_b^r \neq VMP_b^p$.

b. $MRP_b^r \neq MRP_b^p$.

c. $w_b^r \neq w_b^p$.

d. $MRC_b^r \neq MRC_b^p$.

(a) ____ 2. If the capital-to-labor ratio for a given kind of labor is greater in Ripley than in Perkins:

a. the wage rate in Ripley is likely to be higher.
b. the wage rate in Perkins is likely to be higher.
c. there will be unemployment of labor in Ripley.
d. there will be unemployment of labor in Perkins.

(d) ____ 3. A resource is correctly allocated among different employments when in all of those employments its:

a. marginal resource cost is the same.
b. price is the same.
c. marginal revenue product is the same.
d. value of marginal product is the same.

(a) ____ 4. One would expect that, in general, the movement of labor from low wage employments to high wage employments would:

a. increase national income.
b. have no effect on national income.
c. increase costs of production economy-wide.
d. be contrary to the underlying philosophy of a capitalistic system.

(b) ____ 5. If units of a given resource are correctly allocated, then:

a. for each firm in the economy marginal cost equals marginal revenue.
b. the resource is making its maximum contribution to national income.
c. its marginal revenue product is the same in all uses.
d. its price is the same in all uses.

(d) ____ 6. If pure competition exists, resource A is used in making two products, X and Y, and resource A is initially correctly allocated, an increase in demand for X will cause:

    a. $VMP_a^x < VMP_a^y$.

    b. $VMP_a^x = VMP_a^y$.

    c. $MRP_a^x < MRP_a^y$.

    d. $p_a^x > p_a^y$.

(c) ____ 7. For common labor, lower wage rates in rural areas than in urban areas indicate that:
    a. farm employers tend to exploit labor monopsonistically.
    b. farm employers tend to exploit labor monopolistically.
    c. labor supply relative to demand for it is larger in rural than in urban areas.
    d. capital-labor ratios are higher on the farm.

Questions 8-12 are based on the following information:

Suppose that there are three geographic areas, each constituting a short-run competitive market for common labor. In the long run, both labor and capital can move among them. Initially, labor is paid $6 per hour in Market I, $10 per hour in Market II, and $14 per hour in Market III.

(c) ____ 8. In the long run it would be expected that labor would:
    a. move from Market I to Market III, decreasing wage rates in Market III, and by demonstration effects, decreasing wage rates in Market II.
    b. move from Market I to Market II and Market III and from Market II to Market III, raising wage rates in Market I and decreasing wage rates in both Market II and Market III.
    c. move from Market I to Market II and Market III and from Market II to Market III, raising wage rates in Market I, decreasing wage rates in Market III, and having uncertain effects on wage rates in Market II.
    d. move from Market I to Market II and Market III and from Market II to Market III, raising wage rates in Market I and Market II and decreasing wage rates in Market III.

© 1988 The Dryden Press

(d) ____ 9. A minimum wage rate of $10 per hour, effective
in all three markets, would in the short run:
a. cause short-run unemployment in Market I.
b. not affect employment in Market II.
c. not affect employment in Market III.
d. all of the above

(d) ____ 10. A minimum wage rate of $10 per hour, effective
in all three markets, would in the long run block
labor out of:
a. both Market II and Market III, causing unemployment in Market I.
b. Market III only, causing unemployment in
Market I.
c. Market II only, causing unemployment in Market I.
d. Market III with a possibility, but not a cer-
tainty, of unemployment in Market I.

(b) ____ 11. A minimum wage rate of $14 per hour would:
a. restrict employment in Market II to current
levels.
b. cause unemployment in Market I.
c. reduce employment in Market III.
d. all of the above

(d) ____ 12. In the long run, capital would tend to:
a. remain in the high wage market.
b. migrate to Market I only, raising the wage
rate in Market I.
c. migrate to Markets I and II, raising the wage
rate in both markets.
d. migrate from Market III to Markets I and II
and from Market II into Market I, raising
the wage rate in Market I but with uncertain
effects on the wage rate in Market II.

(b) ____ 13. A partial explanation of the historic North-South
wage differential is that:
a. Southern textile mills are unionized.
b. Northern labor has had larger quantities of
cooperating resources per unit of labor to
work with.
c. Southern workers are exploited monopsonistically.
d. capital has migrated to the South.

(c) ____ 14. If there is some degree of monopsony on the part of each purchaser of a resource and if the resource is mobile among the employers:
   a. the supply curve will be perfectly elastic for each firm.
   b. the resource will have equal marginal resource costs for each employer.
   c. the price of the resource will be the same for each employer but marginal resource costs will differ if elasticities of supply are different for each of the employers.
   d. the marginal revenue products of the resource will be the same for each employer.

(c) ____ 15. In an economy with pure competition in resource purchases and with elements of monopoly and elements of pure competition in product sales, which of the following is not so?
   a. A unit of a given resource will contribute more to national income in the employment of a monopolist than in the employment of a pure competitor.
   b. The price of a given resource is the same for all users.
   c. If there is full employment of a given resource, neither monopolists nor pure competitors can be said to restrict its employment.
   d. Monopolists will use too little and pure competitors will use too much of any given resource for Pareto optimality.

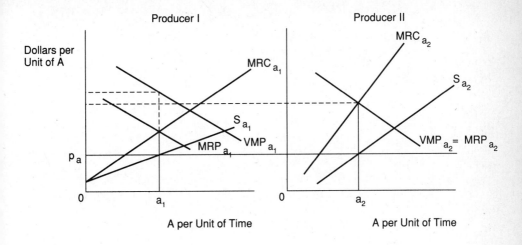

Producer I

Producer II

Dollars per
Unit of A

MRC_{a_1}

MRC_{a_2}

S_{a_2}

S_{a_1}

MRP_{a_1}

VMP_{a_1}

$VMP_{a_2} = MRP_{a_2}$

P_a

0

a_1

0

a_2

A per Unit of Time

A per Unit of Time

(d) _____ 16. In the preceding diagram, in which Producers I
and II are the only users of resource A:
a. Producer I uses too little of resource A and
Producer II uses too much.
b. a reallocation of A from Producer I to
Producer II will increase national income.
c. a reallocation of A from Producer II to Producer I will increase national income.
d. both (a) and (c) above

(a) _____ 17. The FAA's prohibition of airline scheduling committee discussion of flight origins and destina-
tions and bargaining over individual landing slots
before 1986 caused:
a. an inefficient allocation of slots at each
airport.
b. an inefficient allocation of slots at the
airport in question but not at the other
airports.
c. an efficient allocation of slots at each
airport.
d. an efficient allocation of slots at the airport in question but not at the other airports.

(d) _____ 18. The FAA's landing-slot allocation system before
1986 caused:
a. older, larger airlines to remain too large.
b. newer, smaller airlines to remain too small.
c. inefficient allocation of slots among airports
and among airlines.
d. all of the above

(d) _____ 19. Property rights in waste pollution set up by the
EPA could be:
a. reallocated by exchange from lower-valued uses
and users to higher-valued uses and users.
b. structured by the EPA to increase or decrease
the total level of pollution allowed, depending on the seriousness of the pollution situation.
c. sold by those firms that had more pollution
rights than they wanted, thus encouraging them
to economize on such rights.
d. all of the above

(d) _____ 20. Which of the following are consequences of the
Davis-Bacon prevailing wage law?
a. higher wages in the nonunion sector of the
labor market
b. more unionized employees in the unionized
sector
c. more expensive federal projects at a cost to
all taxpayers
d. all of the above

CHAPTER 17

DISTRIBUTION OF INCOME AND PRODUCT

Chapter Outline

Individual Income Determination
Personal Distribution of Income
   Distribution among Spending Units
   Income Equality and Income Differences
Causes of Income Differences
   Differences in Labor Resources Owned
   Differences in Capital Resources Owned
   Price Manipulations
Movements toward Less Inequality
   Resource Redistribution
   Minimum Prices
   The Negative Income Tax
   Income Redistribution and the Price System

Applications

The New Jersey-Pennsylvania Experiment
The Minimum Wage in Practice

Chapter Objectives

There is much myth and emotion attached to the issues of product distribution, and the primary purpose of this chapter is to
dispel as much of it as possible. First of all, we take a look
at the facts of income distribution—functional and personal.
Next, we examine the causes of income differences. Finally, we
analyze various means of assisting those at the bottom of the
income scale.

Suggestions for Teaching

Data on the personal distribution of income are most useful to
students in getting at the nature of income distribution problems. The functional distribution shows primarily that the bulk
of income is generated by labor resources. Students seem to
think visualization of income distribution through Lorenz curves
helps them understand the magnitude of the problem.

Many students find it hard to believe that income distribution
rests basically on the relative economic worths of different

© 1988 The Dryden Press

households. In the first place, despite the principles they have
learned in Chapters 14, 15, and 16, they are reluctant to think
that most people earn in accordance with the respective marginal
revenue products of their resources. They prefer to believe in
some sort of exploitation theory—that employers exploit employees and engage in wholesale sex, race, and nationality discrimination. Some examples demonstrating the economic costs to firms
of such discrimination among resource units of equal quality are
useful.

We think it important to show students that price fixing for
both products and resources usually will result in a worse,
rather than better, distribution of income. Monopoly in product
sales and monopsony in resource purchases seem to be rare, but
even in these cases, the question arises as to who will set the
prices and on what criteria they will be set.

The federal minimum wage application discusses a policy that the
public believes improves the position of low-income workers but
is reluctant to believe that it does so on the shoulders of other
low-income workers. University students seeking summer jobs who
are hampered by the minimum wage can identify with the application.

Much controversy has surrounded negative income tax schemes.
Although economists generally agree on their merits as a means
of redistributing income, the public, including our intermediate
price theory students, tends to oppose them. Some facts and
figures on government transfer payments and some comparisons between the actual amounts transferred and the amounts that would
need to be transferred to totally eliminate poverty if transfers
were made only to the poor can be persuasive. Our application
describes the operation of a massive experiment with a negative
income tax scheme.

Many students view income transfers to the poor as "socialistic." We spend some time attempting to demonstrate that a price
and market system can take very substantial transfers in stride.
Taxes and subsidies may indeed alter patterns of consumption and
production but they certainly do not preclude the general use
of prices and markets to organize economic activity.

Problems and Questions for Discussion

1. Check the latest issues of the sources cited in text Table
    17.2 and bring the functional distribution of income of
    Table 17.2 up to date. Explain each item in the function-
    al distribution indicating the resource category(ies) to
    which it belongs.

© 1988 The Dryden Press

2. Obtain the latest data available on the size distribution of income. Find the latest definitions of the poverty level of income for an urban family of four and for an unattached individual. What percentage of the U.S. population lives in poverty using the latest definitions?

3. What are the sources and the relative sizes of those sources of your family's annual income?

4. Do you think that national income should be equally distributed among individuals of the economy (consider a family as a collection of individuals)? Why or why not?

5. In a private enterprise economy, what determines the distribution of income?

6. Explain the determinants of the distribution of labor resources. Are there any forces in a private enterprise system that tend toward diminution of differences in labor resource ownership? Explain. Are there any forces that tend to prevent movements toward smaller differences?

7. What kinds of measures do you think should be taken to reduce income differences to tolerable levels? Explain these carefully.

8. Draw the diagram consistent with an expectation among economists that the New Jersey-Pennsylvania Experiment would cause the amount of work supplied to decline.

9. One could make a case that the New Jersey-Pennsylvania Experiment was so limited in scope that it is too risky to draw any inferences from it about how well or poorly a negative income tax policy would work. What were the major deficiencies of the experiment? Can you see how overgeneralization might carry risks to policy makers?

10. The U.S. Supreme Court decided in 1983 that it is unconstitutional for an insurance company to pay out a smaller monthly amount to a female pensioner than a male pensioner even if the "average" female is expected by actuarial tables to live longer than the "average" male. Now that "unisex" pension payouts are going to be adopted, which of the following groups would you expect to be gainers and which losers: (a) single women pensioners; (b) single men pensioners; (c) nonworking women married to men who collect a pension; (d) nonworking men married to women who collect a pension? Explain your answers carefully.

© 1988 The Dryden Press

11. Based on text Figure 17.7, list as many reasons as you can that would explain why the demand for teenage employees would be relatively elastic as is shown by $D_c'D_c'$ instead of relatively inelastic as is shown by D_cD_c in Figure 17.7.

12. The U.S. House of Representatives defeated a subminimum legal wage for teenagers in 1977 by just one vote, but the idea has been under consideration by each presidential administration since then. For example, one proposal would lower the legal minimum wage rate by 25 percent for workers aged 18 to 22 who were hired during the summer months only. This is favored by businesses but opposed by unions because approximately 70 percent of low-wage workers are adults. (Joann S. Lublin, "Lower Minimum Wage for Youth Opposed in Presidential Panel Report to Congress," The Wall Street Journal, May 22, 1981; "Reagan Weighs Minimum Wage Cut for Youths," ibid., January 11, 1983.)
    a. Explain the effect that the subminimum wage rate for teenagers would have on the employment of teenagers and adults.
    b. No national lobbying effort by teenagers or their parents has been mounted to obtain a subminimum wage for teenagers. Explain why this behavior probably is economically rational.
    c. Encourage a class discussion of student employments in recent summers. How many worked at jobs that paid more than the legal minimum wage? How many worked at jobs that paid less? How many worked as independent contractors?

13. Construct an argument relating increases in the national legal minimum wage rate with increased enrollments in 2-year community colleges and some 4-year colleges by average or below-average students who cannot find full-time market work.
    a. Contact your college admission or employment office and determine whether the college is free to hire students for part-time work at less than the legal minimum wage rate. If known in advance, would this fact lead some students to quit searching for full-time market jobs and become "employed" in obtaining an education while working part-time? Explain.
    b. If supported by the evidence, what would be the implication of your theory for the reliability of U.S. data on unemployment? Explain.

© 1988 The Dryden Press

14. In March 1987, Congressional Democrats proposed increasing the minimum wage to $4.65 by 1990 in a series of three annual steps, with automatic increases to occur thereafter. Supporters said that the present minimum wage rate of $3.35 established in 1981 has been eroded by inflation. One of its sponsors, Senator Edward Kennedy (D., Mass.) said that the legislation is intended to "make the minimum wage a living wage...the most important poverty program that we in this Congress can pass—without adding one nickel to the deficit." Labor Secretary William Brock said that "the [Reagan] administration cannot stand by while some in Congress propose an action which will further deny opportunity to America's young men and women." He said that a higher minimum wage would result "in the loss of job opportunities for thousands of kids," and repeated the administration's proposal for a subminimum wage rate for teens. (Cathy Trost, "Democrats Seek Higher Minimum Wage and White House Quickly Opposes It," The Wall Street Journal, March 26, 1987.)

   a. Which of these arguments, or parts of them, are supported by the economic evidence presented in the text?

   b. Check indexes to The New York Times or The Wall Street Journal for articles over the past year explaining the state of play in Congress for a higher national minimum wage rate or a subminimum wage rate for teenagers. Which groups favor or oppose them, and how do these positions appear to square with their economic interests? Do you see pressure on Congress to enact either proposal? If the issues were voted upon, explain the pressures that led to their success or defeat.

15. U.S. minimum wage laws also apply to Puerto Rico. Explain whether you would expect the effects on employment in Puerto Rico to be less or more severe than in the continental United States if each of the following conditions applied to Puerto Rico:

   a. the ratio of high- to low-wage laborers was lower
   b. the price of labor relative to capital was lower
   c. the level of labor productivity was lower

Solutions to Problems and Questions for Discussion

1. Depends on facts discovered.

2. Depends on facts discovered.

3. Depends on facts discovered.

© 1988 The Dryden Press

4. This is a normative question that each voter must decide individually. We would not support equal distribution because it would weaken incentives to produce.

5. The distribution of income in a private enterprise economy is determined primarily in accordance with marginal productivity theory—where each resource unit is paid its marginal revenue product.

6. Labor resources differ according to, among other things, the willingness to work, aptitudes and abilities, training and education (human capital), and inherited advantages. Horizontal movements of labor from areas of lower- to higher-wage opportunities tend to diminish income differences. Blockage of vertical movement of labor into higher-level occupations perpetuates income differences.

7. This is another normative question that each voter must decide individually. Typical measures to reduce income differences include progressive tax rates, subsidies, wage and price controls, and redistribution of resource ownership. Setting questions about their effectiveness aside, our view is that redistribution, if attempted, must be done gingerly. Experience shows that when societies become overly concerned about the distribution of shares of net national income among groups, they often adopt redistributional schemes that weaken the incentives of productive people to increase net national income. In the long run, the "economic pie" available for redistribution becomes smaller. But we strongly favor removing legal restrictions and other impediments to horizontal and vertical mobility so that the price system over time will reduce income differences. We also favor the use of a negative income tax to bring about whatever income redistribution the society deems desirable.

8. Review the discussion of text Figure 17.6. In panel (a) and (b), the negative income tax preserves some work incentives, although these incentives are not as strong as those provided by the market alone.

9. The experiment excluded families headed by a woman only and its duration was for only three years. This may have been too little time for some families to adjust, and for others significant adjustments may not have been worth while for benefits available for three years only.

10. a. They benefit as a group from the higher monthly payout because they tend to live longer after retirement.
    b. They lose as a group from the lower monthly payout because they tend to live shorter periods after retirement.
    c. They lose as a group because their husbands get smaller monthly payouts and tend not to live as long as they do.
    d. They benefit as a group because their wives get a higher monthly payout.

11. Teenagers seeking full-time jobs tend to have relatively low skills, so capital or older workers can be substituted for them at relatively low cost. Often they also work in competitive industries where the elasticity of product demand is high, which increases the elasticity of labor demand. Students seeking part-time summer employment also have many substitutes.

12. a. In the teenage market, the lower minimum wage rate raises employment to a degree. This reduces employment and raises wage rates in uncovered markets. The minimum wage rate for adults in covered markets does not change. Competition from teenagers reduces adult employment in covered markets. Adults shift to uncovered markets and reduce wage rates there. Generally, teenagers gain relative to adults, although the gains are greatest for teenagers with the greatest productivities relative to adults.
    b. We are not certain why it occurs, but the lobbying costs may exceed the potential gains for teenage students seeking summer employment only. Teenagers seeking full-time jobs may not vote, and their families may not realize the effects of the minimum wage law.

13. One study of the effects of minimum wages offered this
    theory. To a degree, market work and education are substi-
    tutes. The legal minimum wage law does not permit employers
    to lower the rate for teenagers with low skills while they
    acquire on-the-job training. Thus, the law pushes teenagers
    into such nonmarket activities as education. The alterna-
    tive cost (foregone earnings) for the unemployed is zero.
    Teenagers who would not otherwise have gone to college may
    enroll in two-year community colleges to get sufficient
    training to break out of the minimum wage barrier.
    a. Student employees of public schools, colleges, and
       universities were exempt from the minimum wage law in
       1986. Thus, teenagers may pursue education and part-
       time work jointly.
    b. The theory is supported by evidence. Over time, school
       enrollments increased whenever the minimum wage rate was
       increased or coverage was expanded. Hence the minimum
       wage laws increase unemployment indirectly by encourag-
       ing youths to leave the labor market for schooling. To
       the degree that these include average or below-average
       students who would not otherwise have continued school-
       ing, then the skill level of entering college students
       may decline. One study speculated that the minimum wage
       may have contributed to the declining median score on
       college entrance examinations. (J. Peter Mattila, "The
       Impact of Minimum Wages on Teenage Schooling and on
       the Part-Time/Full-Time Employment of Youths," in Simon
       Rottenberg, ed., The Economics of Legal Minimum Wages,
       Washington, D.C. and London: The American Enterprise
       Institute for Public Policy Research, 1981, 61-87.)

14. a. The proponents of a higher minimum wage are correct
       that inflation has eroded the $3.35 wage rate. They are
       also correct in arguing that higher minimum wage rates
       make employees who keep their jobs better off. As op-
       ponents point out, however, this is accomplished at the
       expense of employees who are forced to search for new
       jobs in the covered sector or to take inferior jobs in
       the uncovered sector. Teenagers are hurt: each 10 per-
       cent increase in the minimum wage rate reduces hiring
       of teenagers by some 2 to 3 percent. President Car-
       ter's Minimum Wage Study Commission found that "an ex-
       plicit purpose of the minimum wage was, and is, to
       protect adult workers from low wage competition from
       youth." (Michael S. Bernstam, "Minimum Wage: Bulwark
       of the Privileged," The Wall Street Journal, June 15,
       1987.) Such adverse effects are not confined to teen-
       agers. As Finis Welch showed, low-wage workers in
       other age groups are also affected.
    b. Depends on facts discovered.

15. (a), (b), and (c) all make the consequences more severe for Puerto Rico. (Simon Rottenberg, "Minimum Wages in Puerto Rico," in Simon Rottenberg, ed., The Economics of Legal Minimum Wages [Washington, D.C., and London: The American Enterprise Institute for Public Policy Research, 1981]:327-339.)

True-False Questions

(T) _____ 1. If consumers spend all of current income on goods and services currently produced, neither saving nor dissaving, the distribution of income determines the distribution of the economy's output.

(T) _____ 2. If product demand curves and resource supply curves are highly elastic, then resource owners tend to be paid approximately what their resources contribute at the margin to national income.

(T) _____ 3. A consuming unit's monthly income depends upon the qualities and quantities of the resources it can put into productive processes, together with the prices received for those resources.

(F) _____ 4. Income differences have been a constant source of strife and trouble throughout history and serve no useful economic purpose.

(T) _____ 5. Most families are substantially better off today than they were in 1947.

(F) _____ 6. Monopoly in the product market causes resources employed by monopolists to be paid less than they are paid by purely competitive sellers.

(F) _____ 7. Capital resources account for a much larger share of national income than do labor resources.

(F) _____ 8. Almost all of the poor live on income from labor while almost all of the rich live on income from capital.

(F) _____ 9. In the United States, the poverty problem is getting worse over time.

© 1988 The Dryden Press

(T) _____ 10. Workers having skills that produce goods and services highly valued relatively by the public and whose skills are in short supply tend to have high incomes.

(T) _____ 11. The incomes of some people are low because they are denied access to opportunities to develop their labor resources.

(T) _____ 12. Movement of a person from lower skill levels to higher skill levels ordinarily increases national income.

(F) _____ 13. Generally speaking, limitations on the number of persons who can enter medical school hold national income above what it would be if there were more doctors and lower prices for their services.

(F) _____ 14. In a capitalistic economy, national income can always be increased by blocking the upward mobility of the lower classes, keeping their services in the form of common labor.

(T) _____ 15. Inheritance plays a very large role in the distribution of both labor and capital resources.

(T) _____ 16. In redistributing income, direct redistribution in the form of taxes and cash subsidies usually will interfere less with incentive and economic efficiency than will indirect redistribution in the form of price and wage fixing.

(T) _____ 17. Attempts to increase the incomes of the poor by fixing minimum wage rates are likely to result in unemployment.

(T) _____ 18. Incomes tend to vary directly with educational levels and skill levels.

(T) _____ 19. A long-term narrowing of income differences must be based primarily on a narrowing of the differences in resource ownership.

(F) _____ 20. The reduction in employment caused by a hike in the legal minimum wage rate is exactly equal to the increase in unemployment that it causes.

(T) ____ 21. A higher legal minimum wage rate creates inefficiency and a lower net national product since it
causes the marginal revenue product of labor in
the covered sector to diverge from that in the
uncovered sector.

(T) ____ 22. The inefficiencies caused by increases in the
legal minimum wage rate are difficult to measure
owing to the number of workers who drop out of the
labor force rather than search for jobs.

(F) ____ 23. The New Jersey-Pennsylvania Experiment suggests
that the negative income tax proposal, as a device
for ameliorating poverty, has little applicability
to the United States.

(T) ____ 24. The fact that the families included in the New
Jersey-Pennsylvania Experiment knew that it would
be of short duration tends to cloud the value that
researchers and policy makers may attach to the
experiment's results.

(F) ____ 25. The New Jersey-Pennsylvania Experiment produced
no surprises to the researchers who had designed
and implemented it.

(F) ____ 26. All firms subjected to an effective minimum wage
level will adjust to increases in that level by
laying off workers.

(T) ____ 27. Adverse effects of minimum wage legislation are
not limited to teenagers and minority groups, but
are likely to extend to other low-skilled workers.

Multiple-Choice Questions

(b) ____ 1. The marginal productivity theory of income distribution:
a. is unable to take monopoly and monopsony into
account.
b. holds that resource owners in a competitive
economy tend to be paid what their resources
are worth at the margin in the production
process.
c. has been empirically disproved.
d. makes the alleviation of poverty impossible.

(d) ____ 2. The underlying basis of poverty in the United
States is that:
a. businesses refuse to pay workers as much as
they are worth to the businesses.
b. the economy is much too agriculturally oriented.
c. labor unions do not have a large enough proportion of the labor force organized to exert
the power needed to raise low wages.
d. the poor have relatively small quantities
of low-grade resources that frequently do not
find their way into their most productive
uses.
e. there is large-scale importation of goods
made with cheap foreign labor.

(c) ____ 3. The functional distribution of income provides:
a. little information on the extent of poverty in
the economy.
b. good information on the extent of poverty in
the economy.
c. some information, but not complete information, on the shares of national income going
to labor resources and to capital resources,
respectively.
d. complete information on the shares of national
income going to labor resources and to capital
resources, respectively.

(d) ____ 4. The share of national income earned by labor resources is:
a. less than 30 percent.
b. between 30 percent and 50 percent.
c. between 50 percent and 75 percent.
d. over 75 percent.

(d) ____ 5. Vertical mobility of labor:
a. is not related to educational levels.
b. has been of little importance in the United
States over time.
c. will do little to increase the level of national income.
d. is often blocked by restrictions on entry
into specific professions such as medicine.

© 1988 The Dryden Press

(c) ____ 6. Horizontal and vertical differences in labor resources do not:
  a. create incentives for reallocation and training of labor that will tend to reduce income inequality.
  b. account for income differences.
  c. increase labor's share of national income.
  d. result from differences in labor training opportunities.

(c) ____ 7. It is generally correct to say that:
  a. the poor do not receive income from capital.
  b. the rich derive most, but not all, of their income from capital.
  c. both the rich and the poor derive income from both labor and capital.
  d. both (a) and (b)

(b) ____ 8. Social inheritance——the culture in which one grows up——
  a. has little to do with income distribution—— we are all familiar with the rags to riches cases.
  b. has an important bearing on the quality of labor resources that one will develop.
  c. is primarily a factor in the distribution of capital resources.
  d. can be easily modified through inheritance laws.

(a) ____ 9. The personal distribution of income:
  a. refers to the numbers of persons and families in each of several income classifications.
  b. helps alleviate poverty.
  c. shows that labor earns more than capital.
  d. is derived from the functional distribution of income.

(b) ____ 10. Persons with higher skills tend to earn higher incomes than those with lower skills because:
  a. they charge more in order to recoup the costs of their training.
  b. they perform services more valuable to society, and the supply of them on the market tends to be smaller.
  c. they are more plentiful.
  d. they work harder.

(c) ____ 11. Which of the following has least to do with a person's holdings of physical capital?
a. income in previous years
b. the propensity to accumulate
c. physical inheritance
d. material inheritance

(a) ____ 12. Minimum wage laws:
a. may increase income differences by generating unemployment.
b. have done much to reduce income differences in the society.
c. tend to offset monopolistic exploitation of labor.
d. are especially beneficial to minority groups in the economy.

(b) ____ 13. Which of the following would be most effective in redistributing income to the poor?
a. the setting of minimum wage rates for labor through either legislation or collective bargaining
b. measures that increase the quantities and qualities of resources owned by the poor
c. food stamps programs
d. old age, survivor's, and dependent's insurance

(a) ____ 14. The establishment of minimum wage rates may be effective in raising both the levels of employment and income of workers where:
a. monopsony prevails.
b. pure competition prevails.
c. monopoly prevails.
d. oligopoly prevails.

(d) ____ 15. Attempts to redistribute income toward the poor via wage fixing and price fixing:
a. are generally successful.
b. tend to overcompensate the poor.
c. prevent the poor from being exploited.
d. interfere with the efficiency of the economy and do little for the poor as a group.

(b) ____ 16. Large incomes earned by top professional athletes:
a. disprove marginal productivity theory.
b. result from great demand for and small supplies of the skills that they possess.
c. show that the price system does not work.
d. are irrational in economic terms.

(c) _____ 17. Low incomes of grape pickers in California result largely from:
    a. exploitation by grape growers.
    b. low prices of wine and grape jelly.
    c. large supplies of unskilled labor available for grape picking.
    d. alternative employment opportunities available to grape pickers.

(a) _____ 18. The negative income tax as embodied in the New Jersey-Pennsylvania Experiment:
    a. is only one of several possible forms that such a scheme might take if implemented on a permanent basis through legislation in Congress.
    b. yielded results that were precisely what the research designers predicted.
    c. was of little value to economists and illustrates that academic experiments in general are not well designed.
    d. none of the above

(d) _____ 19. Several sources of the reduction in real output that society suffers each time the legal minimum wage rate is increased are:
    a. increased idleness of workers.
    b. inequality of marginal revenue products between covered and uncovered sectors.
    c. higher prices of final goods and services than would otherwise have occurred.
    d. all of the above

(d) _____ 20. Teenagers are particularly vulnerable to increases in the legal minimum wage rate because:
    a. their skill levels and productivities are low.
    b. they often take jobs in industries that are susceptible to the business cycle.
    c. the range of jobs that are not covered by the legal minimum wage has fallen.
    d. all of the above

(a) ____ 21. The full economic effects of increases in the
legal minimum wage rate are difficult to ascertain
because:
a. each increase is small relative to the other
    economic forces that are at work in labor mar-
    kets at the same time.
b. the change in the minimum wage rate is the
    only major variable at work in the markets for
    teenagers.
c. the primary effects of the higher legal mini-
    mum wage rate are large relative to the sec-
    ondary effects.
d. the demand for labor of low-wage persons is
    relatively elastic.

(d) ____ 22. The increases in the legal minimum wage rate generally cause the following effects in the work-
place and amenities of those affected:
a. an increase in the pace of work
b. substitution of high-skilled persons for low-
    skilled persons
c. a reduction in fringe benefits such as vaca-
    tions and pleasantness of workplace surround-
    ings
d. all of the above

PART SIX

HOW THE PIECES FIT TOGETHER

This part, a single chapter, summarizes in broad outline the framework of microeconomic theory. We use it to tie the course together. It is especially important that students learn to distinguish between optimum welfare conditions and the conditions of general equilibrium. Achievement of the latter does not necessarily, and in most cases will not, result in the former.

CHAPTER 18

WELFARE AND EQUILIBRIUM

Chapter Outline

The Concepts of Welfare and Equilibrium
   Welfare
   Equilibrium
The Conditions of Optimum Welfare
   Maximum Consumer Welfare: Fixed Supplies
   Maximum Efficiency in Production: Given Resource Supplies
   Optimal Outputs of Goods and Services
   Summary of Optimum Welfare Conditions
Private Enterprise and General Equilibrium
   Consumer Equilibrium: Fixed Supplies
   Producer Equilibrium: Given Resource Supplies
   Product Output Levels: Given Resource Supplies

Applications

The Welfare Core of the Applications

Chapter Objectives

In this chapter we pull together the most important principles
of microeconomics, putting them in a welfare economics context.
Its purpose is not to teach welfare economics, but rather to fit
the various parts of the book into a logical coherent framework.
We review first the concept of equilibrium—partial and general.
Then we consider the optimum welfare conditions for <u>any</u> kind of
economic system. Finally we address the question, under what
circumstances, if any, would a <u>market system</u> in general equilibrium yield Pareto optimal conditions?

Suggestions for Teaching

Many students confuse general equilibrium with optimum welfare.
We take especial care to separate these very different concepts.
The former is positive in nature, showing us where an economic
system, left to its own devices, will go. The latter may be a
normative goal—an "ideal" situation—independent of the type
of economic system that exists.

After defining the equilibrium and welfare concepts, we go
step-by-step through the conditions of optimum welfare, first

for consumers, assuming fixed supplies per unit of time of products. Then we bring producers into the picture, assuming fixed
supplies of resources. Next, we consider the optimal outputs
of goods and services.

The step-by-step process seems to work well, so we use it to
show the conditions of general equilibrium in a private enterprise economic system. At each step we pose the question: Are
optimum welfare conditions achieved? Why or why not? In particular we examine the effects of different market structures
both in product sales and in resource purchasing on deviations
of general equilibrium conditions from those of optimal welfare.

Most discussions of general equilibrium and welfare are ab-
stract. To increase students' interest—and knowledge—we have
culled the welfare implications from the applications sections
of each chapter, presenting them here as the welfare core of
the applications. Oddly enough, our students like it!

Problems and Questions for Discussion

1. Distinguish carefully between the partial equilibrium
    position of a purely competitive industry X and general
    equilibrium for the economy as a whole. (It may be help-
    ful to consider another purely competitive industry Y as
    representative of every other industry in the economy.)
    Is it possible for X to be in equilibrium even though
    the rest of the economy is not? Explain.

2. Suppose that a large decrease in the supply of crude oil
    occurs. Trace through the partial equilibrium adjustment
    of the gasoline refining industry. Now, trace through the
    effects on the automobile industry and electric utilities.
    Finally, trace through the effects on industries produc-
    ing alternative sources of energy; e.g., coal or nuclear
    energy.

3. Suppose that we know the indifference maps of two students,
    J and M, for onions and other goods and services. The
    supplies available to them are given. Initially, they are
    off the contract curve in such a way that J's consumption
    of onions is too small and M's consumption of onions is
    too large for them to be on the contract curve. Addition-
    al consumption of onions by J results in a decrease in M's
    well-being. What are the implications of moving toward
    the contract curve?

4. If there are no externalities in consumption, would you expect the price system to lead to maximum community welfare:
    a. under conditions of pure competition in the sale of goods and services?
    b. under conditions of monopoly in the sale of goods and services?

    Illustrate with a diagram and explain your answer in each case. Use a two-good, two-consumer model.

5. In a two-product, two-resource production model, explain the derivation of the transformation curve.

6. In a two-product, two-resource production model with no externalities, will the price system bring about a most efficient allocation of resources between the two goods if there is:
    a. pure competition in product sales and resource purchases?
    b. monopsony in resource purchases?

    Illustrate and explain in each case.

7. Why is the slope of a transformation curve for two goods, X and Y, at any given point measured by MC_x/MC_y?

8. Suppose in a two-good, two-person model at the existing product mix that for each consumer $MRS_{xy} < MRT_{xy}$. Under conditions of pure competition, what is the nature of the forces set in motion? Explain the equilibrium position, assuming that there are no externalities.

9. In an isolated community there are two kinds of land and
    wheat is the only product produced. There are 100 farms
    of each grade. The labor supply is homogeneous—i.e., all
    workers are equally efficient. There is private property
    in land and free contract for labor. Labor services are
    bought and sold only in units of one laborer per year.
    The markets for both labor and land (unless otherwise spe-
    cified) should be assumed to be freely competitive. All
    workers prefer employment to unemployment at any wage
    rate above zero.

    The table below shows the amounts of wheat that can be
    obtained from one single farm of each grade, with differ-
    ent numbers of laborers per year.

Number of Laborers	Output on A-grade Farm	Output on B-grade Farm
1	500	400
2	1,200	1,000
3	2,100	1,300
4	2,700	1,500
5	3,100	1,600
6	3,400	1,650

a. The labor population (supply) is 240:
    (1) What will be the wage rate per year in bushels?
    (2) What will be the rent per farm of each grade?
    (3) Explain both wages and rents in terms of produc-
         tivities.

b. The labor population (supply) is 550:
    (1) What will be the wage rate per year in bushels?
    (2) Why cannot the wage rate be higher? lower?
    (3) What will be the rents on each grade of land?
    (4) What would be the effect on wages and rents of an
         output (excise) tax of 10%?
    (5) Suppose a land tax of 100 bushels per farm is
         levied on the A-grade farms (B-grade are exempt).
         What are the effects on wages? on amounts paid as
         rent by tenants?
    (6) Suppose a minimum wage of 650 bushels per year
         is legally prescribed and enforced. What are the
         effects on employment? on rents?
    (7) Suppose that instead of a legal minimum wage rate
         being imposed, workers on the A-grade farms or-
         ganize and enforce a wage rate of 650 bushels—the
         market for labor remaining fully competitive on
         the B-grade farms. What are the effects?

10. What impact on consumer welfare would you expect from a government requirement that <u>all</u> automobiles be equipped with air bags? Explain your answer. Illustrate with diagrams if you can.

11. Suppose that in the United States economy those persons comprising the highest 20 percent of income receivers receive 50 percent of the annual income of the economy while those comprising the lowest 20 percent receive 5 percent of the annual income of the economy. General equilibrium exists but because of (1) externalities in production and consumption, and (2) imperfections in market structures, Pareto optimality does not.

    Suppose now that through a progressive tax-subsidy program, 10 percent of the economy's annual income is transferred from the highest 20 percent of income receivers to the lowest 20 percent.

    Apart from those paying the taxes and those receiving the subsidies, <u>who</u> is made better off and <u>who</u> is made worse off by the program? Determine this by tracing through as thoroughly as you can the effects of the transfers as the economy moves to a new general equilibrium position. It may be helpful to use a few real-world industry examples in your analysis.

    In a short paragraph, explain what happens to welfare in the economy and why.

12. Analyze the effects of each of the following on the level of consumer welfare:
    a. a law that prohibits the production and sale of artificial sweeteners
    b. a law that prohibits the scalping of Olympics tickets
    c. governmental subsidies to Amtrak when revenues do not cover marginal costs

13. Poland is a planned economy where political party officials set prices and wages. Food is heavily subsidized and prices to consumers are set so low that queues are the rule rather than the exception. Poland's factories produce steel and other goods that typically are not competitive in Western markets; the state-owned tractor factory produces about two and one-half tractors per employee per year, whereas the Western-owned factory under construction in 1981 was expected to produce ten per employee per year. Typically, one factory produces the entire national supply of things like tractor tires and batteries. Battery shortages equal about a half-year's production. The price of gasoline to consumers is twice the price to factories. Seventy-five percent of Poland's industrial capacity is underutilized in spite of a labor force that is highly skilled plus farmland and mineral deposits that are rich and extensive. Between 1977 and 1980, Poland's gross national product fell by 25 percent and was expected to drop another 17 percent in 1981. (Robert Ball, "Poland's Economic Disaster," _Fortune_, September 7, 1981.) Explain what changes in Poland's policies might halt the fall in its standard of living.

14. In an attempt to halt the decline in their standard of living, Polish government officials were considering letting factory managers determine wages of employees, prices of their goods, and the extent of capital investments out of profits that their enterprises created or bank loans that they could negotiate individually. (Robert Ball, "Poland's Economic Disaster," _Fortune_, September 7, 1981.) Explain what effect this single change in economic policy might be expected to have on Poland's standard of living.

15. Explain to what degree the absence of competitive bidding for M.B.A. classes at the University of Chicago, as described in the text on pp. 95-98, violated one or more conditions of optimal welfare. Explain the degree to which these conditions were remedied by permitting students to compete for seats with play money.

Solutions to Problems and Questions for Discussion

1. Partial equilibrium may exist for industry X, even though other parts of the economy are in disequilibrium. Decision makers in X may have adjusted fully to the external facts as they see them. Changes in the rest of the economy may change those external facts and thus change the partial equilibrium position of X. The primary difference between partial equilibrium and general equilibrium is one of focus. Are we looking at one segment of the economy and how it adjusts to the facts it faces? Or are we looking at all parts of the economy simultaneously to observe how all of them together adjust to disequilibrium forces?

2. Higher crude oil prices raise the cost of oil refining, reducing the output of refineries in the short run, and perhaps closing higher-cost refineries in the short run. Higher prices of such refined products as kerosene and gasoline raise operating costs of electric power plants and raise electricity rates. Consumers adjust to higher electricity prices in the short run by reducing the quantity of electricity that they demand and in the long run by purchasing fewer energy-intensive appliances like air conditioners. Higher gasoline prices raise the cost of driving and lead in the short run to a smaller quantity of gasoline demanded. The prices of energy-intensive cars fall in the short run, and prices of energy-conserving cars rise, just enough to account for the differences in their gasoline utilization rates. Over the long run, consumers demand more smaller cars relative to larger cars, and the mix of production shifts accordingly. Finally, higher crude oil prices lead to higher prices of coal and nuclear energy substitutes in the short run depending upon their availability. In the long run, the demand for coal and nuclear energy plants and the resources used to make them rise.

3. Review the discussion of text Figure 18.2. The combined welfare of the two persons may be higher (Pareto optimal) at a point off the contract curve.

© 1988 The Dryden Press

4. a. Yes. Review the discussion of condition 18.3 on pp. 594-595 of the text. Each consumer's marginal rate of substitution between two goods is equal to the ratio of their prices, which is also equal to the ratio of their marginal costs, which is the marginal rate of transformation in production. Condition 18.3 is met and community welfare is maximized.

    b. No. Review the discussion of condition 18.4 on p. 595 of the text. Consumers equate their marginal rates of substitution between two goods to the ratios of the market prices of the two goods. But profit maximization leads a monopolist to produce an output rate for which marginal cost equals marginal revenue, which is less than price. Thus, too little of the monopolized good is produced and too much of the other good is produced for optimum welfare to be achieved.

5. Review the discussion of text Figures 18.3 and 18.4. In Figure 18.3, fixed supplies of two resources are used to produce two products. When the supplies are distributed between the two products in combinations that lie along the contract curve, at a point like E, condition 18.2 is satisfied. A maximum efficiency allocation of resources is achieved because neither product's output can be increased unless some of the other is sacrificed. The infinite number of efficiently produced combinations of the two products shown by the contract curve in Figure 18.3 is also shown by the transformation curve of Figure 18.4.

6. a. Yes. Review the discussion surrounding condition 18.2 on p. 592 of the text. Under pure competition in resource markets, when marginal revenue product of each resource equals its marginal resource cost, the value of marginal product of each resource equals its price. When each firm employs resources in profit-maximizing quantities, condition 18.2 will also be satisfied.

    b. No. Review the discussion surrounding condition 18.2 on p. 593 of the text. Under monopsony, when the elasticity of supply of a resource to one firm differs from that of another firm, at whatever the supply price of the resource to both firms may be, then the marginal resource costs of the resource will differ between firms. When each firm employs resources in profit-maximizing quantities, condition 18.2 will not be satisfied.

7. The slope of the transformation curve at any point is the change in Y produced per unit of time divided by the change in X produced per unit of time. The value of the quantity of X sacrificed to produce another unit of Y equals MC_y, and the value of the quantity of Y sacrificed to produce another unit of X equals MC_x.

8. If $MRS_{xy} < MRT_{xy}$, then $MC_x > p_x$ and $MC_y < p_y$. The price system will bring about a reduction in the output of X and an expansion in the output of Y, increasing MRS_{xy} and causing p_x to rise and p_y to fall. As MRT_{xy} falls, MC_x decreases and MC_y increases until $MC_x = p_x$ and $MC_y = p_y$, and $MRS_{xy} = MRT_{xy}$.

9. In solving this set of problems, keep in mind that if wage rates are above zero and there is unemployed labor, competition among workers, if possible, will drive wages down. If there are idle farms and rents are above zero, competition among farms will drive rents down. If wage rates are uncontrolled, they must be uniform. Rents on A-grade farms must be uniform if uncontrolled. Rents on B-grade farms must be uniform if uncontrolled. We must compute the MPP_1 schedule for each grade of farm.

Number of Laborers	Output on A-grade Farm	MPP_1 on A-grade Farm	Output on B-grade Farm	MPP_1 on B-grade Farm
1	500	500	400	400
2	1,200	700	1,000	600
3	2,100	900	1,300	300
4	2,700	600	1,500	200
5	3,100	400	1,600	100
6	3,400	300	1,650	50

a. (1) Wage rates = 700 bu.
   (2) Rent = 0 on each type of farm.
   (3) Common sense must prevail here. Bidding must be superimposed over simple marginal productivity theory. But suppose we start initially with marginal productivity theory. Let 60 A-grade farms each employ 4 workers each at 600 per worker. Total wages would be 2,400, thus 300 is left for each farm as rent. No B-grade farm can afford to employ workers at this wage rate (note that at 2 workers total wages would be 1,200 and rent would be negative). But now there are 40 idle A-grade farms. Paying slightly more than 600 they can bid workers away from the other 60 and can make positive rents. Incentives of this sort exist until the wage rate is bid up to 700 bu. Eighty farms will now be employ-

© 1988 The Dryden Press

ing 3 workers each. Rents will have declined to 0 for all eighty. Twenty A-grade farms will be idle and thus also earn 0 rent. Wage rates cannot exceed 700 at any employment level because at such a higher rate the total wage bill of a farm would exceed total output, leaving negative rent.

b. (1) Wage rate = 500 bu. One hundred A-grade farms each employ 5 workers and 25 B-grade farms each employ 2 workers.

(2) At a higher wage rate there is no incentive for B-grade farms to bid for labor since their rents would be 0 or negative for all possible employment levels. Unemployment would drive the wage rate down to 500. At a lower wage rate, say 400, 25 idle B-grade farms can bid wage rates up and earn rent with 2 workers per farm. But competition with the other 75 B-grade farms continues to drive the wage rate up until at 500 the rents of all B-grade farms would become 0.

(3) A-grade farm rent = 600 bu.
B-grade farm rent = 0.

(4) Wage rates drop to 450. There are no employment changes.
A-grade farm rent = 540.
B-grade farm rent = 0.

(5) There is no effect on the employment pattern or the wage rate. A-grade rent is reduced from 600 to 500. B-grade rent remains at 0.

(6) One hundred A-grade farms employ 3 workers each at 650 bu. Two-hundred fifty are unemployed.
A-grade farm rent = 150.
B-grade farm rent = 0.

(7) One hundred A-grade farms employ 3 workers each at 650 bu. Fifty B-grade farms employ 2 workers each at 300 bu. Fifty B-grade farms employ 3 workers each at 300 bu.
B-grade farm rent = 400.

10. If some consumers would not voluntarily have purchased an air bag at marginal cost when they ordered their new car, then apparently they do not value the air bags at marginal cost. Condition 18.3 is violated. In text Figure 18.6, the combination of air bags and other goods that are produced will not be optimal.

11. The income transfers will change demand patterns in the economy, increasing the demand for such staples as housing, clothing, and basic food products while decreasing the demand for items that are generally purchased by wealthier people. Let X be a composite of the items for which demand increases and Y be a composite of those for which demand decreases.

Those who furnish resources to produce X will be made better off while those who furnish resources to produce Y will be made worse off. Diagrammatically, one could trace through the short-run and long-run effects on both X and Y under the various selling market structures.

It is impossible to determine what happens to general welfare, since there is a different Pareto optimal distribution of goods and services for every different income distribution. The general equilibrium conditions that initially prevailed would be disturbed and the economy would move toward a new equilibrium position, but we cannot determine whether it is better or worse in terms of welfare.

12. a. Consumers differ in their willingness to bear risk, and therefore will differ in their marginal rates of substitutions between sugared and diet drinks. Prohibiting exchange violates condition 18.1.
    b. Consumers differ in their willingness to incur the extra costs required to buy tickets through the inconvenient procedures that the Olympic committee established. Prohibiting subsequent voluntary exchanges (i.e., scalping) among consumers whose plans and preferences have changed perpetuates differences in their marginal rates of substitutions between Olympics tickets and cash. Condition 18.1 is violated.
    c. Subsidizing Amtrak prices distorts the relative prices between Amtrak trips and other things. Marginal rates of transformation between Amtrak trips and other things depend upon marginal cost ratios, and marginal rates of substitution among consumers between Amtrak trips and other things depend upon price ratios, so the two marginal rates will not be equal. Amtrak trips are over-produced relative to other things and condition 18.3 is violated.

13. Satisfying conditions (18.1), (18.2), and (18.3). In practice this is enormously difficult because planners lack the necessary information. An alternative is to move toward a decentralized private enterprise system in which profit-maximizing resource owners have stronger incentives to obtain information and to allocate their resources accordingly.

© 1988 The Dryden Press

14. It will probably resolve only part of Poland's problems. What incentives will factory managers have to allocate resources so that conditions (18.2) and (18.3) are satisfied if managers may not keep at least some of the resulting profits?

15. Without bidding, consumers (students) could not engage in mutually-beneficial exchange of goods in fixed supply as depicted in text Figure 18.1. Condition (18.1) is violated. Play money is not real money, so allowing bidding improves the allocation of seats in courses without regard to choices between further schooling versus other goods and services in the economy.

True-False Questions

(T) _____ 1. Definition of a unique optimum welfare position for an entire community would require that interpersonal comparisons of satisfaction be made.

(T) _____ 2. Partial equilibrium refers to the equilibrium position of a sub-unit of the economic system in response to variables endogenous to that sub-unit.

(F) _____ 3. If one were to study the repercussions of energy supply limitations on every industry in the economy, the appropriate framework would be partial equilibrium analysis.

(T) _____ 4. If one were to study the impact of environmental controls on the automobile industry, the appropriate framework would be partial equilibrium analysis.

(F) _____ 5. If an economy were to attain a general equilibrium adjustment, it would also be in a position of Pareto optimality.

(F) _____ 6. In the absence of externalities, whenever two persons are on their contract curve, it is always possible to increase their joint welfare by exchanges between them.

(F) ____ 7. In the absence of externalities, with pure competition in the purchase of goods and with an initial random distribution of fixed supplies of goods among consumers, free exchange and the introduction of a price system will most surely result in decreased welfare for some persons.

(T) ____ 8. Smith is a neighbor of Jones. If Smith's consumption of charcoal-broiled steaks annoys Jones, there is an externality involved in Smith's consumption.

(F) ____ 9. In order for two goods to be optimally allocated among consumers, the marginal rate of transformation of one good for the other must be the same for each consumer.

(T) ____ 10. If $MRS_{xy}^{j} > MRS_{xy}^{s}$ for consumers Smith and Jones, and $MRS_{xy}^{j} = P_x/P_y$, forces will be set in motion to increase P_y and reduce P_x.

(T) ____ 11. Effective price controls will usually prevent an optimum allocation of goods and services among consumers from being attained.

(F) ____ 12. In order to determine an efficient allocation of resources among products, it is necessary to know the optimal product mix.

(T) ____ 13. A firm which imposes external costs on the economy will tend to overproduce from the point of view of economic welfare.

(T) ____ 14. If for all consumers MRS_{xy} is the same and if $MRS_{xy} = MRT_{xy}$, where X and Y are the only goods produced in the economy, the output mix is optimal.

(F) ____ 15. If the economy is producing an optimal output mix and distributing that output mix among consumers in an optimal way, there cannot be another output mix that is optimal.

(F) ____ 16. Monopoly in the sale of products will prevent resources from being allocated efficiently in the production of those products.

(T) ____ 17. Monopsony in the purchase of resources will prevent resources from being allocated efficiently in the production of products.

(F) ____ 18. The slope of a transformation curve for X and Y at any point on the curve is measured by P_x/P_y, regardless of the type of market in which the goods are sold.

(T) ____ 19. The price mechanism can be expected to move the economic system toward general equilibrium.

(F) ____ 20. Movements toward general equilibrium in the economic system will always be movements toward Pareto optimality.

Multiple-Choice Questions

(a) ____ 1. An analysis of the impact of a technological breakthrough in the production of miniature calculators on the price and output of calculators is an example of:
   a. partial equilibrium analysis.
   b. general equilibrium analysis.
   c. welfare analysis.
   d. cutthroat competition.

(b) ____ 2. Partial equilibrium analysis:
   a. provides little information that is of value to economists.
   b. will help in predicting the impact of import duties for crude oil on the price at the pump of gasoline.
   c. will help in predicting the impact of import duties for crude oil on prices and outputs of the whole array of industries of the U.S. economy.
   d. is of especial value in explaining inflation.

(c) ____ 3. General equilibrium analysis:
   a. uses exogenous variables only.
   b. will help in predicting the impact of import duties for crude oil on the price at the pump of gasoline.
   c. will help in predicting the impact of import duties for crude oil on prices and outputs of the whole array of industries of the U.S. economy.
   d. is of especial value in explaining inflation.

(a) ____ 4. If two goods, X and Y, are to be efficiently allocated among consumers, then:
   a. MRS_{xy} must be the same for all consumers and the distribution must be complete.
   b. all consumers must receive equal quantities of each good.
   c. income distribution among consumers must be equal.
   d. MRT_{xy} must be the same for all consumers.

(c) ____ 5. In the absence of externalities, which of the following is <u>not</u> a necessary condition for an efficient allocation of resources A and B among products?
   a. $MRTS_{ab}$ is the same in all employments.
   b. All of the available quantities of the resource are employed.
   c. $MRC_a = MRC_b$.
   d. All firms using the resources are on the contract curve.

(d) ____ 6. The contract curve of two consumers for goods X and Y shows:
   a. that there is only one distribution of the goods between the consumers that is efficient.
   b. the prices at which the goods will be efficiently distributed.
   c. the terms under which the consumers are willing to trade with each other.
   d. that there are many distributions of the products that are efficient.

(c) ____ 7. If producers of X and Y purchase resources A and B competitively, we would expect that:
   a. $MPP_{ax} = MPP_{ay}$.
   b. $MPP_{ax}/P_a = MPP_{bx}/P_b = MPP_{ay}/P_a = MPP_{by}/P_b$.
   c. $MPP_{ax}/MPP_{bx} = P_a/P_b = MPP_{ay}/MPP_{by}$.
   d. both (b) and (c)

(b) ____ 8. If products X and Y are sold monopolistically by firms that use resources A and B, these resources will:
   a. not be allocated efficiently between the two products.
   b. be allocated efficiently between the products if $MRTS_{ab} = P_a/P_b$ for each firm.
   c. be allocated efficiently between the products if $MRP_{ax} = MRP_{ay}$ and $MRP_{bx} = MRP_{by}$.
   d. both (b) and (c)

© 1988 The Dryden Press

(d) ___ 9. The price system can be expected to bring about an efficient allocation of resources among products under conditions of:
a. pure competition in product sales and resource purchases.
b. monopoly in product sales and pure competition in resource purchases.
c. pure competition in product sales and monopsony in resource purchases.
d. both (a) and (b)

(a) ___ 10. If resources are efficiently allocated among products, it follows that:
a. the firms producing them are on the contract curve.
b. the distribution of goods among consumers will be optimal.
c. the product mix is optimal.
d. there is no monopoly in product sales.

(a) ___ 11. If producers of X and Y are monopsonists in the purchase of resources A and B, the supply curves of A to each firm have different elasticities at each resource price, the supply curves of B have different elasticities at each price of B, and both resources are mobile between the employers, then we would expect in equilibrium that:
a. $MRTS^x_{ab} = MRC_{ax}/MRC_{bx}$.
b. $MRTS^x_{ab} = MRTS^y_{ab}$.
c. $MRC_{ax} = MRC_{ay}$.
d. both (a) and (c)

(d) ___ 12. At an optimal output mix for two products, X and Y, we would expect:
a. $MRS_{xy} = P_x/P_y$.
b. $MRT_{xy} = P_x/P_y$.
c. $MRT_{xy} = MC_x/MC_y$.
d. all of the above

Questions 13-26 are based on the following choices:

    a. For all consumers, marginal rates of substitution are the same for each and every good or service.

    b. For all goods or services, marginal rates of technical substitution between any pair of resource inputs are the same for each and every use.

    c. The product mix is such that the marginal rate of transformation between any pair of goods or services is the same as the marginal rate of substitution between that pair.

    d. Resource prices are not equal to marginal revenue products of resources.

(a) _____ 13. Which were violated by the prohibition of jitneys?

(a) _____ 14. Which were violated by the restriction on eyeglass advertising?

(a) _____ 15. Which were violated by price discrimination in medicine?

(b) _____ 16. Which were violated by preventing exchange of airport landing slots?

(b) _____ 17. Which were violated by minimum wage laws?

(b) _____ 18. Which were violated by the Davis-Bacon Law?

(d) _____ 19. Which were violated by the baseball reserve clause?

(c) _____ 20. Which were violated by OPEC's pricing of oil?

(c) _____ 21. Which were violated by agricultural price supports?

(c) _____ 22. Which were violated by a failure to establish exclusive and transferable rights in mobile fish and game?

(a) _____ 23. Which were violated by a failure to price organ transplants?

(a) _____ 24. Which were fulfilled by "pricing" M.B.A. classes at the University of Chicago?

(c) ____ 25. Which were violated by a failure to price medical care to senior U.S. government officials?

(a) ____ 26. Which were violated by agricultural marketing
and   orders for Canadian eggs and California-Arizona
(c)   citrus?

SOLUTIONS TO EVEN-NUMBERED PROBLEMS FROM THE TEXT

Chapter 1

2. "Reality" is a complete description of all phenomena associated with an event. Theory is concerned with the causal
relations among the most important phenomena of the event.
Theory is always a simplification of reality, intended to
enable one to understand and predict, not just to describe.

4. Deductive reasoning is by far the more common. The number
of consumers and firms is enormous, and the number of transactions among them and within each group is still greater.
The mind boggles at the thought of trying to construct a
theory of consumer behavior, for example, by interviewing
each consumer. Further, it is difficult to design questions
that will yield unambiguous answers—particularly if self-
interests are at stake.

Chapter 2

2. We would expect them to increase. The attainment of
higher levels of education enables persons to move out of
lower-value, lower-paying jobs into higher-value, higher-
paying ones.

4. The system hastens all civil trials and benefits everybody.
Parties who hire the "rent-a-judge" rather than wait ten
years for a regular trial obviously consider themselves
better off, or they would have waited. In complex cases,
finding an impartial retired judge with previous experience
in the subject shortens trials and saves on attorneys' fees.
Removing these cases from the court docket enables remaining cases to be tried sooner.

6. If none were clearly priority cases, rationing could be
done by age, favoritism, bribery, or in many other ways.
Actually it was done by lot, which made it unnecessary for
hospital officials to decide which patients were more de-
serving. Stiff penalties would probably rule out bribery.
Shortages are more likely in public hospitals since costs
of hospitalization cannot be used to ration space to patients as they can be in private hospitals.

8. The extent of oil reserves. The price of oil. The number
of countries seeking to establish claims. The relative
bargaining powers of the competing countries. Environmental issues.

10. It is unlikely that this problem will be resolved with a
    voluntary transaction through the price system. The bene-
    fits to society of more knowledge about the cosmos versus
    the use of different street lights will be extremely diffi-
    cult to calculate. Some solutions affect many parties, so
    bargaining costs are likely to be high. If we were making
    the decision, however, we would attempt to avoid the great-
    er economic harm by estimating (1) which use generated the
    higher gain to society, (2) which party could adjust at
    lower cost, and (3) whether the cost of adjustment exceeded
    the gain.

    Owing to these problems it is more likely that the dispute
    will be settled through the judicial or political system,
    where the astronomers have done well so far. San Diego
    adopted sodium lights for new residential areas and park-
    ing lots, and required billboards and some businesses to
    cut lighting for nonsecurity purposes (Ralph Frammolino,
    "San Diego Accedes to Astronomers, Votes to Shut Off Some
    Lights," Los Angeles Times, September 24, 1985). In Ari-
    zona, where some of the world's best telescopes are threat-
    ened, twenty-five cities reduced lighting, and Phoenix was
    considering curbs like San Diego's. (Bill Curry, "Astron-
    omers in Fight for Night; Arizona Cities Seeking to Curb
    Light Pollution," Los Angeles Times, January 30, 1984.)

Chapter 3

2. a. It is very unlikely that the higher price brought
        larger sales. The container's size and shape is one of
        the variables held constant for a given state of demand.
        The more attractive shape increased demand.
    b. It is not all psychological. At the lower price, quan-
        tity demanded would be greater.
    c. Although shoppers may not know much about the price of a
        good purchased infrequently, one can be fairly certain
        that they will buy less at higher prices than they would
        buy at lower prices.
    d. The statement does not say over what period of time the
        same number of sets was sold. Selling 50 sets in one
        month at $60 is a greater rate than selling 50 at $70
        over six weeks. If price is unimportant, why not raise
        it to $170?

4. a. Demand <u>never</u> equals supply. At some price, quantity demanded equals quantity supplied.
   b. Two corrections are possible. The most likely is "Price Soars Here because Supply of Lettuce Dwindles." Alternatively, a soaring price would cause the <u>quantity</u> of lettuce supplied (but not the supply) to <u>increase</u>. Stating the correct relation between price and the quantity of lettuce supplied appears to alter the meaning, however.
   c. Should read "quantity demanded," not "demand."
   d. "Supply" and "demand" never come into line. Quantity supplied and quantity demanded come into line at the correct price, although to do so they must move in opposite directions.

6. a. If the demand for labor is inelastic.
   b. Higher wage rates reduce quantity demanded causing unemployment.
   c. No. Only if labor demand is inelastic.

8. The wholesale demand appears to be inelastic in this price range—about 0.33. The retail demand is more inelastic—about 0.83.

10. a. The best tickets. The "package deal" the Committee used is often referred to as a tie-in sale: the consumer must buy the less-desired item to get the more-desired item. This raises the effective price of the more-desired item above its stated price.
    b. We would expect that the best tickets had a less elastic demand in the relevant price range than the cheaper tickets. This is consistent with our argument that the prices of the best tickets could have been raised to yield more revenue.

Chapter 4

2. In Figure 4.1, draw a new and flatter demand curve through the intersection of DD with SS. Thus, for the price support level p_1, the reduction in quantity demanded will be greater along the new curve. Assuming the supply curve does not change, the new surplus will be greater than X_1X_2.

© 1988 The Dryden Press

4. a. Large sums of money move cheaply and easily among
        states. Funds for lending dried up in states with lower
        ceilings. The ensuing shortages induced them to raise
        or abolish the ceilings.
    b. We doubt it. There is much competition among lenders.
        Consider not only the number of banks but the finance
        companies and credit unions, which helped keep bank
        rates competitive. Customers going outside the local
        area for loans strengthened the inducements to banks to
        hold rates down. The local car-loan market is prob-
        ably competitive.

6. a. Shortages.
    b. Encourages apartment owners to convert to condominiums.
    c. Hastens demolition of old buildings to escape controls.
    d. This is usually the aftermath of growing shortages.
    e. Apartments will be converted to condominiums, new
        private-sector buildings will be constructed, and new
        public housing will be supplied at higher rates than
        would have occurred otherwise. This means that average
        cost will rise.

8. Figure 4.3 shows that incidence of the tax is the same for
    given supply and demand schedules no matter who it is col-
    lected from.

10. a. At the lower end. Such substitution opportunities as
        small cars had not yet been adopted in the United States
        so the United States would be toward the lower end.
    b. This answer would support the argument for decontrol.
        We favored decontrol at the time and still do.

Chapter 5

2. a. Measuring units of food on the vertical axis and
        units of clothing on the horizontal axis, satisfaction
        is maximized with the combination at which (1) $MRS_{cf} =
        p_c/p_f$, and (2) $c \times p_c + f \times p_f = I$.
    b. At the selected point $MRS_{cf} > p_c/p_f$. The consumer
        is willing to give up more food to obtain an additional
        unit of clothing than the market requires.

4. a. The person who likes Brand B more relative to Brand A
        has flatter indifference curves at three units of B.
    b. The person who consumes only Brand A chooses quanti-
        ties along the X-axis, and the person who consumes only
        Brand B chooses quantities along the Y-axis. The bud-
        get line determines how much is chosen.

6. The preference maps of these senators appear to be like Figure 5.7. Since they prefer more rather than less of both, indifference curves showing higher preferences lie to the northeast. The curves also appear to be convex to the origin. If a combination containing $7,500 of speech income and $300 billion in defense spending lies on the same indifference curve as that containing $5,000 of speech income and $400 billion in defense spending, we would expect that at the former point a senator would be willing to give up more speech income for an extra $10 billion than would be the case at the latter point; that is, MRS_{ds} would be smaller at the latter point.

8. a. In Panel (a) of the following diagram, budget line AB shows the feasible combinations of profits and emoluments per unit of time in a for-profit firm. The manager maximizes satisfaction on U_1 at C.
   b. In Panel (b), prohibiting profits in excess of P_0 removes the dashed segment AE and the area ADE from the manager's set of feasible combinations. The budget line becomes DEB. The manager maximizes satisfaction at E on U_0, which is inferior to the case in Panel (a) where profits were not limited. If the manager's preference for emoluments is relatively strong and the satisfaction-maximizing combination of profits and emoluments was in the EB segment of AB in part a., then the profit limit would not change managerial behavior.

© 1988 The Dryden Press

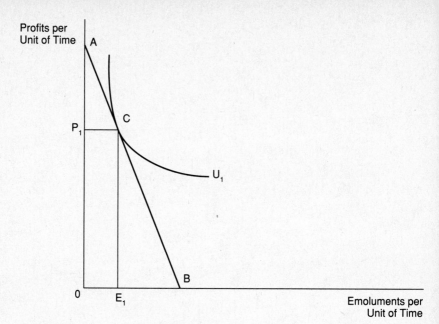

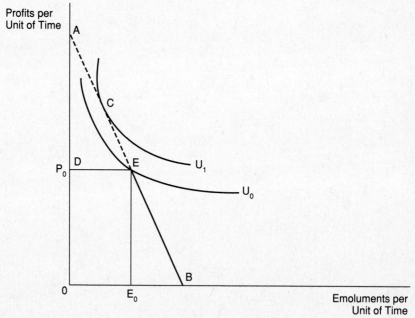

10. Economists and officials at the Bureau of Labor Statistics would agree with Mr. Howard that the CPI overstates an increase in inflation, but this is the root problem with a Laspeyres' price index. BLS economists construct the index and make the monthly calculations, but linking the retirement pay of government officials to changes in the CPI was decided by Congress.

Chapter 6

2. Children could be inferior "goods." This hypothesis is superficially consistent with the tendency for higher-income families to have fewer children. Such families tend to invest more in each child's health and education, however, creating a "quality" effect that may offset the "quantity" effect. Thus, it may be misleading to view the inferiority or superiority of children only in terms of numbers. The economic theory of fertility is controversial and has not been fully resolved.

4. a. The differential is consumer's surplus.
   b. Your diagrams will be like Figure 6.10 if you treat M.B.A. classes as a superior good.

6. a. In Figure 6.11(a), assume that X represents cigarettes and that the analysis is for a light smoker. The quantity of cigarettes the consumer smokes at price p_{x1} along budget line (I_1, I_1/p_{x1}) is zero and he will pay nothing. He achieves satisfaction level U_1. But the quantity he smokes given price p_{x2} along budget line (I_1, I_1/p_{x2}) is x_1 at S on U_2. The consumer is indifferent on U_1 between zero cigarettes at I_1 and x_1 at R. The maximum amount he would pay for the right to purchase x_1 at R when the alternative is to do without cigarettes entirely at I_1 is $I_1 I_4$.
   b. A "heavy" smoker would have a relatively high marginal rate of substitution between income and cigarettes per unit of time. This person's indifference curves between income and cigarettes would be steeper in the vicinity of point S, so the point of maximum satisfaction on the budget line would probably be to the southeast of point S, indicating a greater rate of smoking than for the "light" smoker. Accordingly, the maximum amount that the heavy smoker would pay for the optimum quantity of cigarettes would exceed $I_1 I_4$.

8. Working from Figure 6.2, draw a new budget line from the point I_1/p_{y1} tangent to indifference curve U_2. This tangency will occur at a quantity greater than x_1, because the substitution effect overpowers the opposite income effect. In this case, the negative income effect is insufficient to make X a Giffen good. This is why we say that not all inferior goods are Giffen goods (if indeed any are). A Giffen good case is one in which the negative income effect overpowers the positive substitution effect of a price change.

10. i. Shift A's "other goods" axis to the right by the amount of the gasoline curtailment. This shifts his entire indifference map to the right and a lower and steeper indifference curve of A now passes through point S.
     ii. (a) Price controls on gasoline and other goods fix the budget line at its tangency point with B's indifference curve through point S, thus destroying B's incentive to trade and preventing exchange that could enhance the welfare of both A and B. A has a shortage of gasoline and a surplus of other goods. He would thus be willing to trade other goods for gasoline at the controlled prices.
         (b) Mr. A would bid the price of gasoline up and the price of other goods would fall, increasing the slope of the budget line and inducing B to give up gasoline for other goods. Either or both persons could get on higher indifference curves than distribution S would allow.

Chapter 7

2. With diminishing marginal utility of income, the loss in utility from being $100 poorer would be greater than the gain in utility from being $100 richer. The person would not be expected to bet.

4. The marginal rate of substitution is the ratio of marginal utilities between the two goods. The ratio will decrease if the denominator is rising faster than the numerator, so a decreasing ratio does not depend on both commodities having diminishing marginal utilities.

6. None. Scarcity, however it comes about, keeps marginal utility and hence, value in exchange relatively high.

© 1988 The Dryden Press

8. The assumption in each case is that the shares would be
    sold slowly enough so that market price does not change
    much. Market price would change more if all were sold at
    once.

10. In the following diagram, the initial distribution of in-
    come is I_y of yours and I_x of X's. You achieve indifference
    level U_6 at point g.
    a. The relevant budget line through g is gpj. Its slope
        equals p_x, the "price" of charitable giving (the cost
        per unit for income transfers).
    b. Along gpj, you can reach p by transferring go of income
        to X. This raises X's income by amount op to I_x' and
        reduces your income by go to I_y'. You are better off on
        U_7 than on U_6 even though you have given away $I_y - I_y'$.
        Donating it is also superior to simply tearing up go
        dollars, which would have moved you from g on U_6 to o
        on U_5.
    c. Assume the disaster reduces X's income to I_x'' without
        reducing yours below I_y. Now the relevant budget line
        for transferring income to X is fnh. (Its slope is
        equal to gpj since nothing has changed the market
        "price" of charitable giving.) At f you can reach U_2,
        but you can move to c on fnh by transferring fe so that
        X now winds up with I_x'' in income. Transferring only
        fm (equal to the pre-disaster amount go) would put you
        on U_3 at n, which is inferior to U_4 at c. (As before,
        throwing away income makes you worse off than by do-
        nating it to X.) Thus, indifference curve analysis
        shows that the income you transfer to X after a disas-
        ter exceeds the pre-disaster amount—the same result
        achieved with marginal utility analysis. (Louis De
        Alessi, "A Utility Analysis of Post-Disaster Coopera-
        tion," Papers on Non-Market Decision Making 3 [Fall
        1967]:86.)

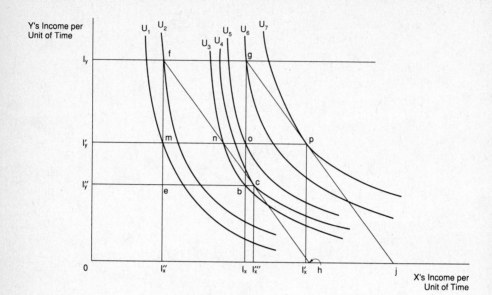

Chapter 8

2. No distinction between "actual differences" between goods
    as opposed to differences that consumers think exist is
    necessary. What consumers think is <u>all</u> that matters. It
    is consumers' willingness to purchase at different prices,
    consumers' expectations, consumers' incomes, and consumers'
    determination of what constitutes substitutes and comple-
    ments that underlie market demand curves facing sellers.

4. Advertising may be profitable for any firm facing a down-
    ward-sloping demand curve. Monopolists have incentives to
    use it to try to push their demand curves to the right and
    to make them less elastic. Oligopolists may find it' use-
    ful in increasing their individual market shares; however,
    they often find it degenerates into competitive advertising
    that at best may only preserve market shares. In monopo-
    listic competition product differentiation through adver-
    tising may help the individual firm sell a little more or
    charge a price a little higher than before.

    Advertising may or may not be in the best interests of
    consumers. It may be beneficial if it makes them better
    informed with respect to the qualities of the advertised
    product.

6. A few nationwide aspirin brands probably make this market
    oligopolistic, but less so than it used to be owing to the
    introduction of various aspirin substitutes and the sale
    of generic pain relievers in pharmacies and grocery stores.
    Haircuts are probably monopolistically competitive owing
    to numbers of barbers with different hairdressing skills.
    Wheat is purely competitive (except for government price
    controls). Retail gasoline is either oligopolistic or mo-
    nopolistically competitive depending on the number of in-
    dependent gas stations in each community. Domestic car
    production among the "big three" is an oligopoly, but for-
    eign producers have made the market more competitive. The
    same applies to retail automobile dealerships. Steel pro-
    duction is oliogopolistic, but foreign producers are im-
    portant here too. Nationally advertised pantyhose brands
    are relatively few, but some retail chains sell their own
    brands—it is probably an oligopolistic industry at retail.
    Contract construction is either oligopolistic or monopo-
    listically competitive depending on the number of firms
    in the market, as are restaurants and laundries.

8. Foreign aircraft producers sell actively in the United
    States, and the world's airlines are experienced, knowl-
    edgeable buyers.

10. a. Concentration will be the lowest in the states that
         prohibit branching and highest in the states that do
         not limit branching.
     b. It will probably lower local concentration as commer-
         cial banking organizations are allowed to invade ter-
         ritories from which they were previously prohibited.
         Some banks are bound to raise their market shares as
         a result of such competition, which could increase
         nationwide concentration. This is why concentration
         ratios can be a poor index of competition.

Chapter 9

2. Probably not. Labor was abundant and relatively cheap.
    Capital was extremely scarce and relatively expensive. This
    would induce the use of high ratios of labor to capital so
    that the MPP_l would be relatively low and the MPP_k would be
    relatively high. See Figure 9.4.

4. a. Plot hours spent in improving grades per week on the
        horizontal axis and hours spent in interviews per week
        on the vertical. Output can be thought of as better
        job opportunities, represented by higher isoquant curves
        lying to the northeast. Along a given isoquant, the
        marginal rate of technical substitution represents the
        extra amount of time spent studying per week that is
        required to compensate for less time spent interviewing
        per week to maintain a given level of job opportunities.
        Each student's isoquant map reflects his or her pro-
        ductivity in making these substitutions.

    b. The position of the isocost line depends on the pro-
        portion of a student's week that is devoted to job-en-
        hancing efforts versus other activities. The greater
        this proportion, the farther from the origin the iso-
        cost line will lie. Obviously, the position of the iso-
        cost line will differ among students. The slope will
        be minus one, however, since the same number of hours
        can be devoted wholly to either activity. The opportu-
        nity cost of an hour of studying is an hour of inter-
        viewing.

    c. A corner solution is unlikely. Few seniors can grad-
        uate and get jobs with zero studying. Most seniors
        will do zero interviewing only if they intend to go to
        graduate schools, family businesses, or self-employ-
        ment. If the hours available for studying and inter-
        viewing are allowed to change, analogous to the changes
        in total outlay in Figure 9.6, the student will choose
        an input combination on expansion path GFH between the
        ridge lines OC and OD where neither input is generating
        a negative marginal product. Any combination on GFH
        minimizes the cost of achieving a given level of job
        opportunities.

6. a. For an efficient allocation of resources the ratio of
        the marginal physical products of the resources must be
        the same for tractors as it is for airplanes. Setting
        the problem up as an Edgeworth Box, the resource allo-
        cation between the uses must lie on the contract curve.
    b. The transformation curve is derived from the contract
        curve of the Edgeworth Box and the isoquants for air-
        planes and tractors.
    c. It would be downward-sloping because producing more of
        one product would require producing less of the other.
        In addition, the marginal rate of transformation will
        usually rise as the rate of output of one good is in-
        creased and that of the other is decreased. This occurs
        because resources more specialized or more efficient in
        producing the good being decreased in quantity must be
        used increasingly in the expansion of production of the
        other.

8. The substitution can be conceptualized with Figure 9.9.
    Draw separate diagrams for "Diet Coke," which used aspar-
    tame and saccharin, and for other diet drinks, which used
    aspartame only.

10. Following Figure 9.10, plot aluminum per unit of time
    along the X-axis and steel per unit of time along the Y-
    axis. If T_1 is the initial total outlay and the price of
    aluminum rises, the new isocost line rotates inward from AB
    to AC. The expansion path changes from one like GH to one
    like SJ. Less aluminum and more steel are used for each
    output rate and total outlay.

Chapter 10

2. a. None of these so-called economic concepts measures the
        economic effects of migration. Each ignores the goods
        and services emigrants leave for remaining citizens to
        consume, the income emigrants send home to families,
        and current transfers from host to home countries.
    b. "Historic cost" exaggerates compensation since the cost
        and quality of education is higher in the host country.
        "Opportunity cost" and "discounted present value" exag-
        gerate it further. They are based on host-country jobs,
        which pay more because of better training and more cap-
        ital.
    c. Whichever one gives the lowest estimate.

4. a. The long-run total cost curve in Figure 10.6(b) is
        generated from the expansion path OF in Figure 10.6(a).
        Total cost at each isocost is divided by the output
        rate of the isoquant tangent to it. The spacing of iso-
        quants, resulting from economies and diseconomies of
        size, determines the shape of the long-run total cost
        curve.
    b. In Figure 9.5, $b_1 J$ is the short-run "expansion path"
        when the quantity of resource b is held constant at b_1
        units. If Figure 9.5 showed a long-run expansion path,
        the point at which the short-run and long-run paths
        intersect would yield an output rate at which short-run
        and long-run total costs were equal. The short-run
        total variable cost curve is generated from the iso-
        quant-isocost map along the short-run "expansion path"
        just like the long-run total cost curve in Figure
        10.6(b) is generated along the long-run expansion path.
        Total fixed cost must be added to it to obtain short-
        run total cost.

6. The long-run total and unit cost curves shift down. Trace
    out the steps as we did in the answer to Problem 5. First
    make the necessary changes in the isoquant-isocost diagram,
    and then adjust the cost curves accordingly.

8. The SAC curve will be tangent to the LAC curve at the
    designated output rate. It is a less than most efficient
    size of plant. The SMC curve cuts the SAC curve at mini-
    mum SAC (to the right of the tangency). The LMC curve cuts
    the LAC curve at minimum LAC. The SMC curve intersects
    the LMC curve at the designated output rate (below the
    point of tangency of SAC and LAC).

10. Average cost curves need not be U-shaped. Much research
    suggests that a flat segment is common. We use U-shaped
    curves because they illustrate short-run increasing returns
    and diminishing returns and long-run economies and dis-
    economies of size. Also the single output rate that they
    yield makes analysis somewhat more simple.

© 1988 The Dryden Press

Chapter 11

2. Bond interest, unlike dividends, reduces taxable profits.
    Thus, up to some point, managers have an incentive to sub-
    stitute debt for common stock. But the higher the debt-
    equity ratio, the higher the interest rate the firm must pay
    to expand debt financing and the less desirable debt financ-
    ing becomes. Lenders will not lend to a firm if they think
    its income is insufficient to pay the interest, which puts
    an upper limit on the substitution possibilities.

4. Working from Figure 11.5, low-interest loans will reduce
    operating losses by lowering cost curves. Price ceilings on
    diesel fuel have the same effect for firms able to obtain
    it. For other firms shortages appear and the cost of cir-
    cumvention may increase the cost of doing business. A tar-
    iff reduces supply of shrimp and raises price. This shifts
    up the $d_0d_0 = MR_0$ curve to $d_1d_1 = MR_1$ and cuts the firm's
    losses.

6. More elastic. See the text accompanying Figures 11.2,
    11.10, and 11.12.

8. Whatever the cost of production of the leftover old widgets,
    it is an irrelevant "sunk" cost. With the latest style
    change the old widget is worth less than the new. A's try-
    ing to sell old widgets at the market price relinquishes
    sales to heads-up entrepreneurs who discard worthless in-
    ventories and sell new widgets at market prices.

10. In panel (b) of the following figure, demand for lamb is unchanged because none of the circumstances held constant in defining a given state of demand has changed (e.g., consumer incomes or tastes). The initial market price is p, and the total quantity sold at that price is X. As ranchers sell to feedlots earlier at lower prices, the AC and MC curves in panel (a) shift down to AC_1 and MC_1. This shifts the individual operator's short-run supply curve to the right. The supply of fattened lamb increases to S_1S_1, and market price falls to p_1.

    a. In panel (a), p_1 is less than AC_1 but greater than AVC_1. This operator would run losses but stay in business. Operators who anticipated the drought had smaller losses.

    b. If the cost of transporting live lambs to market exceeds the immediate selling price, or if the present value of the expected future price is less than the expected cost of feeding and transporting them, then p_1 is less than AVC_1. The operator would probably destroy his stock.

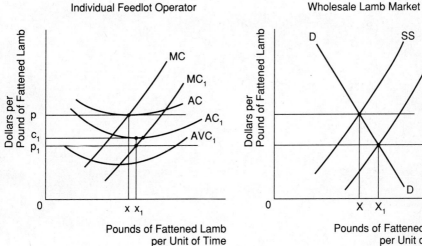

Individual Feedlot Operator

Pounds of Fattened Lamb
per Unit of Time

(a)

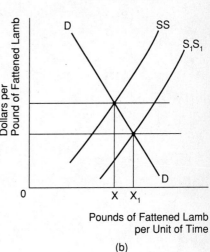

Wholesale Lamb Market

Pounds of Fattened Lamb
per Unit of Time

(b)

Chapter 12

2. Airplanes are a highly mobile form of capital. Monopolizing service at one airport would attract competitors unless most of the "gates" already had been leased by the aspiring monopolist on a long-term basis. This would disadvantage all travellers including many local residents who would, if the monopoly price were high enough, exert political pressure on the local airport authority to establish more competition.

4. (1) In each case the regulated price would be less than the unregulated price and the output in the regulated market would be greater.
   (2) In each case price regulation makes the demand curve and the marginal revenue curve horizontal at the regulated price out to the intersection point with the unregulated demand curve. Consequently, in
      a. there is no shortage or surplus.
      b. a shortage occurs.
      c. there is no shortage or surplus.

6. It appears to be third-degree price discrimination as long as the costs of providing and shipping blood to the two types of hospitals are the same.

8. a. Third-degree discrimination if marginal costs to each group are equal.
   b. Same as a.
   c. Effectively offers a discount for taking additional courses. Second-degree discrimination as long as marginal costs do not decline with additional courses offered.
   d. Senior's demand is less elastic owing to the greater adjustment costs of shifting to another college to finish a degree relative to the sophomore's costs. Third-degree discrimination if marginal costs to each student are the same.
   e. Second-degree discrimination if marginal costs are equal.
   f. A higher price would be charged to the off-campus group if discrimination were the purpose, since they would more likely be living in rooms or apartments with kitchen facilities. However, the purpose may be to discourage on-campus students from cooking in rooms, thus increasing fire risks.

10. The factors would include the speaker's prominence; connection with scandals; previously published books; appearances on "talk shows"; and differentiation from those already on the lecture circuit.

© 1988 The Dryden Press

Chapter 13

2. a. The contract terms suggest that the interests of schools
        with nationally prominent teams were underrepresented.
        The NCAA has 870 members, most of them smaller schools.
        Even within its Division I schools having million-dollar
        athletic budgets, where entry costs are high but not
        prohibitive, the interests of schools diverge according
        to their athletic success.
    b. The NCAA tries to cartelize by limiting under-the-table
        payments to athletes, but it is unable to stop them.
        It has never been a centralized cartel because it has
        lacked any mechanism to equalize marginal costs among
        producers. Television contracts have been its main de-
        vice for pooling and dividing revenue.
    c. The number of televised games trebled, and the networks
        emphasized stronger athletic conferences and teams. Big
        schools with nationally prominent teams gained. (Rob-
        ert Friedman, "Court Ruling Still Scrambles Picture for
        Broadcasting College Football Games," The Wall Street
        Journal, July 23, 1984.)

4. Each oligopoly situation is unique, so classification is
    difficult without more information about the industry's
    behavior over a period of years. The available evidence
    suggests imperfect competition. Apparently an attempt at
    cartelization was made and, failing to achieve that, the
    five firms were relying heavily on their price leadership
    capabilities.

6. A joint sales agency would reduce chiseling, but it would
    not resolve the problems of determining the profit-maximiz-
    ing price for countries with diverging interests, ration-
    ing quotas, or preventing entry.

8. This is unlikely. With price increases, marginal wells
    that were closed when the price fell below $20 would become
    economical to reactivate, and fields that are known to have
    recoverable oil could begin production. Also, if the price
    should rise the United States could sell oil at a profit
    from its Strategic Petroleum Reserve.

10. Both cartels generate overproduction and idleness. But the
    USDA can get the Department of Justice and federal courts
    to enforce LAC's prorate and quotas. As the editors of The
    Wall Street Journal said, "Sheik Yamani must be envious"
    ("The Squeeze on OLEC," August 20, 1985).

12. a. In the short run, the board must reduce total output enough to yield the profit-maximizing egg price for the group, allocate quotas for the allowable output, and prevent chiseling. In the long run, existing growers will expand if the output reduction leads to economic profits, and new growers will enter.
    b. We would follow the model of the centralized, tight cartel with output quotas or allotments that are freely and fully exchangeable. This would minimize total production costs.
    c. We would prefer a competitive market, essentially the status quo. This avoids the welfare losses of cartelization.

14. a. Different skills and locations of dentists put them in the category of monopolistic competition.
    b. Probably to reduce competition from younger, entrepreneurial dentists to older, established dentists.

Chapter 14

2. Marginal physical product of feed is 0.35 gallons of milk when 8 units of feed are used instead of 6. When milk is worth $1 per gallon, each of these two units of feed has a value of marginal product (marginal revenue product) of $0.35, which is equal to the price (marginal resource cost) of feed per pound.

4. Following Equation 14.4 let resource L represent labor. Hold its price (and MRC_l) constant. A reduction in the quantity of labor used will increase MPP_l and thus lower MRC_l/MPP_l. Hiring less labor reduces the productivity of complementary resources, inducing the firm to decrease its use of that resource, so MRC_s/MPP_s also falls. This reduces the marginal cost of cars.

6. The monopolist hires workers up to the point at which the wage rate equals marginal revenue product, whereas the competitive firm hires workers up to the point at which the wage rate equals marginal revenue and value of marginal product. Marginal revenue product is less than value of marginal product for the monopolist because its marginal revenue is less than price. Commutative justice is not attained; however, if workers are mobile between the two firms, the monopolist must pay a wage equal to what they can earn elsewhere, i.e., from the competitive firm.

© 1988 The Dryden Press

8. The conditions that give rise to monopsony—isolated re-
    source markets, single employers, or effective collusion
    among employers—are rare. We describe what was once the
    most important American monopsony in the next chapter.

10. a. The following diagram depicts the VMP_a and MRP_a curves
        of a monopolist as well as its supply curve, $s_a s_a$. Un-
        constrained, the monopolist would hire a units of the
        labor at p_a where the wage rate equals marginal revenue
        product. Monopolistic exploitation is $p_a v$. Imposing
        a minimum resource price of p_{a1} leads the monopolist to
        hire a_0 units of labor, but does not eradicate monopo-
        listic exploitation equal to $p_{a1}v'$.
    b. In Figure 14.9, a minimum resource price of p_{a1} induces
        the monopsonist to hire a_1 of A, where the wage rate
        equals marginal revenue product. We would not expect
        such pricing to be successful since a regulatory author-
        ity is unlikely to know the intersection point of the
        MRP_a and the $s_a s_a$ curves. Thus, increasing the minimum
        resource price by too much will reduce employment.

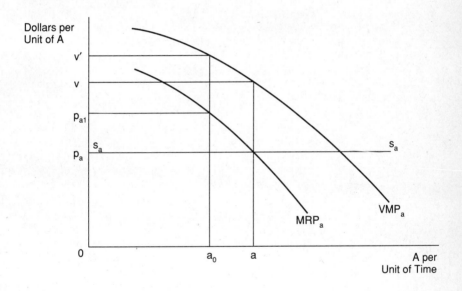

12. See Equation 14.6 and the accompanying explanation.

2. The insurance cost is analogous to imposing an excise tax
   if it is a fixed sum per worker regardless of the wage rate.
   Refer back to Figure 4.3(b) and the discussion accompanying
   it. Assume that the wage rate is plotted along the vertical
   axis and labor per unit of time along the horizontal. The
   farm owners are buyers of labor and the workers are sellers.
   If the insurance cost is collected from buyers, the demand
   curve shifts down by that amount. The wage rate paid by
   buyers rises by less than the insurance cost, so a portion
   of the cost is borne by sellers in the form of reduced employment and a lower wage rate net of the insurance cost.
   Whether buyers or sellers bear the greater incidence depends on the elasticities of demand and supply.

4. If Americans are less enthusiastic about the kinds of
   nonagricultural jobs taken by aliens at current wage rates,
   then the S_d curve in Figure 15.2(a) would lie to the left
   of its present position. This indicates that a higher wage
   rate is required to induce each quantity of domestic workers to take so-called dead-end jobs. Blocking aliens from
   this market would raise wage rates further. If domestic
   workers do not want these jobs at present wage rates, why
   block aliens from filling them? The answer, of course, is
   to obtain even higher wage rates for those Americans who
   do accept the jobs.

6. a. Economic rent.
   b. Pilots who have the lowest-valued, next-best job alter-
      natives will suffer the greatest losses of rent.

8. a. Collusion among hospitals.
   b. Depends on facts discovered.
   c. Yes, although it is not an automatic remedy for reasons
      we describe in the text.

10. a. In the question 9 answer diagram, the wages of workers
       who keep jobs rise by w_1w_2AB. The wages of workers who
       lose jobs fall to zero.
    b. BAC.
    c. $w_1w_2AB - DBC$.
    d. w_2D_BA.

12. a. pp'BA.
    b. X_1X_2GH.
    c. It is simply a means of transferring income from con-
       sumers and taxpayers to those who furnish resources,
       labor and capital, to the domestic shoe industry. As
       such it is much less efficient than direct transfers
       to poverty-stricken shoe workers would be.
    d. Auctions distribute quotas to importers who can use
       them most productively and minimize rent-seeking costs.
       Removing uncertainty over whether imports can be sold
       will dampen the rise in shoe prices.

Chapter 16

2. a. The costs of transporting oil from Oklahoma to New York.
   b. Not unless the shipment of oil is restricted, thus rais-
      ing the New York price artificially.
   c. It would no longer be economical to transport to New
      York and oil would be inefficiently allocated.

© 1988 The Dryden Press

4. a. In Alpha rent levels will be lower than in Omega and
        shortages will occur. Those unable to obtain apartments
        in Alpha at the controlled price go to Omega, increasing
        demand, rent levels, and quantities of apartments in
        Omega. The number of apartments in Alpha will not in-
        crease.
    b. Accentuates the results described in a.
    c. In the following diagram, the market-clearing rent in
        Alpha is p_m and the controlled rent is p_c. The shortage
        is X_1X_2. Removal of the control for new apartments
        yields the kinked supply curve p_cABS'. X_1X' housing can
        be rented at p' and that $0X_1'$ is rented at p_c. This re-
        duces demand and rents in Omega.

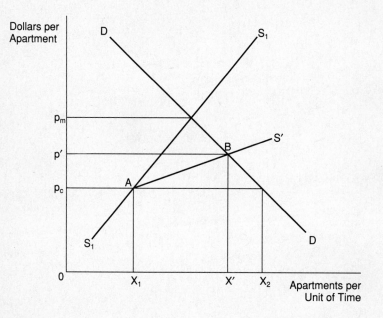

6. a. The nonexempt market has a shortage at the controlled
        price (interest rate), and price is at the market-clear-
        ing level for exempt lenders. Efficient resource use
        requires that the two markets have the same price.
    b. Restrictions on lending in California tend to increase
        the supply of loanable funds and lower interest rates
        elsewhere.
    c. It reduced the distortions indicated in a and b.

© 1988 The Dryden Press

8. Two-thirds of the income difference is accounted for by fewer hours worked, and one-third by lower wages. The wage rate in smaller communities must be sufficiently high to offset the apparent preference of most physicians for "the bright lights" of urban life. Physicians who prefer small-er communities get economic rents.

10. a. Creates a misallocation unless these carriers would have paid the highest prices in competition for these slots.
    b. Same as a. It is more likely that commercial air car-riers would have outbid private aircraft owners.
    c. This "use-it-or-lose-it" provision forces an airline to waste resources to preserve a right when temporary idleness might be more economical. Why not let slots lie idle transitionally as long as an airline incurs the opportunity cost of sacrificing a sale? (Are vacant land and voluntary unemployment analogies?)

12. We do not agree. The opportunity cost of hoarding is the receipts that could have been obtained from selling the rights. Hoarding must be most efficient in some situations.

Chapter 17

2. a. Restricting supply in one market leads workers to shift to unaffected markets. Society sacrifices a higher marginal revenue product for a lower marginal revenue product from the workers who shift. The incomes of one group are improved at the expense of the incomes of others. Income distribution is made less rather than more equitable.
   b. Workers who keep their jobs after licensing restricts entry gain at the expense of workers who must shift to next-best alternatives and consumers who must now pay higher prices for smaller quantities of goods and ser-vices. Employers also incur a deadweight loss from hiring fewer workers.

4. Employment will fall if the wage rate rises and the demand for labor is unchanged. The amount depends on elasticity, which is probably high for low-skilled labor for which capital can be easily substituted. Wage receipts fall if elasticity exceeds unity.

6. a. An effective minimum wage rate generates unemployment
        among those with the lowest skill levels. Those made
        unemployed may seek employment in uncovered employ-
        ments, increasing supply and reducing wage rates in
        those employments. It has done little if anything to
        reduce poverty levels. In comparison, a negative in-
        come tax benefits low-income workers without making
        some groups among them worse off.
    b. The worker must weigh (i) the benefits to be obtained
        from the negative income tax against (ii) the possi-
        bilities of a higher total wage from a minimum wage
        rate, tempered with the possibility of being laid off
        because of the minimum wage. Most workers see little
        or no connection between the minimum wage and employ-
        ment levels (neither do members of Congress, appar-
        ently). They tend to think exploitation is diminished
        and independence from government support is obtained
        by a minimum wage rate.

8. On economic grounds one would expect members of Congress
    from (b) and (c) to oppose, and from (d) to favor a high
    minimum wage rate. States in the (b) and (c) categories
    stand to lose employment. States in the (d) classification
    see it as a means to stop industry from migrating to low-
    wage areas. Those in (a) and (e) are less affected by it.
    But congressional decisions are not always made on econom-
    ic grounds!

10. a. Without wage ceilings, shortages in the rigorous eco-
        nomic sense cannot be sustained. Sometimes people say a
        shortage occurs whenever supply falls and price rises
        rapidly.
    b. As demand rises, the excess supply resulting from the
        legal minimum wage rate will decline. Eventually wage
        rates may exceed the legal minimum levels and surpluses
        will tend to disappear.
    c. Higher wage rates for lower-wage, less-skilled workers
        tend to reduce disparities in the distribution of in-
        come.

Chapter 18

2. We would want to raise questions as to whether with subsidized housing

$MRS_{ho} = MRT_{ho}$?

$MRS_{ho} = P_h/P_o$?

Are there externalities to consider?

Are there alternative methods of income redistribution that will lead to better welfare results; i.e., a negative income tax system, subsidized education for the poor, etc.?

4. See Equations (18.3) and (18.4). The output of X is too small relative to that of Y to achieve optimum welfare. In a competitive, private-property, profit-maximizing economy, profits and losses will lead to greater output of X and smaller output of Y until $MRS_{xy} = p_x/p_y = MRT_{xy} = MC_x/MC_y$.

6. a. In the following diagram, the input combinations along expansion path EF are generated by market-determined prices of inputs p_c/p_1 that are assumed to prevail throughout the economy. The regulation that considers profits to be earned on the use of capital but not labor would artificially lower the price of capital that regulated firms face from p_c to p_{cr}. This generates the new expansion path JK, along which the regulated firm employs more capital than previously for each output level. Since the ratio of input prices for the phone company differs from their ratio in producing other products, condition (18.2) for the efficient allocation of two resources between two products is violated. (Harvey Averch and Leland L. Johnson, "Behavior of the Firm under Regulatory Constraint," American Economic Review 52 [1962]:1052-1069. For elaboration and a discussion of qualifications to the theory, see Alfred E. Kahn, The Economics of Regulation: Principles and Institutions, vol. 2 [New York and other cities: John Wiley & Sons, Inc., 1971]:49-59.)

   b. Condition (18.3) is not met if AT&T prices its equipment to phone companies in excess of marginal cost, or if it requires phone companies to buy more or different equipment than they would take under competitive conditions of supply.

   c. This is third-degree price discrimination if the price differences are not justified by marginal cost differences. It yields suboptimal welfare distributions of these and other goods and services among consumers, and violates condition (18.1).

   d. Same as b. if all consumers pay the same rental fee.

© 1988 The Dryden Press

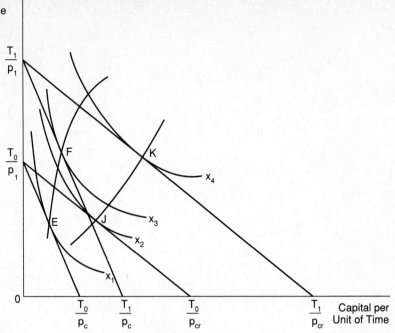

8. Violates condition (18.2) if the relative who is hired (a) gets the same wage as another person who is more productive, or (b) is paid more than another person of equal productivity. Nepotism should be more common in organizations where managers do not bear much of the costs of the inefficiency that nepotism creates. Owners of for-profit firms bear more of these costs, and in any case are spending their own money when they indulge themselves.

10. Bread was used as animal feed. This violates condition (18.2).

12. Both situations violate condition (18.3). Subsidizing health care results in a greater quantity demanded than otherwise and in the production of too much health care relative to other goods and services. Preventing consumers from bidding for organs keeps marginal costs above prices and leads to too few transplants. The failure to price organs also violates condition (18.1) because one patient is prohibited from selling a place in the queue to another patient.

328   © 1988 The Dryden Press